NEW

CUTTING EDGE

PRE-INTERMEDIATE

STUDENTS' BOOK

sarah cunningham   peter moor

with jane comyns carr

PEARSON

Longman

CONTENTS

Leisure and lifestyle

▶ Revision of question forms
▶ Present simple
▶ **Vocabulary:** Leisure activities
▶ **Reading:** *Unusual ways of keeping fit*
▶ **Pronunciation:** Sentence stress in questions, Intonation in *Wh-* questions
▶ **Task:** Compile a fact file
▶ **Real life:** Questions you can't live without

Vocabulary and speaking
Leisure activities

1 **a** **MD** Look at the pictures. Which of the leisure activities can you see?

clubbing	football
going for a run	going to the gym
playing the guitar	rollerblading
skateboarding	skiing
snowboarding	surfing the Internet
swimming	yoga

b Discuss the following questions in pairs or small groups.

• Which of these things do you enjoy?
• Which of these things don't you enjoy?
• What else do you do in your free time?

2 **T1.1** Listen to the results of a survey of leisure activities among people aged sixteen to thirty and complete the missing information on page 7.

We asked 100 people between the ages of sixteen and thirty this question:

Which of these things do you enjoy doing?

Here are the results.

playing video games	____%
going _____ / _____	28%
going to the cinema	____%
renting a video / DVD	____%
reading a _____ / _____	100%
going for a _____	93%
going to a _____	____%
listening to the _____	71%
playing a _____	____%

3 According to the survey, which activities are the most/least popular? Which results are surprising/different from your country?

4 Look back at the phrases in exercises 1 and 2 and complete the diagrams below with verb + noun combinations. Pay attention to phrases which have *the*, *a*, *to* and *for*.

a (GOING TO) — the gym

b (GOING FOR A)

c (GOING + -ING) — swimming

d (PLAYING) — video games

e (DOING)

f (other verbs) — renting a video

5 Work with a new partner. Make a list of **six** leisure activities that you both do. Compare your list with other students. What are the differences?

> We both like going to the cinema.

Language focus 1
Revision of question forms

SPORTS AND GAMES

a **What** do the letters NBA mean?

b **Which** of these countries has never won the football World Cup: Argentina, England, France or Japan?

c **When** were the Olympic Games in Sydney, Australia?

d **What kind** of ball do they use in the game of rugby?

e **How often** do the Winter Olympics happen?

f **Where** does the sport of judo come from?

g **How many** spots are there on a dice?

h **Who** starts in a game of chess: the black player or the white player?

i **Why** are there fifty-two cards in a normal pack?

1 Discuss the following questions.

- Which sports and games are popular in your country? Make a list of ten.
- Which sports do you play?
- Which sports do you watch on TV?
- Do you play any games like chess or cards?

2 **MD** How much do you know about sports and games? Answer as many of the questions in the quiz as you can in **five** minutes.

3 **T1.2** Listen and check your answers. How many questions did you answer correctly?

Grammar

Question words

Look at the question words in bold in exercise 2. Which question word(s) do we use to ask about:

1 a person? ___who___
2 a place? _____
3 a thing? _____ / _____
4 a time? _____
5 a period of time? _____
6 the class or type of thing? _____
7 the number of times you do something?
   _____
8 the way you do something? _____

Word order in questions

Put the words in the correct order to make questions.

1 good at / Is / James / sport ?
2 football / play / your friends / Do ?
3 start / the match / does / When ?

▶ Read Language summaries A and B on page 148.

(handwritten notes)
- page 8 & 9 Cutting Edge
- Present Style people des
- how not to learn English
- Short autobiographies

What colour is the shirt worn by the race leader in the Tour de France?

Practice

1 Find the correct answers to the questions in the boxes below.

a 1 **When** do you **play football**?
2 **Who** do you **play football with**?
3 **Where** do you **play football**?
4 **Why** do you **play football**?

My friends from college.	On Sunday mornings.
Because it's fun and it's good exercise.	In the local park.

b 1 **How often** do you **have English lessons**?
2 **How long** are the **lessons**?
3 **Which days** do you **have lessons**?
4 **How many teachers** do you **have**?

Two.	Twice a week.
Tuesdays and Thursdays.	Ninety minutes.

c 1 What **time** is it?
2 What **time** does the **train leave**?
3 What **day** is it?
4 What **date** is it **today**?

The sixteenth of May.	Monday.
Nearly three o'clock.	Five forty-five.

Pronunciation

1 **T1.3** Look at the list of questions in exercise 1. Notice the words which are stressed (these are in bold). Listen and practise the stressed words.

2 **T1.4** Now listen and practise the whole question.

2 a Write the questions for the answers below.

Example:
I get up **at nine o'clock** at the weekend.
What time do you get up at the weekend?

1 I go to the cinema **once a month**.
2 I come to school **by bus**.
3 My birthday is **in August**.
4 I like **rock and jazz**.

5 **My favourite colour** is blue.
6 There are **five** people in my family.
7 **My journey to school takes** about half an hour.
8 I would like to visit **India and Australia**.

b Ask the questions to your teacher or another student. Think of other questions as well.

> What time do you get up at the weekend?

> About seven o'clock.

> Seven o'clock! Why do you get up so early?

> Because I always go for a run before breakfast.

9

Reading

1 What are your favourite ways of keeping fit? What other ways of keeping fit are popular in your country?

2 **MD** What are the people in the pictures opposite doing? Read the three paragraphs and match them to one of the pictures.

UNUSUAL WAYS OF KEEPING FIT

KORFBALL

A mixture between handball and basketball, korfball is a fast, exciting game. The main difference is that men and women play on the same team. It's also a great way to keep fit! The game began in the Netherlands about 100 years ago, and there are now korfball
5 clubs in more than forty countries around the world. There are eight players on each team – four male and four female – and each player tries to throw the ball (similar to a soccer ball) into the 'goal' which is a bit like a basket but bigger. You can't touch your opponent, kick or run with the ball, and men can only attack against men and women
10 can only defend against women. A game lasts for sixty minutes and the teams change ends after every two goals. 'It's a terrific sport and a great way to meet people,' says Paul Dicks of the British Korfball Association.

TAI-CHI

15 Tai-Chi is a Chinese martial art which goes back thousands of years. It is different from most forms of exercise in that it is very gentle. It consists of a series of slow movements which you must do very carefully and exactly. The big advantage is that you can do it anywhere, anytime, and you don't need to be a member of a club or
20 use any expensive equipment – all you need is a qualified teacher! Tai-Chi fans say it is an excellent way of getting rid of stress. Early in the morning, you can see people doing the gentle movements of Tai-Chi in parks all over China, and it is now common in the West, too. So what's the secret of Tai-Chi? 'Mind and body working
25 together,' says one enthusiast.

GAMING FOR FITNESS

Most people don't see playing video games as a way of keeping fit. You sit on the floor, or on the sofa, you look at the screen … and the only part of your body that moves is your thumb. But that's all
30 changing … Thanks to a brand-new game from Japan called Dance Dance Revolution, gamers are now getting onto the exercise floor. In this case, the floor is a grid of nine squares. You put one foot in the centre and move your other foot in time to the dance music that gets faster and faster as you go through the levels. 'Most gamers
35 just want to go to a fantasy world when they play a video game, but why not have games which are physical as well?' says one DDR fan. So, who knows? Perhaps the gamers in the future will be fit and healthy people – thanks to Dance Dance Revolution.

3 Read the text and make a note of the following for each activity.

- Where it began
- When it began
- Adjectives/Phrases to describe it

4 Here are some phrases from the texts. What do the words in bold refer to?

a **It's** also a great way to keep fit! (line 3)
b **It's** a terrific sport and a great way to meet people … (line 11)
c … **it** is very gentle. (line 16)
d … **it** is an excellent way of getting rid of stress … (line 21)
e … you can do **it** anywhere, anytime … (line 18)
f … when **they** play a video game … (line 35)

5 Work in pairs. Discuss these questions.

- Would you like to try any of these ways of keeping fit? Why?
- Do you know of any other unusual ways of keeping fit?

Language focus 2
Present simple

1 Look at the photos below of three sportspeople. Can you guess who:

a has a big lunch (with lots of beer) and then goes to sleep for a few hours?
b doesn't eat very much?
c runs 8 km at least four times a week?
d trains for eight hours every day?
e usually trains before breakfast?
f weighs about 40 kg?
g weighs about 175 kg?
h is 1.5 m tall?
i is 1.95 m tall?
j earns about $50,000 a week?
k receives money from his/her parents every month?

2 `T1.5` Listen and check your answers. Whose life sounds the most difficult? Why?

Grammar

Present simple

1 Which of the following sentences describes:
 • a habit? • something that is always true?
 a *Ania **comes** from Lublin in Poland.*
 b *He **has** a big lunch and then **goes** to sleep for a few hours.*

2 Put each sentence into:
 • the question form. • the negative form.

How often?

1 The phrases below tell us how often things happen. Match the two halves of each phrase.

every	a week
on	Sundays
five times	month

2 Here are some more phrases that tell us how often things happen. Number them from 1 (most often) to 6 (least often).

> sometimes   often   usually   always 1   never   occasionally

---

▶ Read Language summaries C and D on page 148.

Ania, from Poland, is a champion gymnast.

Toshi, from Japan, is training to be a sumo wrestler.

João, from Brazil, is a professional footballer. He plays for a top Italian club.

Practice

1 Use the prompts below to make more sentences about the three athletes on page 11.

Example:
eat / Ania / a healthy diet / always
Ania always eats a healthy diet.

a   for many hours / all of them / train / every day
b   much money / Ania and Toshi / not earn
c   Ania / at seven / get up / usually
d   never / before midnight / go to bed / she
e   live in / Toshi / a special training camp called a *Heya*
f   on the floor / he / sleep / often
g   lots of fan letters / receive / every week / he
h   not play / João / in every match
i   two sports cars / own / he
j   miss / he / his family in Brazil
k   phone / about four times a week / he / his mother

2 a You are going to interview your partner. Work in groups, A and B.

Group A looks at the text below.
Group B looks at page 140.

Complete the gaps with *are you?* or *do you?*

HOW ENERGETIC ARE YOU?

1   .... usually get up as soon as you wake up?

2   .... slow getting ready in the morning, or .... usually leave the house quickly?

3   .... walk to school or work, or .... go by car or bus?

4   How often .... run upstairs?

5   .... often sleepy after lunch?

6   .... energetic when you come home in the evening, or usually tired?

7   How often .... stay up very late or all night?

b Work in pairs with a person from the other group. Ask and answer the questions.

> What time do you usually get up?

> Normally about half-past six. How about you?

Task: Compile a fact file
Preparation: reading

1 Look at the pictures of Orlando Bloom. Do you know why he is famous?

Either Make a list of **five** things you know about Orlando Bloom (films he has made, nationality, age, etc.).

Or Write **five** questions about Orlando Bloom (Where was he born? Is he married?, etc.).

2 MD Read the fact file about Orlando Bloom. Either check the information you wrote or find the answers to your questions.

3 Work out what questions the interviewer asked Orlando Bloom.

Example:
Question: *What's your full name?*
Answer: *Orlando Bloom.*

Task: speaking

1 You are going to interview another student in your class for a fact file like the one on page 13. You can add extra topics if you want to. Spend a few minutes planning and practising your questions.

▶ Useful language

ORLANDO BLOOM FACT FILE

FULL NAME	Orlando Bloom.
JOB	Actor.
NICKNAMES	Orli, O.B.
BORN	January 13th 1977, Canterbury, England.
HEIGHT	1.80 m.
HAIR COLOUR	Brown.
FAMILY	Mother, Sonia. One sister, Samantha – two years older than him. His father died when he was only four.
RELATIONSHIP	Girlfriend – Kate Bosworth.
EDUCATION	Attended St Edmund's School in Canterbury and the Guildhall School of Music and Drama, London.
HOBBIES	'When I was a kid, I wanted to become a professional football player – but I wasn't good enough. Today I'm a fan of Manchester United. I like sports like bungee-jumping, biking and surfing.'
PETS	'When I phone home, the first thing I want to know is how our dog Maude is.'
FAVOURITE FOODS	'Anything without meat – I'm a vegetarian. When I go out to eat, I mostly have pizza or pasta.'
FAVOURITE BANDS	'I'm not up-to-date. My favourites are people like David Gray and Bob Dylan!'
FAVOURITE CLOTHES	'My favourite clothes make is GAP.'
FAVOURITE FILM(S)	*Stand By Me, Amélie.*
HERO	'Johnny Depp. He's cool!'
AMBITIONS	'I'd like to be in different kinds of movies – not just action!'

2 Work in pairs with someone you don't normally work with in class. Ask and answer the questions to complete your fact files.

FACT FILE

FULL NAME	
JOB	
NICKNAMES	
BORN	
HEIGHT	
HAIR COLOUR	
FAMILY	
EDUCATION	
HOBBIES	
PETS	
FAVOURITE FOODS	
FAVOURITE BANDS	
FAVOURITE CLOTHES	
FAVOURITE FILM(S)	
HERO	
AMBITIONS	

3 Tell the class **two** things you discovered about your partner.

Useful language

What's your … (full name)?

What are … (your ambitions)?

How old/tall …?

When/Where … (were you born)?

When/Where did you … (go to school)?

Have you got … (a nickname/any pets)?

Who is your … (hero/favourite singer)?

Tell me about your … (family/hobbies).

What about …?

Optional writing

Write your fact file, and put it on the wall for other students to read.

In the street

Filling in a form at the bank

In a restaurant

In the classroom

In a shop

When you start talking to someone for the first time

Real life
Questions you can't live without

1 Look at the pictures above. Discuss which questions in the box below you might hear or ask in each situation.

What's your date of birth?	Where are you from?
How long are you going to stay?	What time is it?
Where's the nearest (bank)?	Can I help you?
Which part of (Poland) are you from?	Where are the toilets, please?
Sorry, could you repeat that, please?	Do you speak English?
How much does this cost?	How do you spell ...?
Can we have the bill, please?	Anything else?

2 a **T1.6** Listen to **three** conversations. Match the conversations to three of the situations above.

b Listen again. Tick (✓) the questions from the box that you hear.

Pronunciation

1 **T1.7** Listen and write down the **eight** questions.

2 Look at the tapescript on page 162 to check.

3 Notice that when we ask questions beginning with *When, Where*, etc., our voice usually goes down at the end of the sentence. Listen again and practise saying the questions.

STUDY...

Using the mini-dictionary (1): Checking word class

1 **Add more words to the lists below.**

Adjectives
hot, cold _____, _____

Adverbs
quickly, slowly, _____, _____

Modal verbs
might, must, _____, _____

Nouns
newspaper, time, _____, _____

Verbs
play, enjoy, _____, _____

Prepositions
for, to, _____, _____

2a **The sentences below are from the text on page 10. What 'word class' are the words in bold?**

fit /fɪt/ *adjective* when your body is in a healthy and strong condition: *What do you do to keep fit?* • *Will plays a lot of tennis – he's very fit.*

1 It's also a great way to keep **fit**!
2 ... men can only attack **against** men ...
3 ... women **can** only defend against women.
4 You can't **kick** ... or run with the ball ...
5 ... movements which you must do very carefully and **exactly**.
6 ... you don't need ... any expensive **equipment** ...
7 ... you can see people doing the **gentle** movements of Tai-Chi ...
8 ... the only part of your body that moves is your **thumb**.
9 ... gamers are now getting **onto** the exercise floor.

b **Now check your answers in the mini-dictionary.**

PRACTISE...

1 Question words ☐

Complete the questions with question words.

a '_____ were you born?' 'In 1986.'

b '_____ did the journey take?' 'About two hours.'

c _____ colour do you prefer: red or green?

d '_____ is that young woman?' 'That's my sister!'

e '_____ did you get here today?' 'I walked.'

f '_____ music do you like?' 'R & B. How about you?'

g _____ does this word mean?

h '_____ do you live?' 'In Beijing.'

i '_____ colour are his eyes?' 'Blue.'

j '_____ did you come here this evening?'
'Because I wanted to talk to you.'

k '_____ do you go to the gym?' 'Every day.'

l '_____ children does he have?' 'Three, I think.'

▶ **Need to check? Language summary A, page 148.**

2 Word order in questions ☐

Put the words in the correct order to make questions.

a at the concert / be / tomorrow night / Will / you ?

b Cristina / Does / like / skateboarding ?

c Can / football / play / tomorrow night / you ?

d late / the train / this morning / was / Why ?

e did / have lunch / today / Where / you ?

f at home / Is / today / your brother ?

▶ **Need to check? Language summary B, page 148.**

3 Present simple ☐

a Put the following sentences into the negative form.

1 I like wet days.

2 My brother lives in the town centre.

b Put the following sentences into the question form.

1 You know my cousin.

2 Your friend likes snowboarding.

c Change the sentences to She ...

1 I speak perfect Spanish.

2 I fly home once a year.

3 I have lunch at home.

4 I catch the early train to work.

▶ **Need to check? Language summary C, page 148.**

4 How often ...? ☐

Put the words in brackets into the correct place.

a We go to our holiday home a month. (once)

b I go for a walk before going to bed. (always)

c I am tired when I get home. (usually)

d We go to the beach day in summer. (every)

e Juana is late for class. (never)

f We go swimming before breakfast. (often)

▶ **Need to check? Language summary D, page 148.**

5 Leisure activities ☐

Match the word(s) in A with the word(s) in B to make phrases.

A	B
a play	1 a video / DVD
b go to	2 run
c rent	3 yoga
d go for a	4 the gym
e go	5 a video game
f do	6 swimming

▶ **Need to check? Vocabulary, page 7.**

6 Questions you can't live without ☐

Match the phrases in A with the phrases in B to make complete questions.

A	B
a Anything	1 are you from?
b Can we have	2 the bill, please?
c How do	3 does this cost?
d How much	4 else?
e Can I	5 help you?
f Where's	6 the nearest bank, please?
g Which part of Mexico	7 repeat that, please?
h Could you	8 you spell that?

▶ **Need to check? Real life, page 14.**

Pronunciation spot

The sounds /w/ and /v/

1 **T1.8** The letters 'w' and 'wh' are usually pronounced /w/ in English. Listen to the sound.

T1.9 The letter 'v' is pronounced /v/. Listen to the sound.

2 **Write in the missing letters in the words below: 'w', 'wh', or 'v'.**

a _ eekend

b _ ideo games

c _ en

d _ isiting

e _ omen

f _ egetarian

g _ atch

h _ ords

i _ ich

j _ ery

3 **T1.10** Listen and check. Practise saying the words, paying attention to the /v/ or /w/ sounds.

REMEMBER!

Look back at the areas you have practised. Tick the ones you feel confident about. Now try the MINI-CHECK on page 158 to check what you know.

Important firsts

- ▶ Past simple
- ▶ Time phrases often used in the past: *at, on, in, ago*
- ▶ Vocabulary: Words to describe feelings
- ▶ Pronunciation: *-ed* endings, Word stress
- ▶ Wordspot: *feel*
- ▶ Task: Tell a first time story
- ▶ Writing: Linking ideas in narrative

Language focus 1
Past simple

1 How often do you watch television? Which programmes / TV channels do you prefer? Which of these do you sometimes/never watch?

- soap operas
- adverts
- cookery programmes

2 **T2.1** **MD** Read and listen to the first part of the article about some TV firsts. What was the nationality of:

- the 'father' of TV?
- the inventor of TV?
- the first person to appear on TV?
- the first TV chef?

TV Firsts

a The first person to appear on TV was William Taynton – a young Englishman who worked with Scottish inventor, John Logie Baird, the inventor of television.

b Many people call Vladimir Zworykin, a Russian who went to live in the United States in 1919, 'the father of television'. He invented the first 'electronic' TV in 1929.

c In 1936, the BBC (the British Broadcasting Corporation) made its first TV programmes. Not many people watched them as not many people had a TV!

d Cookery programmes were popular even in the1930s. Frenchman Marcel Boulestin became the first TV chef in 1937.

▶ Read Language summary A on page 149.

Practice

1 **T2.2** Read the rest of the article *TV Firsts* below. Complete the gaps with the correct past form of the verbs in the box. Then listen and check your answers.

be (×2) begin buy come cost last make

a The first TV soap opera _____ in 1947. Its name _____ *A Woman to Remember*.

b The first TV advert – for a Bulova clock – _____ just 20 seconds and it _____ only $9 to make!

c Colour TV _____ to Europe in the 1960s. The first colour TVs _____ very expensive, so not many people _____ them.

d The Japanese company JVC _____ the world's first VHS video recorders in the mid-1970s.

More to enjoy

Motorola TV

It's enough to turn anyone's head. Takes quite a picture to steal the stage from a young lady like this. Motorola TV does it with the sharpest, brightest picture ever. Just tap the on-off button. Picture and sound come on, already tuned. Sit wherever you please — the set swivels to face you. In so many ways, you get More to enjoy from Motorola—World's largest exclusive electronics manufacturer.

McE

---

1 **MD** Look at the pairs of regular Past simple forms below. If necessary, check the meaning in your mini-dictionary.

2 **T2.3** Listen to the pronunciation of the past forms below. Notice the different pronunciation of the -ed endings.
a /d/ called appeared
b /t/ looked worked
c /ɪd/ ended lasted

3 **T2.4** Listen to the pronunciation of some more past forms. If the pronunciation of -ed is the same, write S. If it is different, write D.
a worked watched S
b opened invented
c asked stopped
d travelled started
e lived closed
f walked wanted
g laughed arrived

4 Practise saying the verbs. Pay attention to the pronunciation of -ed.

---

2 Complete the questions in the quiz with *did, was* or *were*.

★ ★ Important Firsts ★ ★

1 Where .... the first female police officer from?
a London   b Los Angeles   c Rome

2 *Toy Story* was the world's first 100% computer-generated movie. When .... it come out?
a in 1990   b in 1995   c in 2000

3 What .... the first animal in space?
a a cat   b a dog   c a monkey

4 Where .... the world's first traffic lights?
a in Australia   b in Germany   c in the USA

5 Where .... the Tamagotchi – the world's first virtual pet – come from?
a China   b Japan   c Taiwan

6 Who .... the first man to walk on the moon?
a Neil Armstrong   b Neil Legstrong   c Neil Headstrong

7 Where .... the first McDonald's in Europe open?
a in France   b in Germany   c in the UK

8 Where .... the first World Cup finals of the twenty-first century?
a in Argentina and Chile   b in Japan and Korea
c in Portugal and Spain

---

3 How many questions can you answer? Discuss your answers in pairs. Then check your answers on page 140.

4 **a** Write **one** sentence about each of the following. Three of the sentences should be true and two should be false.

* something you did yesterday
* a place you went to last year
* something you bought last week/month
* something you didn't do last year
* something you didn't like when you were a child

b Read out your sentences to a partner. Your partner decides which sentences are true and which are false.

> Yesterday, I went swimming with my brother.

> Yes, that's true.

c Who guessed the most answers correctly?

Language focus 2
Time phrases often used in the past: *at, on, in, ago*

1 Look at the sentences below. Which ones are true?

a I started learning English **six months ago**.
b The weather was hot **last weekend**.
c I had an English lesson **on Monday morning**.
d I began school **in the 1990s**.
e My birthday was **in November last year**.
f I was at home **two hours ago**. 1
g I was in bed **at eight o'clock this morning**.
h I played football **yesterday afternoon**.
i I was born **in 1985**.
j I went to a party **on January 1st this year**.
k People started using mobile phones **100 years ago**.
l Our teacher was born **in the nineteenth century**.

2 Number the phrases 1–12, starting with the most recent.

3 Rewrite the sentences so they are true for you.

Grammar

1 Complete the phrases with *in, on, at* or *ø*.
  a Times: ___ eight o'clock ___ 12.15 ___ midnight.
  b Days/Dates: ___ Wednesday ___ New Year's Day ___ June 14th
  c Months, seasons, years, decades, centuries: ___ June ___ winter ___ 1998 ___ the 1990s ___ the twenty-first century
  d Phrases with *last* and *yesterday*:
  I saw him ___ yesterday.
  We arrived ___ last night.
  They left ___ yesterday morning.

2 Which of these phrases is wrong with *ago*?
  ten weeks ago   a long time ago
  ten thousand years ago
  a few minutes ago   years ago
  the summer ago

▶ Read Language summary B on page 149.

Practice

1 T2.5 Listen and answer the questions a–j using the time phrases in the box in your answers.

2 Complete the sentences below with information about yourself. Then work in pairs and compare your sentences.

> The last exam I took was ...

> The last time I stayed up late was ...

> The last time I lost something important was ...

> The last wedding I went to was ...

> The last time I went for a run was ...

> The last long journey I went on was ...

> The last time I went to a restaurant was ...

> The last time I sang was ...

> The last video I rented was ...

> The last cup of tea/coffee I had was ...

> When did you last go to a wedding?

> The last wedding I went to was my sister's wedding about two years ago.

Vocabulary
Words to describe feelings

1 **MD** How do the people feel in each of the pictures? Choose one of the adjectives from the box. (There may be more than one answer.)

> angry bored disappointed embarrassed excited impatient
> in a good mood nervous relaxed scared surprised worried

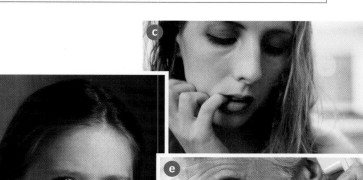

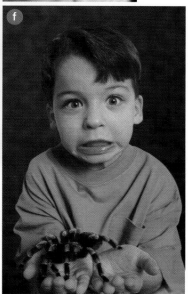

2 **T2.6** Listen to **eight** short conversations. Where are the speakers in each conversation? How do you think the second speaker feels in each case? Use one of the adjectives from exercise 1.

3 Use the words from exercise 1 to answer the questions below. Ask your partner the same questions.

How do you normally feel:

* when you are at home watching TV?
* just before an important exam?
* when you can't remember someone's name?
* if you have to speak in front of a lot people?
* if you have to wait for a long time in a shop?
* if you lose your purse/wallet?
* if you go to a big rock concert?
* if you miss your train or bus?
* if you see a big spider?
* if your English lesson is cancelled?

Pronunciation

T2.7 Listen to the words and mark the stress.

angry disappointed
embarrassed excited
impatient   in a good mood
nervous   relaxed
surprised   worried

Wordspot
feel

1 The diagram below shows some common uses of *feel*. Tick (✓) the phrases that you already know. Write (?) next to the ones you are not sure about.

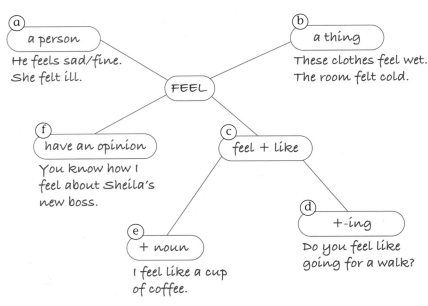

(a) a person
He feels sad/fine.
She felt ill.

(b) a thing
These clothes feel wet.
The room felt cold.

FEEL

(f) have an opinion
You know how I feel about Sheila's new boss.

(c) feel + like

(e) + noun
I feel like a cup of coffee.

(d) +-ing
Do you feel like going for a walk?

2 a Match a sentence from A with a sentence from B.

A
1 How's your mum today?
2 What do you feel like doing tonight?
3 What time did you go to bed last night?
4 How do you feel about our new boss?
5 Ooh, your hands feel cold!
6 Do you feel like a rest after your journey?
7 How was work?
8 I feel terrible about what I said to Tina.

B
a Oh, before nine. I felt really tired.
b Don't worry – I'm sure she wasn't upset.
c No, it's OK, I slept a lot on the plane.
d Oh, she's feeling much better, thanks.
e Oh, terrible. Sometimes I feel like walking out.
f I think he's OK. He's got some good ideas.
g I don't know … what's on at the cinema?
h I know – I left my gloves at home.

b (T2.8) Listen and check your answers.

3 Work in pairs. Student B closes his/her book and Student A reads out a sentence from list A above. Student B tries to remember the answer from list B above. Then change over.

Task: Tell a first time story
Preparation: listening

1 a Do you have a good memory?
How many things can you remember? Tick (✓) the appropriate boxes.

- your first day at school, college or work ☐
- the first time you travelled alone or went abroad ☐
- the first time you met someone important in your life ☐
- the first time you drove a car ☐
- your first English lesson ☐
- your first pet/car ☐
- the first time you went shopping or bought something alone ☐
- another important first ☐

b Which of these do the pictures show?

2 (T2.9) **a** You will hear two people, Helen and Josh, talking about the first time they did something. Listen and say which pictures illustrate their stories.

b (MD) Can you remember which phrases below come from each story? What did Helen and Josh say about these things?

crowded	embarrassing
secondary school	a get together
a video camera	a big smile

3 (T2.9) Listen to the stories again and answer these questions.

a Where and when did it happen?
b Who else was in the story?
c How did they feel?
d What happened in the end?

Task: speaking

1 Choose **one** of the two tasks below.

Task 1 Talk about your own important firsts. (See below.)

Task 2 Tell the story of an important first using some pictures. (See page 141.)

Task 1

1 Choose two or three 'important firsts' from Preparation for task, exercise 1 that you can remember.

2 Spend a few minutes thinking about your answers to these questions.

- Which 'important first' are you describing?
- Where/When did this happen?
- How old were you at the time?
- Who was with you?
- How did you feel before/after?

▶ Useful language a

2 Work in small groups. Listen/Tell your stories to each other. Which was:

- the funniest story?
- the saddest story?
- the strangest story?

Useful language

a Telling your own story

I'll never forget the first time I …

I remember my first / the first time I …

I was … years old at the time.

I was in …

I was with my …

I felt very … because …

At first …

Then …

In the end …

Writing
Linking ideas in narrative

1 **a** Read what Marcos wrote about his first trip abroad and complete the text below with the phrases 1–9.

1 <u>and</u> I went with three friends
2 because for all four of us it was our first time away from home
3 and I bought a silver ring for my sister
4 because I couldn't find it when I got on the coach that evening!
5 but I got up early and went to
6 so we decided to travel by coach.
7 but we didn't mind
8 so we went to Hyde Park for a game of football
9 then we went shopping in Oxford Street

b Underline the linking words in exercise 1a.
Example:
1 <u>and</u>

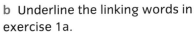

The first time I went abroad was when I went to London. It was in the summer holidays about five or six years ago (a) _____. The plane and train were quite expensive, (b) _____. We left at five o'clock in the morning and the journey to London took about sixteen hours (c) _____: we were all very excited (d) _____.

We stayed in London for three days, in a youth hostel not far from the centre. While we were there we walked a lot. First we went to see all the famous sites – Big Ben, Piccadilly Circus, Buckingham Palace, (e) _____. On the last morning my friends stayed in bed late, (f) _____ Camden Market. You can buy all kinds of jewellery and clothes there, (g) _____. It was really hot and sunny in the afternoon, (h) _____. Unfortunately, I think the ring fell out of my pocket during the game, (i) _____.

I've been back to London several times since then, but I don't think I'll ever feel as excited as I did that first time.

2 Write the story that you told in the Task on page 21. Use at least **three** linking words.

Using the mini-dictionary (2): Word stress

1 Write the number of syllables next to each word in the box.

angry colourful electronic expensive popular inventor programme

2 In the mini-dictionary, (') appears before the syllable which has the main stress. Look up the words in the box in the mini-dictionary and mark the main stress.

angry /ˈæŋgri/ *adjective* if you are **angry**, you have strong feelings because you are not pleased about something: *My parents will be angry if I am late.* • *My flatmate* **makes me angry** *when he doesn't help with the housework.*

Pronunciation spot
Stress and the /ə/ sound

1 T2.10 In many words, syllables which do not have the stress are pronounced /ə/. Listen to these examples.
winter police remember

2 T2.11 Mark the stress on the words below. Then listen and check. Mark the /ə/ sounds.
inventor afternoon November summer Japanese television person colour

3 Practise saying the words, paying attention to the stress and the /ə/ sound.

PRACTISE...

1 Past simple ☐

Put the following sentences into the Past simple.

a The programmes are extremely popular.

b Do you watch television?

c I take my exams.

d My brother stays up late.

e I don't get home until midnight.

f I buy presents for everyone in my family.

g We watch a video in the evening.

h Renate sings beautifully.

i The match begins at 8.30.

j I feel so tired.

▶ **Need to check? Language summary A, page 149.**

2 Time phrases with *at*, *on*, *in* and ø ☐

Put the phrases in the box in the correct place in the table.

a year ago	2002	a minute ago	the 1990s
last night	June 18th	last year	eleven o'clock
Friday afternoon		the twentieth century	

at	on	in	ø
			a year ago

▶ **Need to check? Language summary B, page 149.**

3 Words to describe feelings ☐

Put the letters in bold in the correct order to make words to describe feelings.

a I was so **e r v u s o n** before I took my driving test I couldn't speak.

b My sister was really **d e c r a s** of the dark as a small child.

c Everyone was very **d i e p o n d i t s a p** when we lost the match.

d I was really in a **d o g o d o m o** when I got home.

e Are you **p u r d r i e s s** by what she said?

f Donna is very **i r o d r e w** about her exams next week.

g I was so **r e d o b** I nearly fell asleep.

h The children are very **t e x i d e c** – we're going on holiday tonight.

i I felt **b r a s s r a m e e d** at making such a stupid mistake.

▶ **Need to check? Vocabulary, page 19.**

4 *feel* ☐

Choose the correct alternative.

a I'd like to know how people feel about / for / of the new plans.

b Whenever I remember what happened, I always feel sad / sadly / unhappily.

c How are you today? Are you feeling as well as / better / like better now?

d Let's rent a video: I don't feel like go / going / to go out tonight.

e After eating so much food, I began to feel like bad / badly / ill.

f I took a couple of aspirin, and an hour later I felt fine / finely / the finest.

▶ **Need to check? Wordspot, page 20.**

5 Linking words ☐

Complete the sentences with *and*, *so*, *because*, *then* or *but*.

a We didn't have any money _____ we couldn't go to a restaurant.

b He closed all the doors and windows, and _____ he left the house.

c I was feeling very tired, _____ I went to bed very early.

d Romina is usually on time, _____ tonight she arrived half an hour late.

e I couldn't sleep _____ there was a party next door.

f I phoned all my friends _____ invited them to come to my house.

g It was very cold outside, _____ I put on my warmest clothes.

h We couldn't go out _____ the weather was so bad.

i He looked through the window for a minute or two, _____ went inside.

▶ **Need to check? Writing, page 22.**

REMEMBER!

Look back at the areas you have practised. Tick the ones you feel confident about. Now try the MINI-CHECK on page 158 to check what you know!

At rest, at work

- ▶ *should, shouldn't*
- ▶ *can, can't, have to, don't have to*
- ▶ Vocabulary: Daily routines, Jobs
- ▶ Reading: *Early to bed, early to rise*
- ▶ Pronunciation: *should/shouldn't, can/can't,* Polite intonation in requests
- ▶ Listening: Training to be a circus performer
- ▶ Task: Choose the right job
- ▶ Real life: Making requests and asking for permission

Vocabulary
Daily routines

1 What time of day do you like best?
Why? Compare your ideas with a partner.

2  Check the meaning of the phrases in bold in your mini-dictionary. Do these things normally happen in the morning, the afternoon or the evening? Put them in order for a normal day.

- you **dream** about something
- you **fall asleep**
- you feel tired
- you get dressed
- you get into bed
- you get out of bed
- you have a bath/shower
- you have something to eat
- you **set** your alarm
- you **switch off** the alarm
- you **turn off** the light
- you **wake up**
- your alarm **goes off**
- you go to school/work
- you come home

3 What time do you usually do these things? Find out about your partner. How similar are your daily routines?

Reading and speaking

1 Discuss the following questions with a partner.

- Do you ever have problems falling asleep or getting up in the morning? How about other people you live with?
- What helps you to fall asleep?
- Do you ever wake up in the middle of the night?
- What helps you to wake up in the morning?
- Do you often remember your dreams?
- Do you know anyone who:
  – snores?
  – talks in their sleep?
  – sleepwalks?

2  The text opposite gives advice about falling asleep and waking up. Write *F* next to the items about falling asleep and *W* next to the items about waking up.

Early to Bed, Early to Rise ...

Get an alarm clock, and put it as far away from the bed as you can. If you don't have to get out of bed to turn it off, then it's no good having one. And remember that two is better than one ... but set the second clock ten minutes later than the first one, and put it in the same place as the first one! W

Don't spend longer than thirty minutes trying to fall asleep. If you can't get to sleep after half an hour, get up and do something quiet, like reading. Only go back to bed when you feel tired.

Drink a glass of warm milk fifteen minutes before you go to bed – it helps you to relax – or have a light snack. But avoid coffee, tea or alcohol: they contain chemicals which will make it difficult for you to sleep.

Make sure all the clocks in the house are ten minutes fast before you go to bed (and try to forget you did this when you wake up the next morning).

Get a friend to phone you early in the morning. And hope that your friend is better at waking up than you are ... and is able to have an interesting conversation at 7 a.m. to help you wake up.

Go to bed earlier. It may be difficult at first, but they say that an hour of sleep before midnight is as good as two hours after midnight.

Have a warm bath – it's a great way to relax. But you shouldn't stay in there too long. More than twenty minutes and you will lose all your energy. And the bath isn't the best place to fall asleep!

Listen to some music – or even specially recorded CDs of relaxing sounds like waves. However, if you have to get up and turn the cassette player off when the music finishes, it's not going to work!

Pretend your alarm has gone off. Imagine you have to get up, have a (cold!) shower, make breakfast, etc. The more you imagine it, the more you want to go to sleep!

nice, calming music will make you want to stay in bed even longer ... but the horrible sound of static (the electronic noise you get between stations) is enough to get anyone out of bed ... to turn it off!

3
Look at the phrases below from the text. Match the words/phrases in bold in A with the words/phrases which mean the same in B.

A
a   **Get** an alarm clock
b   have a **light** snack.
c   ten minutes **fast**
d   **Get** a friend to phone you
e   **they** say that an hour of sleep
f   it's a **great** way to relax
g   But **avoid** coffee, tea or alcohol

B
1   Buy / Set / Switch on
2   cheap / late-night / small
3   after the correct time / at the correct time / before the correct time
4   Ask / Find / Look for
5   people in general / your friends / your parents
6   big / expensive / wonderful
7   drink / do not have / try

4   Discuss these questions.

• Which advice do you think is most useful?
• Can you think of any other ways to get to sleep / wake up?
• Have you ever got into trouble because you didn't get up in time for school/work?

Language focus 1
should, shouldn't

1 **MD** Bruce is studying for some very important exams. Look at his room and find the things in the box.

the bin   some rubbish   an ashtray   a cigarette end   his files
his notes   a computer game   a dressing gown

2 Tick (✓) the statements you agree with and put a cross (✗) next to the ones you disagree with.

a   He **should** start work earlier.
b   He **should** tidy up his notes.
c   His coffee cup **shouldn't** be on the computer.
d   He **should** get dressed before he starts studying.
e   He **shouldn't** listen to the radio when he's studying.

Grammar

1 Underline the correct ending to the rule.
We use *should/shouldn't* when:
a   it is/isn't necessary to do something.
b   it is/isn't a good idea to do something.

2 We use *should/shouldn't* to give or ask for advice (often with *I think …*)
I think you **should** get up earlier.
You shouldn't leave your coffee on the computer.
Should I revise everything?

3 We can also give advice like this:
Why don't you **get up earlier**?
Try **getting up earlier**.

► Read Language summary A on page 149.

Practice

1 a Make **eight** more sentences about what Bruce should/shouldn't do.

b **T3.1** Listen and compare your ideas with the ones on the recording.

Pronunciation

1 Notice the pronunciation of *should* and *shouldn't*. Which is stressed in the sentence?
He should tidy up his books.
   /ʃʊd/
He shouldn't smoke so much.
   /ʃʊdənt/

2 **T3.1** Listen again and practise the sentences.

2 Read about the situations below. Discuss what each person should/shouldn't do.

Carla is a student and she's very bad with money. She spends everything on clothes and going out and doesn't have any money to buy books, etc. Her parents are annoyed with her and don't give her any extra money, but Carla's grandmother gives her extra money every time she sees her.

Examples:
Carla should try to spend less money.
Carla's grandmother shouldn't give her any more money.

Chris recently started a new job in the advertising industry. The money is good, but he has to work very long hours. He never goes out with his girlfriend in the evening anymore, saying he is too tired and all he wants to do is stay at home and watch videos. Chris' girlfriend says he must choose between her and the job.

Oliver dreams of becoming a professional footballer. He spends all his time training and playing for his local amateur team. He is now eighteen years old, and he wants to leave school and become a professional footballer. His parents want Oliver to go to university and study to be a doctor.

Language focus 2
can, can't, have to, don't have to

1 **T3.2** Mayo is in London, studying to be something unusual. Look at the pictures above. What do you think she is studying? Check your answer by listening to the first part of the interview.

2 **T3.3** Listen to the rest of the interview. Mark the following sentences *True* or *False*.

a   You need a lot of special qualifications to start her course.
b   She is studying more than one subject.
c   She only studies in the afternoon and evenings.
d   There are no holidays.
e   She is going to do a show before she graduates.
f   All the other people on her course are English.

Grammar

1 Look at the sentences below from the interview. Complete the sentences with *have to, don't have to, can* or *can't*. Then check the tapescript on page 163.
  a   *You _____ have any special qualifications.*
  b   *You _____ be very enthusiastic.*
  c   *If you want to, you _____ stay later in the evenings.*
  d   *There are a lot of Spanish people, but I _____ speak Spanish.*

2 Complete the sentences below with *can, can't, have to* or *don't have to*.
  a   _____ means that something is necessary.
  b   _____ means that you are able to do something.
  c   _____ means that something is not necessary.
  d   _____ means that you are not able to do something.

▶ Read Language summary B on page 149.

Practice

1 Look at the list of activities below. Think about a normal day for you. Write sentences with *have to, don't have to, can* or *can't*.

a   wait for other people to use the bathroom.
   I don't have to wait for other people to use the bathroom.
b   leave home after eight o'clock
   I can leave home after eight o'clock if I want to.
c   catch the bus or train

d   make my own breakfast
e   study in the evening
f   send e-mails
j   cook a meal for my family

h   work in the evening
i   stay out after eleven in the evening
g   sit in front of a computer
k   go to the supermarket

2 Compare your answers with another student.

Pronunciation

T3.4 Listen to **eight** sentences. Does each speaker say *can* or *can't*? Look at the tapescript on page 164 to check.

Vocabulary
Jobs

1 **MD** Add one job to each letter below. Use the pictures to help you.

A is for **a**rchitect and …
B is for **b**arman and …
C is for **c**ivil servant and …
D is for **d**octor and …
F is for **f**armer and …
J is for **j**ournalist and …
L is for **l**awyer and …
N is for **n**urse and …
P is for **p**sychologist and …
S is for **s**hop assistant and …
T is for **t**axi driver and …
W is for **w**riter and …

2 Look at the sentences below. Which job(s) do they refer to?

- You can make a lot of money doing this.
- This can be dangerous.
- You have to study a long time to do this.
- You can work at home.
- This is a job where you can really help people.
- You have to be very patient to do this.
- You have to be good at languages to do this.
- You have to be very good with people to do this.

3 Think of a job, but do not say what it is. Describe the job by saying what you *can/can't* or *have to* do. Can other students guess what job you are describing?

4 Divide the jobs in exercise 1 into the three categories below. Compare your ideas with other students. Which jobs are the most/least popular?

- Jobs I'd like to do
- Jobs I wouldn't like to do
- I know someone who does this job

Task: Choose the right job
Preparation: listening

T3.5 Listen to the four people below talking about themselves and complete the column about interests in the table below.

Morgan, 17, from Australia   Luke, 20, from England

Carmen, 26, from Mexico   Jong, 23, from South Korea

Task: speaking

1 a Look at the jobs on page 28 and think of ideas of your own. Suggest two or three possible jobs for each person. Complete the Possible Jobs and Reasons columns in the table below.

b Compare your answers in groups. Do you agree on the best job for each person?

► Useful language a and b

2 Present your ideas to the class. Do other groups agree?

3 **T3.6** Listen to each person talking about the job they want to do in real life. Are you surprised by any of their answers?

Useful language

a Comparing your ideas

I think (Morgan) should become a (nurse) because she can …

I (don't) think Carmen will be a good (librarian) because …

Jong is very (hard-working) so he'll be a good (accountant) or perhaps he should …

b Agreeing and disagreeing

What do you think?

Do you agree?

I'm not sure.

I don't know.

Maybe he should be a …

Person	Interests	Possible Jobs	Reasons
Morgan			
Luke			
Carmen			
Jong			

Real life
Making requests and asking for permission

1 **a** Look at the conversations below. Where are the people? What does each person want? Can you guess the missing phrases in each gap?

1 A: Yeah?
   B: Hello, _____ turn the music down, please? It's one o'clock and I'm trying to sleep.
   A: Oh, sorry. Is that better?
   B: Yes, _____. Perhaps I can get some sleep now. Good night.

2 A: I'm sorry, _____ leave early today? I'm going to take my cat to see the vet.
   B: You're going to take your cat to the vet? What's the matter with her then?
   A: Him. I don't know. That's why I'm going to take him to the vet's.
   B: Oh, I see. Sure, _____. Thanks for _____.

3 A: David, do you have your mobile phone with you?
   B: Um … yes. Why?
   A: _____ it, please? I need to make a quick call to my mother.
   B: OK, _____.

4 A: _____ change seats?
   B: Yes, all right. _____?
   A: I can't see because of the sun.
   B: OK, then. Why don't you sit there, next to Andrea.

b **T3.7** Listen to the conversations and check your answers. Which speakers are:

- making requests?
- asking for permission?

Pronunciation

1 It is very important to use the correct intonation when we make requests and ask for permission. Look at the tapescript on page 164.

2 **T3.8** Listen and repeat the sentences.

2 With a partner write four-line conversations for **four** of the situations below. Act out your best conversation for the class.

- It's very hot in the room and you would like to open the window.
- You need to borrow some money from a friend because you have lost your bus fare.
- Someone's mobile phone is always ringing during a film.
- You didn't understand the address someone gave you and you would like them to spell it for you.
- The person behind you is talking all the time during the lesson.
- You are watching the TV but you can't hear because the volume is very low. Your friend has the remote control.
- You would like someone to take a photo of you and your friend in front of a famous monument.
- You can't see the timetable at a train station because a stranger is standing in front of it.

STUDY...

Class rules

1 Here is a list of ideas for class rules. Tick the rules that you would like to see in class. Discuss which rules you have chosen with your class.

The teacher:

a should always begin and end the lesson on time.

b should correct all the students' mistakes.

c should give homework every week and return it quickly.

d should use the course book in every lesson.

e should speak slowly.

The students:

f should always listen carefully to the teacher, and to each other.

g should do all the homework which the teacher gives them.

h should be prepared to work in pairs/groups as well as listen to the teacher.

i should speak English as much as possible, and not their own language.

j should try to arrive on time, remember books and homework, etc.

2 Write a list of rules for teachers and students and put it on the classroom wall. See if you can keep to the rules for the rest of this course!

Pronunciation spot

Silent letters

1 Underline the silent letter/letters (letters which are not pronounced) in each word.

could   friend   half   hour
something   light   should
midnight   calm   interesting

2 [T3.9] Listen and check. Practise saying the words.

PRACTISE...

1 *should, shouldn't* and forms for giving advice ☐

Complete the sentences with one word only.

a _____ don't you ask that man for directions?

b You _____ try to speak English as much as possible in class.

c _____ putting a little salt in the water: it'll taste much better.

d You _____ worry so much. I'm sure everything will be OK.

e _____ I go to the hairdresser's or not? What do you think?

▶ **Need to check? Language summary A, page 149.**

2 *can, can't, have to, don't have to* ☐

Rewrite the phrases in bold using *can, can't, have to* or *don't have to*.

a **You are able to** leave early if you want to.

b **It's not necessary for you to** pay me back today.

c **Is it possible for my friend to** come, too?

d **Is it necessary to** carry my student card with me?

e **It's not possible for you to** see him at the moment.

▶ **Need to check? Language summary B, page 149.**

3 Daily routines ☐

Match the beginnings in box A with the endings in box B.

A

| fall   feel   get   get into   have a set   turn off   wake |

B

| the alarm   asleep   bed   dressed the light   shower   tired   up |

▶ **Need to check? Vocabulary, page 24.**

4 Jobs ☐

Write the name of the jobs next to the pictures.

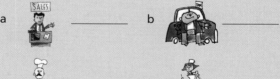
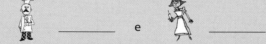

a _____   b _____   c _____

d _____   e _____   f _____

▶ **Need to check? Vocabulary, page 24.**

5 Making requests and asking for permission ☐

Put the words in the correct order to make questions.

a you / please / Could / the / open / window ?

b smoke / I / mind / Do / if / you ?

c borrow / I / your / Can / please / newspaper ?

d later / back / Could / phone / you ?

▶ **Need to check? Real life, page 30.**

REMEMBER!

Look back at the areas you have practised. Tick the ones you feel confident about.
Now try the MINI-CHECK on page 158 to check what you know!

Special occasions

- ▶ Present continuous and Present simple
- ▶ Present continuous for future arrangements
- ▶ Vocabulary: Dates and special occasions
- ▶ Pronunciation: Dates, Polite intonation
- ▶ Reading: *Birthday traditions around the world*
- ▶ Listening: New Year in two different cultures
- ▶ Wordspot: *day*
- ▶ Task: Talk about a personal calendar
- ▶ Real life: Phrases for special occasions
- ▶ Writing: Write an invitation

Vocabulary and speaking
Dates and special occasions

1 Which are your favourite months of the year? Why?

2 a Which of these days do people celebrate in your country? Which month are they in?

Chinese New Year	Father's Day
St Valentine's Day	American Independence Day
Mother's Day	Halloween
Easter	Christmas Day
May Day	New Year's Eve

b **T4.1** Listen and make notes about when they happen in the UK/USA.

Pronunciation

1 **T4.2** Listen and mark the stress on the months, like this:

J́anuary February April July August
September October November December

2 **T4.3** Listen and write down the dates. Look at the tapescript on page 164 to check.

3 Listen again and practise saying the dates. Pay attention to the pronunciation of 'th'.

April <u>the</u> first   July the fif<u>th</u>
      /ð/   /θ/

---

3 a **MD** Match the word(s) in A with the word(s) in B to make phrases connected with special occasions.

	A	B
1	cook a	a cake
2	dress	cards to people
3	eat	flowers
4	exchange	late
5	have a day	out
6	invite people	presents
7	make	relatives
8	send	special meal
9	stay up	to your home
10	visit	up
11	buy	off work

b Which of these things do you / your family / your friends do on the special days in exercise 2a? Think of **one** other reason why people do these things.

Example:
You send a card when people get engaged.

The tradition of birthday parties started a long time ago. People thought that there was a special danger from evil spirits, so friends and family came together to bring good thoughts and wishes and even presents. At one time, only kings had birthday parties but as time went by, children and then adults began to have their own birthday celebrations. There are some traditions – such as sending birthday cards, blowing out the candles on a birthday cake and singing the 'Happy Birthday' song, that you can find almost anywhere, any time. Others are more specific to certain ages ... and certain countries.

Birthday Traditions around the World

1 In China, everyone celebrates their birthday on New Year's Day: they become one year older on that day. On a child's second birthday, family members put a
5 variety of objects on the floor around the child. According to Chinese tradition, the first object that the child picks up tells you what profession the child will choose later in life.

3,5,7 For Japanese children, the third, fifth
10 and seventh birthdays are particularly important. At this age, there is a special celebration called *Shichi – Go – San* (*seven, five, three* in Japanese) when children go to the temple wearing a brand-new kimono. The
15 priest gives them special sweets, and the parents usually organise a party for their friends in their home.

15 In Argentina, Mexico and several other Latin American countries, girls have a special
20 birthday celebration when they reach the age of fifteen. After a religious ceremony, the girls dance a waltz with their father and other boys.

18 Eighteen is the traditional 'coming of age' – the age where you have the right to
25 vote, join the armed forces and (in many countries), drink alcohol and (in the UK) buy a house or become a member of parliament!

21 In many English-speaking countries, a twenty-first birthday cake often has a key on
30 top, or the cake itself is sometimes in the shape of a key. The key means that the young person is now old enough to leave and enter the family home at any time they want to!

30 In the past in parts of Europe, men who
35 reached the age of thirty and were still single, had to clean the stairs of the City Hall. This way every girl could see that the man didn't have a girlfriend. – and how good he was at cleaning the house!

40 **40,50** After the age of thirty, many people prefer to forget their birthdays rather than celebrate them ... children often bring Mum (or Dad) breakfast in bed, and it's traditional to give a bunch of flowers and
45 enjoy a special meal or party. It's also a day when your friends and family have to pay if you go out for drinks or a meal!

Reading

1 **a** When is your birthday? Is this a good month to have a birthday? Why?

What do you usually do on your birthday? What about other members of your family? Which birthday do you remember best?

b MD Look at the picture opposite. Find the things in the box.

| a party dress | a bunch of flowers | a key |
| birthday card | candles | |

2 MD Read the text above about birthday traditions around the world. Tick (✓) the traditions which exist in your country, and put a cross (✗) next to the traditions which are different.

3 Find a word or phrase in the text that means:

a   as someone or something says   *according to*
b   especially
c   completely new
d   a number of
e   a formal, public event
f   The Army, Navy or Air Force
g   the form of something
h   local government building

Language focus 1
Present continuous and Present simple

Carlos
Photographer

Juliet
Editor

Imogen
Personal assistant

1 The people in the picture work for a fashion magazine called *Glitz*. How do you think they spend a normal working day?

Who:

a chooses articles for the magazine?
b makes the coffee?
c earns the most money?
d takes a lot of photographs?
e does the photocopying?
f has a lot of business lunches?
g answers the phone?
h has the most interesting job?

2 Today is a national holiday, so everybody at *Glitz* has the day off. Read about how Imogen is spending her day.

Imogen is spending her day off with her husband, Alex. Imogen and Alex usually go away at the weekend, either to the countryside or to the beach, or they meet friends. But today they aren't doing anything special – they're just sitting at home, relaxing. Imogen likes her job at *Glitz*, but she doesn't want to be a PA all her life: that's why she's also doing a course in fashion design at night school. One day, she wants to have her own design company. She's finding the course really useful.

Grammar

1 Underline the examples of the Present continuous in exercise 2.

2 Choose the correct tense for each rule and add an example from exercise 2.
a We use the Present simple / Present continuous for things that are generally or always true.
Example:

b We use the Present simple / Present continuous for things happening at this moment.
Example:

c We use the Present simple / Present continuous for things happening in the present period, but not at this moment.
Example:

3 Look at the verbs underlined below. Tick (✓) the ones that are correct and put a cross (✗) by the ones that are incorrect.
a <u>I'm not knowing</u> the answer to this question.
b <u>Do you like</u> dancing?
c <u>Are you understanding</u> what it says?
d <u>I don't want</u> any more cake.

▶ Read Language summaries A and B on page 150.

Practice

1
Complete the paragraph about Carlos with the Present simple or Present continuous.

Carlos (1) _____ (spend) his day off with his family. His family (2) _____ (live) quite far away, so he (3) _____ (not see) them very often. But today is a special day: his parents (4) _____ (celebrate) their wedding anniversary. Carlos (5) _____ (spend) most of his free time working on his motorbike. He (6) _____ (not like) his job at *Glitz* very much, so he (7) _____ (look) for another job. He (8) _____ (want) to take photos of motorbikes instead of fashion models!

2
Write some sentences about Juliet, using the picture and the ideas below to help you.

a Juliet is spending her day off with *her mother*.
b At the weekends, she usually …
c Today, she's …
d Her husband is …
e He doesn't …
f Juliet doesn't …
g One day she wants to …

3
a Choose the correct form to complete the sentences: Present simple or Present continuous.

1 I'm learning / learn to drive at the moment.
2 I'm speaking / speak more than two languages.
3 I'm not liking / don't like football.
4 I'm never reading / never read fashion magazines.
5 At the moment, I'm reading / read a very interesting book.
6 I'm wearing / wear black shoes today.
7 I'm going / go to the gym every day.
8 I'm usually spending / usually spend weekends with my family.
9 I'm looking / look for a job at the moment.
10 I'm trying / try to give up smoking right now.

b Which sentences are true for you? Which sentences are not true? Write some more sentences about yourself using the ideas below.

At the moment I'm …

I never …

Today, I'm wearing …

Listening
New Year in two different cultures

1 Is New Year an important celebration in your country? What do people usually do? Where do you usually spend New Year? Who do you spend it with?

2 **MD** You will hear Johnny and Karen talking about New Year celebrations in China and Scotland. Check the meaning of the words below in your mini-dictionary.

> envelopes biscuit coal mushrooms oysters

Karen is from Perth, in West Scotland

Johnny Wong's family live in Hong Kong

3 **T4.4** Listen and complete the information in the table.

	Karen/Scotland	Johnny/Hong Kong
When it happens	December 31st	
Special food/drink		
Things people give to each other		
Other customs		

4 Which things are similar about the New Year's celebrations in the two countries? Which things are different?

Language focus 2
Present continuous for future arrangements

1 It's just before New Year. Read three people's plans. Which verbs below complete each gap?

> cook come go have meet rent

Giacomo from Italy
'This New Year my family
(a) _____ a house
in the mountains. Some
friends of mine
(b) _____ to stay.
It'll be great!'

Nicola from England
'I (c) _____ a
party on New Year's Eve.
I've invited hundreds of
people. I hope they all
come!'

Nestor from Brazil
'My mother
(d) _____ a
special dinner for all the
family. Then, at twelve
o'clock, my friends and I
(e) _____ to the
beach. We
(f) _____ lots of other people for a
big beach party.'

2 **T4.5** Listen and complete the gaps. Whose plans sound the most interesting?

Grammar

Tick (✓) the best explanation.
We use the Present continuous to talk about:
a things we would like to do.
b things we will probably do.
c things we have arranged to do.

▶ Read Language summary C on page 150.

Practice

1 Complete the questions below with verbs from the box.

> cooking doing going (×3)
> having (×2) meeting taking

a Are you _____ out for a meal tonight? Who are you going with?

b Are you _____ anything interesting this weekend? What?

c Are you _____ anyone after this lesson? Who?

d Are you _____ shopping later today? Where? Who with?

e Are you _____ a birthday party soon? When?

f Are you _____ dinner this evening? Who for? What are you _____?

g Are you _____ any important exams in the near future? When?

h Are you _____ abroad soon? Where? Why?

2 *Either* Choose **three** of the questions in exercise 1. Ask them to as many people as possible in the class. Make a note of their answers, then tell the class.

Example:
Susana isn't going home after this lesson – she's going shopping with her friend.

Or Interview your partner, using the questions in exercise 1. Make a note of your partner's answers. Tell the class what you are **both** doing and what **neither** of you is doing.

> We're both going home after this lesson.

> Neither of us is cooking dinner this evening.

Wordspot
day

1 Complete the conversations with a word or phrase from the box to make a phrase with *day*.

the day before yesterday	a day off
Have a good day	every day
go out for the day	bad day
six days a week	one day
the day after tomorrow	all day
the other day	twice a day

a I saw Ahmed _____ . He seemed to be very happy with his new job.

b I'm so tired. What I need is _____ work.

c I'm sure they'll get married _____ .

d It's so boring. We do the same things _____ . I need a change.

e It's my uncle's birthday _____ . I must remember to send him a card.

f 'Right. I'm going. I'll see you tonight.'
   'All right then. _____ ! Don't work too hard!'

g It's Thursday today, and we arrived here _____ – on Tuesday.

h All she wants to do on holiday is sit by the swimming pool _____ and relax.

i You need to take this medicine _____ – first thing in the morning and before going to bed.

j The information centre is open _____ – it's only closed on Sundays.

k After so much time at home, we decided to _____ , so we went to the beach.

l It was a _____ today – I was late for work, had an argument with my best friend and lost my handbag.

2 **T4.6** Listen and check your answers.

3 Put the phrases from exercise 1 into the correct section of the diagram below.

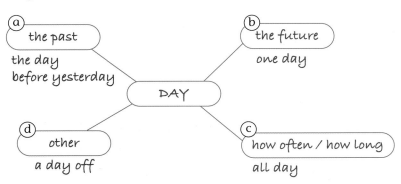

4 Look at the questions on page 140. Write your answers on a piece of paper. Then ask and answer the questions in pairs.

Task: Talk about a personal calendar
Preparation: listening

1 a **T4.7** You will hear some people talking about dates which are important for them. Listen and write in the dates in the *Date* column.

b Listen again and complete the notes about why the date is important.

Task: speaking

1 Work individually. Draw a personal calendar like the one opposite. In the calendar, include as many of these days as you can.

- an important birthday or anniversary
- an important day in your country (Independence Day, a national holiday, etc.)
- an important date from your past
- a day where you've arranged to do something
- a day when something interesting happened to you recently

2 You are going to tell the other students about your personal calendar. Spend a few minutes planning what you are going to say.

▶ Useful language a

3 Work in pairs or small groups. Tell the other students about your personal calendar. Your partners can ask questions. What was the most interesting thing you found out?

▶ Useful Language b

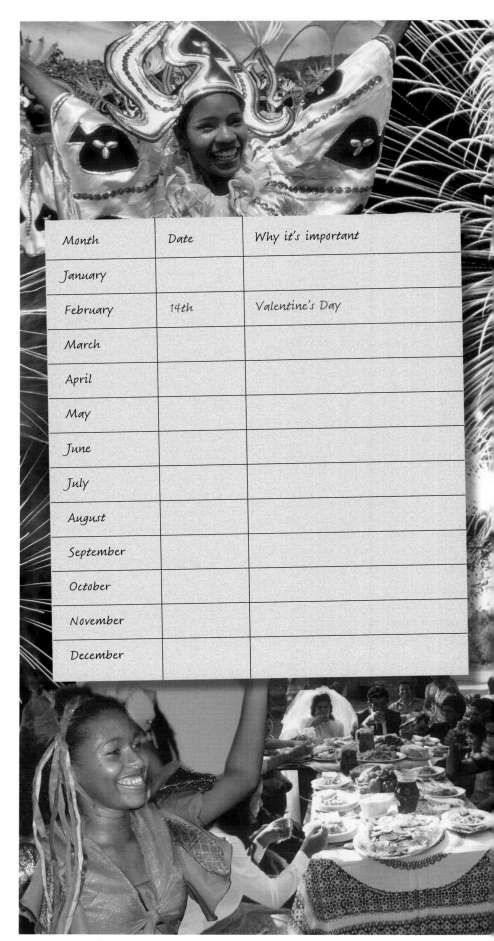

Month	Date	Why it's important
January		
February	14th	Valentine's Day
March		
April		
May		
June		
July		
August		
September		
October		
November		
December		

Useful language

a Explaining your calendar

March 2nd is my mother's birthday.

For (July) I put the 19th because …

July 10th is the day when …

In (Mexico), … is a very important date because …

In May we always go / we're going to / we went to …

b Questions

What happens / happened / is happening on …?

What do you usually do on …?

Why did you put …?

Why is … important for you?

Real life
Phrases for special occasions

New Year

Birthday

Illness

Christmas

Wedding

Wedding anniversary

1 Match the phrases below with the occasions in the pictures. (Some of them can be used with more than one picture.)

Happy New Year!   Happy anniversary!   Thanks for coming.
It's lovely, thank you very much.   Happy birthday!
Merry Christmas!   Congratulations!   Good health!
I hope you'll be very happy!   I hope you feel better soon!
Good luck!   Many happy returns!   Cheers!
The best of luck for the future / your operation / the New Year.

Pronunciation

T4.8 It is important to use friendly, positive intonation with these phrases. Listen and repeat.

2 **T4.9** Listen to the beginnings of some conversations. When you hear a beep, choose the best phrase from the box above.

3 Work in pairs. Practise the conversations using the tapescript on page 165 to help you. Think of similar conversations of your own. Practise them with your partner.

Writing
Write an invitation

1 Read the e-mail below quickly. What is the invitation for?

From: Person [nthom@rvu.uk]

To...	Sofie Jackson
Cc...	
Subject:	summer wedding

Hi Sofie!
How are you? It seems ages since I last saw you – the last time we met I remember you were very busy helping your friend get ready for her wedding – I hope it all went well and the weather stayed fine for you. I've got a new job in the marketing department, so it's more money but more work unfortunately!
Actually, the reason I'm sending you this is to tell you about another wedding. My brother Andy and Anushka (I'm sure you met her one Christmas) have finally set a date for their wedding – 20ᵗʰ August. We'll send you a proper invitation in a few weeks but this is just to let you know in advance.
Anyway, my parents want to celebrate the engagement so they're having a special lunch on Sunday 3ʳᵈ May. We're inviting relatives and close friends, so there'll be about twenty people there. We'd love to see you! It's at Martin's Restaurant – do you know it? It's on the waterfront, so let's hope the weather's good!
I know it's quite a long way for you to come, but Robbie is driving up from Manchester – so maybe you could arrange to come up together? If not, I can meet you at the station – just let me know when your train gets in.
I'm going away for two weeks from tomorrow, but you can phone my parents to tell them you're coming (their number is 0131 445892), or send me an e-mail. I really hope you can come!
Love from Marianne

---

2 Read the e-mail again and put the following things in the order that they appear.

Personal news ☐
Contact details ☐
When the event is happening ☐
Greeting ☑ *1*
Arrangements to meet ☐
Signing off ☐
Where it is and how to get there ☐

3 Write an e-mail to a friend, inviting him or her to a special occasion, real or imaginary. Use the headings in exercise 2 to help you.

STUDY...

Remembering verb + noun combinations

When you learn a phrase with a verb + noun, there are a number of ways to write it down to help you remember it.

- Make a spidergram (like in the Wordspots) and keep it on the classroom wall.

- Make a list of nouns that can be found with a particular verb.

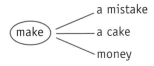

- Keep adding to your list till you have ten/twelve combinations. Then test yourself / each other.

- Write down the verb + noun phrase in a sentence and highlight the combination.

My mother always makes a cake at Christmas.

- Use the mini-dictionary. Common verb + noun combinations are shown like this:

make /meɪk/ *verb* T 1 **make a mistake** to do something that is not correct or that you realize later was not the right thing to do: *She made a big mistake marrying Jim.* 2 **make a decision** to decide: *There are so many choices, it's hard to make a decision.* 3 **to earn** [INFORMAL]: *This is an expensive restaurant so I make good tips as a waitress.* ● *The movie Titanic made a lot of money.*

PRACTISE...

1 Present continuous ☐

Put the following sentences into the Present continuous. Be careful with the spelling of the verb.

a We travel first class.

b It begins to rain.

c My brother is the one who lies on the sofa!

d This train stops at every station.

e They make a lot of noise.

▶ **Need to check? Language summary A, 150.**

2 Present continuous and Present simple ☐

Choose the correct verb.

a Who cooks / is cooking the dinner? It smells great!

b Do you know / Are you knowing what that sign means?

c My parents are coming / come to stay with us every Christmas.

d I don't like / 'm not liking tea.

e Eva comes / is coming home to spend Easter with us this year.

f We have / 're having a birthday party on Saturday. Would you like to come?

g Do you want / Are you wanting any more bread?

h Normally, I take / 'm taking the train to work but this week I walk / 'm walking.

▶ **Need to check? Language summaries A, B and C, page 150.**

3 Dates and special occasions ☐

Cross out the noun that does not go with the verb.

a **buy** a cake / a card / flowers / relatives

b **celebrate** a birthday / Christmas / a meal / an anniversary

c **send** a card / a ceremony / flowers / a present

d **make** a cake / a meal / a party / coffee

e **have** breakfast / a day out / a meal / cards to people

f **visit** friends / a meal / relatives / your family

▶ **Need to check? Vocabulary, page 32.**

4 *day* ☐

Put the words in the correct order to make phrases with *day*.

a I sent the package yesterday / the / before / day, so it's probably there now.

b He won't be here tomorrow, but he'll be back after / day / the / tomorrow .

c Thursday is off / my / day , so I can meet you then.

d Thank you for coming! a / day / good / Have .

e We check the kitchens a / day / twice .

f I felt really fed up after such bad / a / day .

g The tourist office is all / open / day .

h I'm sure that your son will be an international sportsman day / one .

i The postman comes day / ten o'clock / every / at .

j Would you like to for / day / go / out / the / on Sunday? How about the beach?

k I saw Simon in the street other / the / day .

l The restaurant is open a / week / days / six . We're only closed on Mondays.

▶ **Need to check? Wordspot, page 37.**

5 Phrases for special occasions ☐

Complete the phrases with words from the box.

best   better   for   good (x2)   happy (x5)   merry

a _____ anniversary!

b _____ birthday!

c _____ Christmas!

d _____ health!

e _____ New Year!

f Thanks _____ coming!

g I hope you feel _____ soon.

h Many _____ returns!

i _____ luck!

j The _____ of luck for the future!

k I hope you'll be very _____ .

▶ **Need to check? Real life, page 39.**

REMEMBER!

Look back at the areas you have practised. Tick the ones you feel confident about. Now try the MINI-CHECK on page 159 to check what you know!

Appearances

- ▶ Comparative and superlative adjectives
- ▶ Describing people
- ▶ Vocabulary: Physical appearance
- ▶ Reading: *You're gorgeous*
- ▶ Pronunciation: Word stress, Comparatives and superlatives
- ▶ Wordspot: *look*
- ▶ Task: Describe a suspect to the police
- ▶ Song: *His Latest Flame*

You're Gorgeous

Reading and vocabulary
Physical appearance

1 Who do you think is the most attractive man/woman in the world? Why? Which people in the pictures do you think are attractive? Why?

2 **MD** Each heading below summarises one of the paragraphs in the text. Read the text and match the headings to the correct paragraphs.

- Ideas of beauty 200–300 years ago
- The bigger the better
- Pale is beautiful!
- The importance of a long neck
- The perfect modern woman   *1*
- Showing your emotions
- The world's most handsome men

❤1 For many people, German-born supermodel Claudia Schiffer is the perfect beauty: tall and slim, blue-eyed, tanned and athletic-looking with long, blond hair. No wonder people have described her as 'The most beautiful woman in the world'.

❤2 But people have not always had the same ideas about beauty. Until the 1920s, suntans were for poor people, 'ladies' stayed out of the sun to keep their faces as pale as possible. Five hundred years ago, in the times of Queen Elizabeth I of England, fashionable ladies even painted their faces with lead to make them whiter – a very dangerous habit as lead is poisonous!

3 And people in the eighteenth century would certainly not have thought much of Claudia Schiffer's hair! Ladies in those days never went out without their wigs, which were so enormous – and so dirty – that it was quite common to find mice living in them! As for the 'perfect beauties' painted by Rubens in the seventeenth century, if they wanted to be supermodels today they would have to spend months on a diet!

4 Ideas of beauty can be very different according to where you live, too. For the Paduang tribe in South-East Asia, traditionally the most important sign of beauty was a long neck. So at the age of five or six, girls received their first neck ring, and each year they added new rings. By the time they were old enough to marry, their necks were about twenty-five centimetres long!

5 And what about the ideal man? If you ask women today to name an attractive man, most mention someone like Russell Crowe, Mel Gibson or Denzel Washington: someone tall and strong, brave and 'manly'.

6 In the eighteenth century, however, 'manliness' was very different from what it is today. As well as wearing wigs, perfume and lots of make-up, a true gentleman showed his feelings by crying frequently in public. According to one story, when the British Prime Minister, Lord Spencer Percival, came to give King George IV some bad news, both men sat down and cried!

7 And even now, Russell Crowe might not find it so easy to attract women if he visited the Dinka tribe of Sudan. They have always believed in the saying that 'big is beautiful'. Traditionally, each year, men compete to win the title of 'the fattest man'. The winner is sure to find a wife quickly: for a Dinka woman, if a man is fat, it is also a sign that he is rich and powerful!

3 Are these statements *True* or *False*? Explain your answers.

a Pale skin was more popular than tanned skin until the twentieth century. *True*
b Elizabethan make-up was not safe.
c In the eighteenth century, fashionable ladies had mice as pets.
d Women in Rubens' time probably never went on diets.
e Paduang women with short necks couldn't get married.
f In the eighteenth century it was OK for men to cry.
g Dinka women from Sudan think that thin men are very ugly.

4 a Find words in the text that mean:

1 (for hair) light-coloured or yellow. *blond*
2 pleasant to look at.
3 having skin made darker by the sun.
4 of more than average height.
5 (for skin) light-coloured.
6 looking physically strong and good at sport.
7 having the good qualities of a man.
8 thin in an attractive way.
9 having a lot of courage.
10 with blue eyes.

b **MD** Find the opposites to the words in the box below in the answers to part a above.

> cowardly dark-haired fair-skinned fat short ugly

5 Complete the diagram below with words from the text.

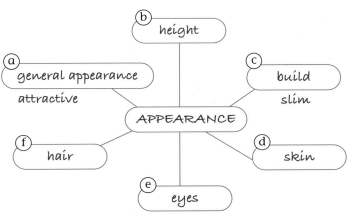

general appearance
attractive
(b) *height*
(c) *build* *slim*
APPEARANCE
(f) *hair*
(d) *skin*
(e) *eyes*

Pronunciation

1 **T5.1** Listen and mark the stressed syllable in each word.

supermodel dangerous attractive powerful

athletic enormous gentleman perfume

fashionable important traditionally

2 Practise saying the words. Pay attention to the stress.

Language focus 1
Comparative and superlative adjectives

1 Look at the four pictures below. Discuss how the girl's clothes change her appearance in each picture, using the adjectives in the box.

casual elegant heavy mature natural
pretty serious sophisticated tall young

2 **T5.2** Listen to Suzanne Weston, a fashion expert, talking about the pictures. Do you agree with her ideas?

3 **a** Complete the sentences below with the correct form of the adjectives in brackets.

1 The glasses make her look much _____ (serious), much _____ (mature).
2 The hair makes her look _____ (young), doesn't it.
3 I think she looks _____ (pretty) in Picture A, to be honest.
4 That tracksuit isn't _____ (elegant) outfit in the world.
5 I'd say she looks _____ (good) in Picture A, definitely.
6 The dress makes her look _____ (tall) than in the other pictures.
7 This is definitely _____ (sophisticated) of the four pictures.
8 I think this is the _____ (good) picture, I really do.

b **T5.3** Listen and check your answers.

Grammar

1 What are the comparative and superlative forms of the adjectives below?

1 syllable	young	tall
2 syllables ending in -y	heavy	pretty
2/3 or more syllables	sophisticated	elegant
irregular forms	good	bad

2 What rules do you know about the formation of comparative and superlative adjectives?

3 Match the beginnings of the sentences in A with the endings in B to make sentences. Notice the prepositions used.

A	B
a She's **older**	**from** the others.
b **The best**	**as** mine.
c It's **the same**	**than** me.
d It's **similar**	**like** me.
e They're **different**	**to** this one.
f She **looks**	**in** the world.

▶ Read Language summary A on page 150.

Practice

1 Write **eight** sentences about people in your class, using comparative and superlative adjectives. Use the ideas below.

big/small hands	young/old
tall	colourful clothes
heavy/light bag	long/short hair
number of brothers and sisters	number of books
	number of rings

Examples:
Vanessa has got the longest hair.
Carla has got the most rings.

2 Complete the sentences about you and your family.

a ___Isabel___ is the youngest person in my family.
b I look very different from _____ .
c People often say I look like _____ .
d My hair is _____ my _____ .
e My eyes are _____ than _____ .
f My mother is _____ than my father.
g I'm more _____ than my brother/sister/cousin.
h My father is the _____ person in the family.
i In my family, my _____ has the most _____ .

3 Tell your partner about the differences between you and your family.

Pronunciation

1 **T5.4** Listen to **eight** sentences. How many comparative and superlative adjectives do you hear?

2 Look at the tapescript on page 165. Listen again and practise saying the sentences.

Language focus 2
Describing people

Match the questions in A with the answers in B.

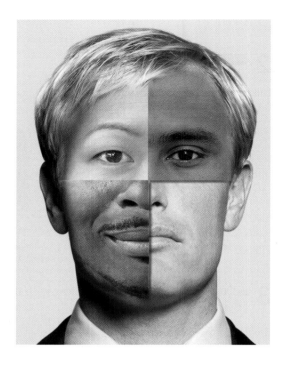

A	B
1 What does he look like?	No. He's clean-shaven.
2 How is he?	About average height.
3 What's he like?	He's fine.
4 How old is he?	He's tall, dark and handsome.
5 How tall is he?	He seems very nice.
6 What colour are his eyes?	Brown.
7 Has he got a beard?	About 22.

Grammar

Which of the questions is about:
a physical appearance?   d features (hair, etc.)?
b height?   e personality?
c health?   f the colour of something?

▶ Read Language summary B on page 151.

Practice

1 Put the words in the correct order to make questions.

1 is / like / new dress / What / your ?
2 are / colour / eyes / her / What ?
3 hair / he / long / Has / got ?
4 dark / fair / hair / her / Is / or ?
5 in / Is / his / thirties / he ?
6 Does / wear / glasses / she ?
7 Is / me / or / she / shorter / taller / than ?

2 **a** **T5.5** Look at the picture on page 46 and listen to the descriptions. Which player is the person describing?

b Look at the tapescript on page 165. What question was the speaker asked in each case? Underline all the words and phrases used to describe people.

3 Work in pairs, Student A and Student B.

Student A: Choose someone in the classroom, someone on page 46 or someone who you both know (for example, a famous person). Be ready to answer Student B's questions.

Student B: Ask questions to find out the person Student A is thinking of. Start like this:

Is it a man or a woman?

It's a woman.

4 Work in pairs or teams.

- Individually, choose a photo of any person in the first five modules of this book.
- Write a detailed description of that person, but do not write who it is or where you found the picture.
- Show your description to your partner. Can he/she find the person?

Wordspot

look

1 The sentences below all have a phrase with *look*. Complete the sentences with a phrase from the box.

> good-looking   have a look   look after
> look at   look for   look good   look like
> look out   look round   look up
> looking forward   strange-looking

a You can use your mini-dictionary to _____ any words you don't know.
b Who's going to _____ your dog while you're away on holiday?
c There was a very _____ man watching us so we ran away as fast as we could.
d Everyone is really _____ to your visit.
e _____ at this website – it's got some brilliant photos.
f Tell me the truth. Do you think I _____ in this new dress?
g _____ ! There's a car coming!
h Will you help me _____ my keys? I can't find them anywhere.
i It's not good manners to _____ your watch every few seconds.
j We'd like a chance to _____ the apartment before we rent it.
k Richard is a very _____ young man and all the girls like him.
l People always say that I _____ my mother.

2 Add the phrases with *look* to the correct part of the diagram.

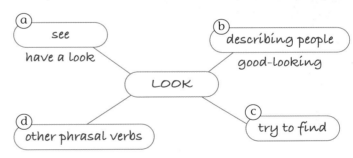

3 Finish the sentences below using your own ideas. Compare your answers with a partner.

a I think _____ is a really **good-looking** man/woman.
b I'd like to **have a look** at _____ .
c I think I **look nice** in black/brown _____ .
d I never/often _____ **look up** words in my mini-dictionary.
e People sometimes say I **look like** _____ .
f I once spent a lot of time **looking for** _____ .
g I think _____ is a very **strange-looking** _____ .
h I'm really **looking forward to** _____ .
i I love / am very bad at / don't mind **looking after** _____ .
j I spend a lot of time **looking at** _____ .
k One building I'd love to **look round** is _____ .
l **Look out** means the same as 'Be _____ .'

Task: Describe a suspect to the police
Preparation: reading

- What has happened?
- Why is the policeman running into the building?

- What are the people in the picture doing?
- What is the man with the moustache looking for?

- Why is the policeman talking to the young woman?
- What do you think she is telling him?

- Who is the man with the policeman?
- What did the policeman do?

1 **MD** Look at the pictures above. Check the following words in your mini-dictionary, then answer the questions about each picture.

arrest fingerprints robbery thief witness

2 Divide into two groups, Group A and Group B.

Group A: Read the card on page 142 and follow the instructions.
Group B: Read the card on page 145 and follow the instructions.

Task: speaking

1 Work in pairs, one person from Group A (a witness) and one from Group B (a police officer). The police officer should ask questions and do one of the following.

Either Make detailed notes about the suspect.

Or Draw a picture of the suspect. Ask the witness questions to check that your drawing is correct.

▶ Useful language a and b

2 a At the end of the interview, B looks at the ten possible suspects on page 147. Decide which was the man in the lift and ask A to say *yes* or *no*.

b If B chooses the wrong man, A must not point to the correct suspect, but he/she should explain why B was wrong.

> He was younger than that and his hair was longer.

c B makes a second and final choice. A says which is the real suspect.

3 How many police officers chose the correct suspect:

- the first time?
- the second time?

Did the witnesses give a good description? Why/Why not?

Optional writing

Write a newspaper report of the robbery. Include the following information.

- Where and when the robbery happened and what was stolen.
- What the police did and who they spoke to.
- What the witness told the police.
- A detailed description of the thief and how/where he was arrested.
- What is going to happen next.

Song
His Latest Flame

1 **MD** Read the words to the song and answer the questions.

- Who are the three people in the song?
- What is the relationship between them?
- How are they all feeling?

His Latest Flame*

A very old friend came by today/yesterday
'Cause he was telling everyone in town
About the girl/love that he just found
And Marie's the name of his latest flame

He talked and talked and I heard him say/tell me
That she had the longest blackest hair
The prettiest blue/green eyes anywhere
And Marie's the name of his latest flame

Though I laughed/smiled the tears inside were burning
I wished him luck and then he said goodbye
He was gone/there but still his words kept returning
What else was there for me to do but cry

Would you believe that the other day/yesterday
This girl was in my arms and swore to me
She'd be mine/there eternally
And Marie's the name of his latest flame

(Pomus/Shuman R & H Music BMI)

* *flame = 1950s slang for boyfriend/girlfriend*

2 **T5.6** Listen to the song and underline the correct word.

3 Below is the 'story' of the song. Complete it with *the singer*, *his friend* or *Marie*.

a Not long ago, __Marie__ promised she would always love <u>the singer</u>.
b _____ came to visit _____.
c _____ described his new girl – he said her name was _____.
d _____ smiled and said 'good luck' to _____.
e _____ said 'goodbye' and went away.
f _____ couldn't stop thinking about _____ and _____.
g _____ started to cry: he knew his romance was over.

4 Tell the story of what happened from the point of view of:

a the singer.   b his friend.   c Marie.

CONSOLIDATION

A Present tenses, *should*, *can*

Complete the gaps in the text below. Use the Present simple, Present continuous, or put *should/shouldn't* or *can/can't* in front of the verbs.

Police officers in Burton (1) _____ (look for) 38-year-old Brian Poole, a murderer, who escaped from prison this morning. 'This man is extremely dangerous,' said Superintendent Michael Walsh earlier today. 'Anyone who (2) _____ (see) him (3) _____ try to talk to him or go near him, but (4) _____ phone the police immediately.'

There is also another man who officers (5) _____ (want) to interview – a witness saw him sitting in a car near the prison, just before the escape. 'We (6) _____ (think) the car was dark blue, but I (7) _____ give you any more details at the moment,' said the Superintendent. 'We would like to hear from anyone who (8) _____ remember seeing a dark blue or black car in that area.'

People who (9) _____ (live) near the prison (10) _____ (ask) how Poole was able to escape from the 'high security' prison. 'It's disgusting,' said mother-of-four, Mrs Jane Thompson, 'the government (11) _____ do something about it – we (12) _____ (not / feel) safe, and we certainly (13) _____ go out after dark. A government representative (14) _____ (visit) the prison tomorrow.

B Vocabulary: Revision

Work in pairs. Read the definitions and find words or phrases from Modules 1–5 (the Module number is in brackets). The first letter of each word is the same as the last letter of the word before.

1 Another word for pretty or handsome. (5) _attractive_
2 Having strong feelings of enjoyment: not calm. (2) e_____
3 His/Her job is to look after your teeth. (3) _____
4 You … your light before you go to bed. (3) _____
5 The opposite of *wake up*. (3) _____
6 Things you give to people on special occasions. (4) _____
7 Afraid. (2) _____
8 Something you imagine when you're asleep. (3) _____
9 Korfball is a … between handball and basketball. (1) _____
10 Someone who plans and builds roads, machines, bridges, etc. (3) _____
11 People in your family. (4) _____
12 Thin in an attractive way. (5) _____

C Comparative and superlative adjectives

Complete the gaps in the article with the correct form of the adjectives.

Found: (1) _____ (big) animal that ever walked the planet

It was (2) _____ (tall) than a giraffe and (3) _____ (heavy) than five elephants. The baluchitherium lived in Asia between 25 and 40 million years ago, and was (4) _____ (large) than any animal that has ever lived on Earth. Scientists who found the graves of twenty of the ancient animals say that this is (5) _____ (important) discovery of its kind and that they now have a (6) _____ (accurate) picture of what the animal looked like than ever before. Adult baluchitheriums were about nine metres long and six metres (7) _____ (tall). They were vegetarians and used their (8) _____ (long) necks to eat leaves from the tops of trees.

D Vocabulary: Pairs

How quickly can you find **eight** pairs of opposites from Modules 1–5 in the box?

terrific	stay up late	excited	great	attractive
awful	fall asleep	dangerous	angry	nickname
candles	wake up	brand new	tanned	disappointed
ugly	slim	often	expensive	go to bed early
cheap	relaxed	enormous	pale	in a good mood

E Real life

Think of an appropriate way of responding in the following situations.

1 Your teacher asks you something, but you didn't hear the question.
2 Your party guests are leaving.
3 You're in a restaurant and you'd like to pay.
4 You want to leave the class early today.
5 Your friends have been married for exactly ten years today.
6 Your friend is going to take her driving test.
7 You want to borrow someone's mobile phone.
8 You want to know the price of something.
9 The sound on your friend's personal stereo is very loud.
10 It's twelve o'clock on December 31st.

F Listening and grammar: Present simple and Past simple

1 You will hear a song called *You are Everything*. What kind of song do you think it is?

2 Match word(s) from A with word(s) from B to make **six** phrases. Do not look at the song yet!

	A	**B**
a	see	the corner
b	feel	memories
c	look	your name
d	turn	your face
e	call out	ashamed
f	bring back	like you

3 **C1** Listen to the song without looking at the words. Number the phrases as you hear them.

4 Listen again and underline the form of the verb you hear.

Today I (1) see / saw somebody

Who (2) looks / looked just like you

He (3) walks / walked like you do

I (4) think / thought it (5) is / was you

As he (6) turns / turned the corner

I (7) call / called out your name

I (8) feel / felt so ashamed

When it (9) isn't / wasn't you

You are everything and everything is you

How (10) can / could I forget when each face that I (11) see / saw

(12) Brings / Brought back memories of being with you

I just (13) can't / couldn't go living life as I do

Comparing each girl with you

When they just won't do

They (14) 're / were not you

You are everything and everything is you.

5 Discuss these questions.

- What was the relationship between the two singers?
- What do you think happened?
- How do they feel about it?

Time off

- ▶ **Intentions and wishes:** *going to, planning to, would like to, would rather*
- ▶ **Predictions:** *will* and *won't*
- ▶ **Pronunciation:** Contractions and weak forms, *will* and *would*, Intonation
- ▶ **Vocabulary:** Holidays
- ▶ **Listening:** The holiday from hell
- ▶ **Real life:** Social chit-chat
- ▶ **Task:** Plan your dream holiday
- ▶ **Writing:** Write a postcard

Language focus 1
Intentions and wishes

1 Discuss the following questions with other students.

- Are you usually free at the weekend or do you have a lot of work/study?
- How many weeks' holiday from work or school do you have every year? Is it enough?
- Do you think people in your country have enough free time, generally? (Think about people in different types of job.)

1 I'm going to walk for more than half an hour today.

2 I'd like to spend my next holiday lying on a beach doing nothing.

3 I'd rather play sport than watch it.

4 I'm not planning to get up before ten tomorrow.

5 I'm going to play an outdoor sport (e.g. tennis, soccer) this weekend.

6 I'd like to spend more time in bed than I normally do.

Are you a **live wire** or a **couch potato**?

7 In a strange city, I'd rather go sightseeing than stay in my hotel room.

8 I'd rather take the lift than walk up a flight of stairs.

9 I'm planning to go skiing and/or surfing sometime this year.

10 I'm going to spend most of this evening in front of a TV/computer screen.

11 I'd like to go on a cycling holiday or climb a mountain one day.

12 I'm planning to buy a more comfortable sofa when I have enough money.

2 **a** Look at the pictures on page 52. Can you guess what a *couch potato* and a *live wire* are?

b Work with a partner and tick (✓) the sentences that are true for you.

3 **a** Count how many blue sentences you ticked, and how many red ones. Blue = couch potato. Red = live wire.

b Compare your answers with the rest of the class.

Grammar

1 Choose the alternative which has the closest meaning to the sentence.

a **I'm going to** buy a new computer.
- I hope I can buy a new computer.
- I intend to buy a new computer.
- I want to buy a new computer.

b **I'm planning to** buy a new computer.
- I have thought carefully about buying a new computer.
- I'd like to buy a new computer.

c **I'd like to** buy a new computer.
- I enjoy buying computers.
- I want to buy a new computer.

d **I'd rather** buy a new computer than a second-hand one.
- I like new computers more than second-hand ones.
- I want to buy a second-hand computer.
- I intend to buy a new computer.

2 What form of the verb do we use after *I'm going*, *I'm planning* and *I'd like*? What form do we use after *I'd rather*?

3 What does *I'd* mean in *I'd like* and *I'd rather*: *I had* or *I would*?

4 Make these sentences into questions.
   a You're going to see it.
   b You're planning to do it.
   c You'd like to see it.
   d You'd rather go home.

▶ Read Language summary A on page 151.

Practice

1 Use the phrases below to make **six** good resolutions for the future with *going to*.

Examples:
I'm not going to argue with my sister any more.
I'm going to spend less money on clothes.

- spend (more/less) time ....-*ing*
- save up money to buy ...
- spend more/less money on ...
- eat more/less ...
- study ... at the weekend
- keep in touch with my ...
- learn to ...
- stop ...
- join ...
- do more ...
- buy a new ...

2 When you have some free time, do you go away for the day/weekend? Use the prompts below to make questions with *planning to, would like* or *would rather*, then ask two other people.

Free time

a (plan/have) any days or weekends away in the near future. Who (plan/go) with?

b Which places near your home (like/visit) for the day?

c Which other parts of your country (like/visit) for a few days?

d For a weekend away, (rather/visit) the mountains, the seaside or a city?

e Which of these cities (rather/visit) for a long weekend: New York, Paris or London?

f Which other cities (would/like) visit one day?

Pronunciation

1 **T6.1** Listen to the recording. Notice how the words are linked together, and notice the pronunciation of *to*.

We are	→ We're	→ We're planning to	→ We're planning to have a party.
You are	→ You're	→ You're going to	→ You're going to see your mother.
He would	→ He'd	→ He'd like to	→ He'd like to go to Dublin.
I would	→ I'd	→ I'd rather	→ I'd rather go by train.

2 **T6.2** Look at the tapescript on page 165. Listen and practise saying the contracted forms.

Vocabulary and speaking
Holidays

1 a Which of these are most important to you on holiday? Discuss these things in groups.

- the weather
- sightseeing/culture
- the food
- the accommodation
- the scenery
- the nightlife
- shops
- who you go with
- other

b What can you see in the photos? Do they show positive or negative things about holidays?

2 **MD** Read the extracts and check the meaning of the words and phrases in bold in your mini-dictionary if necessary. Write *P* if the extract comes from a postcard/e-mail and *B* if it comes from a holiday brochure.

… here I am sitting in the warm sunshine with a cool drink, watching … P

… a short walk from the city centre, this **luxurious** hotel has 400 rooms …

… trouble is you have to **queue** for ages for the most popular …

… there's absolutely **no nightlife** and absolutely nothing to do here except …

… unfortunately, our **flight** was **delayed** for three hours so we had to sit …

… or if you prefer **self-catering accommodation**, there are comfortable …

… there are plenty of **excursions,** where you will have the opportunity to visit …

… has spent most of his time in the **swimming pool** which is OK, but I'd like to …

…the beach is so **crowded** you have to get there very early in the morning if you …

… you can enjoy the **peaceful** and **relaxing** atmosphere of this beautiful old seaside town …

… and I have always wanted **go on a cruise,** so we decided to get away for a couple of weeks …

… there is also a discount of 5% if you **book** your holiday **online** with us …

3 Put the words and phrases in bold into the following categories:

Ideal holiday	Awful holiday	Not sure/Either

4 a Tell your partner about a holiday you have had that was either very good or very bad. Use some of the phrases in exercise 2.

b Listen to your partner's story. Has anything similar ever happened to you?

Listening and speaking
The holiday from hell

* luxurious hotel close to beautiful sandy beach
* three swimming pools, tennis, golf and watersports
* three beach bars and first class restaurant
* average temperatures 28–30°C; average hours of sunshine per day eight to nine hours
* flying time approximately eight and a half hours from London
* airport just fifteen minutes by bus from the hotel

1 Last year Mark and Rosa saved up and booked their dream holiday in the Caribbean. Read what they read on the hotel website above.

2 Work in pairs, Student A and Student B. Act out the following conversation.

Student A: You are Mark/Rosa. Tell a friend about the holiday you are planning (you can invent extra details).

Student B: You are Mark/Rosa's friend. Ask about the holiday.

Where are you planning to go?
What's the hotel like?
How long is the journey?

3 a **T6.3** Unfortunately, Mark and Rosa's holiday was awful. Listen to Part 1 and make a list of the problems Mark and Rosa had:

* at the airport.
* during the flight.

b **T6.4** What do you think happened next? Listen to Part 2 and make a note of the problems they had:

* when they arrived in the Caribbean.
* with the hotel swimming pool.
* with the food at the hotel.
* at the hotel itself.
* with the weather.
* with the sea.

4 Complete as many gaps as you can to tell the story of Mark and Rosa's holiday. Then listen again to check.

Part 1
Mark and Rosa saved up for their dream holiday at a place called San Antonio in the Caribbean – but the dream was more like a nightmare! The holiday cost over
(1) _____ each, but they decided to go for
(2) _____ weeks in the month of
(3) _____ because they heard that the weather was (4) _____ there at that time.

The problems began when the flight was
(5) _____ because of bad weather and they couldn't leave until (6) _____ . They finally got on the plane (7) _____ hours late! Then, they couldn't fly to San Antonio because there was a (8) _____ and they had to fly to the capital city instead, where they stayed in a (9) _____ hotel next to the (10) _____ .

Part 2
The hotel was next to the sea, but it wasn't near a (11) _____ : the sea was so
(12) _____ you couldn't swim in it and the hotel swimming pool was full of
(13) _____ ! To make things worse, the food was terrible, too: for breakfast there were only different types of (14) _____ and the lettuce bowl was full of (15) _____ ! The worst part was when the (16) _____ arrived: they felt really (17) _____ because of the wind and rain. Because of the weather they had to stay another
(18) _____ in the hotel with
(19) _____ to do. They finally arrived in San Antonio (20) _____ days late – and someone told them the weather had been
(21) _____ all the time!

5 a Work in pairs, Student A and Student B. Mark and Rosa are talking to their friend again after the holiday. Start the conversation like this:

STUDENT A: So did you have a good holiday then?

STUDENT B: No, it was awful! It was a nightmare!

STUDENT A: Why? What happened?

b What do you think was the worst part of the holiday?

Language focus 2
Predictions: *will* and *won't*

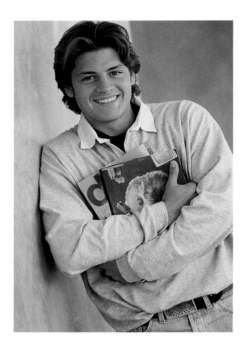

Matt, from London, is visiting the capital city of your country in August. What do you say to him?

a It'll be hot.
b You'll have a wonderful time.
c There'll be lots of tourists.
d You won't see the city at its best.
e It won't be very crowded.
f You'll have to take warm clothes with you.
g There'll be lots of insects.
h You won't be able to find a hotel.

Grammar

1 Tick (✓) the correct answer. Sentences a–h above describe:
a things you plan to do.
b things you expect to happen.
c things you want to happen.

2 a What does *'ll* mean in *It'll be hot*?
b What does *won't* mean in *You won't see the city at its best*?
c Change this sentence into a question.
    There'll be lots of tourists.

▶ Read Language summary B on page 152.

Practice

1 Work in pairs, A (Matt) and B (you). Act out the conversation between you and Matt.

A: I'm planning to visit (name of city) in August next year. What do you think?
B: You'll have a great time – it won't be very crowded. Most people will be away on holiday.
A: Oh, good. What about the weather?

2 Matt may stay in your country for a while. Here are some other things he may do.

> go on a coach tour of the city   go to the doctor
> go to the hairdresser   open a bank account
> travel from the capital to the second city

a Match the beginnings in A with the endings in B to make questions for Matt.

A		B
1	Will I have to make	will the journey take?
2	Will I have to give	will I need?
3	Will I have to	crowded?
4	Will I need to book	an appointment?
5	Will it be very	pay immediately?
6	About how much will	to speak English?
7	Will the people be able	a tip?
8	How long	to sleep?
9	What documents	it cost?
10	Will there be anywhere	a seat?

b **T6.5** Listen and check your answers.

c Work in pairs. Choose **two** things for Matt to do. Which of the questions will he need? Act out the conversation between you and Matt.

> I'm going to go to the hairdresser tomorrow. But I'm not sure what to do …

> OK, how can I help?

> Well, will I have to make an appointment?

Pronunciation

1 **T6.6** Listen to the sentences a–k. What do you hear: *will/'ll* or *would/'d*?

2 Look at the tapescript on page 166. Listen again and practise saying the sentences.

Real life
Social chit-chat

chit-chat *n* informal conversation about everyday things

1 Which of these topics do people normally talk about in the situations on the right?

family   health   holidays   personal problems   plans for the day
reasons for your visit   religion   sport   the weather
what you did at the weekend   where you're from

2 **T6.7** Listen to the four conversations, and tick (✓) the topics you hear discussed.

3 **T6.8** What were the questions for these answers? Look at the tapescript on page 166 and check. Underline any useful phrases.

a   A: _____ ?
    B: Yes, it's lovely.

b   A: _____ ?
    B: No, nothing special. We might go to the park later.

c   A: _____ ?
    B: Yes, she's much better now, thanks.

d   A: _____ ?
    B: Yes I am, actually. It's always nice to get home.

e   A: _____ ?
    B: Yes, it's our first time here.

f   A: _____ ?
    B: Yeah, it was OK. I didn't do much, really.

g   A: _____ ?
    B: Oh, yeah, fantastic, wasn't it? That goal was brilliant!

Pronunciation

T6.9 Listen again to the questions from the dialogue. Notice how the speakers sound interested because of their intonation. Listen again and practise saying the questions.

4 **a** Have a conversation similar to those on the recording. First, decide:

- what your relationship is (friends/colleagues/strangers).
- where you are (in a shop/in the street/in a café).
- which topics you will talk about (health/family/sport).

b *Either* Act out your dialogue for the other students.

Or Write out your dialogue.

neighbours

in a shop

in a taxi

work colleagues

Task: Plan your dream holiday
Preparation: listening

Andy and Fiona King are planning to have a last-minute holiday 'somewhere hot', but they're not sure where to go. They go to the travel agent's to ask for some advice.

1 **T6.10** Listen to the conversation they have with the travel agent. Look at the list of the travel agent's questions below. Make a note of Andy and Fiona's answers.

a   When would you like to go?
b   How long are you planning to go away for?
c   What kind of place would you like to go to?
d   Do you want a beach holiday or something else?
e   Are you looking for somewhere quiet?
f   How many people are going to travel?
g   How much would you like to pay?
h   Do you want self-catering or would you rather stay in a hotel?

2 Look at the information about holidays 1–8. Choose **three** holidays which you think are suitable for the Kings.

1 Spain

Andalucía

14 nights £899

Self-catering villa with swimming pool.
• Quiet mountain village
• 40 minutes' drive from beach

2 Turkey

Bodrum

7 nights £429

5-star hotel
• Next to beach   • Busy nightlife
• 24-hour room service

3 Mexico

Cancún

8 nights £489

3-star hotel
• Fantastic beaches and nightlife   •
15-minute bus ride to beach

4 Dubai

5 nights £689

Self-catering, luxury apartments.
• Fantastic shopping in modern city
• Near beaches

5 Florida

Orlando

14 nights £815

3-star hotel
• Near Disney World and other theme parks and beaches

6 Cuba

Havana

8 nights £779

Self-catering / hotel
• 4 days on beach, 4 days in Havana (capital city of Cuba)

7 Barbados

7 nights £685

3-star hotel
• Quiet resort
• Next to the beach

8 Thailand

12 nights £799

5-star hotel
• Asia's number one holiday resort
• Tropical climate, plenty of nightlife

Task: speaking

1 Work in pairs, Student A and Student B.

Student A: You are a travel agent. Ask Student B questions to find out what kind of holiday he/she would like. You can use the questions in Preparation exercise 1 and add some extra ones if you want to. You can use the holidays here or you can invent some of your own!

► Useful language a

Student B: You are planning to go on a last-minute holiday. Decide:

• who you're going with and for how long.
• what kind of place you would like to go to (beach, mountain, city).
• the kind of accommodation (hotel, self-catering).
• how much you want to pay.

► Useful language b

Useful language

a Asking about holidays

Where/When would you like to ...?

Would you rather ... or ...?

How long are you planning to ...?

b Talking about what you'd like

I'd like to go to ...

We'd like somewhere ...

I'd rather go to ... because ...

We don't want to go to ... because ...

It's too ...

It's not ... enough.

c Telling people about your holiday

We're going to ... for ... days/weeks.

We chose this holiday because ...

2 Work in groups. Tell each other about the holidays you have planned. Decide who has chosen the most interesting holiday.

► Useful language c

STUDY...

Writing
Write a postcard

1 **a** Read the postcard below. In the following pairs of phrases, underline the one that is suitable for a postcard. Why are the other phrases **not** suitable?

a   Hi Tim! / Dear Mr Buchanan,
b   on the 28th November. / when I get home!
c   There are loads of places to go … / The city has more than fifty nightclubs and over 800 restaurants …
d   The food's not too expensive and really tasty … / Meals usually cost around $20 and are of excellent quality.
e   I'm staying in … / My postal address is …
f   Bye for now! / Yours sincerely,
g   It's lovely and sunny, / The weather is warm with an average temperature of 30ºC,
h   I am pleased to inform you that I have arrived safely … / Well, here I am in …

b Complete the postcard with phrases from part a.

AUSTRALIA

(1) _____
(2) _____ Australia! I left
England a week ago and after a short stopover
in Thailand, (3) _____ a nice little
hotel just a few minutes' walk
from Sydney Harbour Bridge, the Opera House
and all the other sights. (4) _____
so I'm getting quite tanned here!
(5) _____ and there's every kind
of restaurant you can think of – Chinese,
Italian, Thai … not too many English ones
though! I think I'll have to go on a diet
(6) _____ . (7) _____
in the evening so I'm never bored!
Give my love to everyone,
(8) _____

Paul

Tim Buchanan

Flat A

156 Rutherford Road

Leeds

LS4 9FT

United Kingdom

2 You are on holiday and you are going to write a postcard to a friend or someone in your family. Decide where you are and who you are going to write to. Include:

• the name and address of the person/people you're writing to.
• a greeting.
• where you are now and some information about it.
• other places you've visited.
• signing off.

Increasing your vocabulary (1): Word families

1 **Even if you know a word, you can increase your vocabulary by learning other words from the same family.**

You probably already know the word *sun*. But do you know:

a   the adjective from *sun*?
b   the nouns for when the sun goes up and comes down?
c   a verb describing the activity of lying in the sun?
d   the word for glasses you wear in the sun?
e   an adjective describing skin which is brown from the sun?

2 Match the dictionary entries below with a–e in exercise 1.

sun·bathe /ˈsʌnbeɪð/ *verb* to sit or lie in the sun to make your body brown
sun·glass·es /ˈsʌnglɑːsɪz/ *plural noun* dark glasses that protect your eyes from the sun
sun·ny /ˈsʌni/ *adjective* sunnier, sunniest a sunny day or place has a lot of sunlight
sun·rise /ˈsʌnraɪz/ *noun* the time when the sun appears in the morning
sun·set /ˈsʌnset/ *noun* the time when the sun disappears at night
sun·tanned /ˈsʌntænd/ *adjective* because you have spent time in the sun

3 You can help yourself to remember word families by:

a   copying out a dictionary definition to show the meaning and whether the word is a noun, adjective, verb, etc.

sunlight (noun) natural light from the sun

b   writing a sentence to show you the word in a context. You can take one from the dictionary, or invent your own (ask your teacher to check this).

The garden looked lovely in the morning sunlight.

c   writing a translation of each word in the word family.

sun = sol
sunny = soleado
sunny day = día de sol
suntanned = bronceado

1 Intentions and wishes: *going to, planning to, would like to, would rather* ☐

Replace the words in bold with the correct form.

a I would like to **visiting** India one day.

b Actually, we'd rather **to take** the early train.

c I'm not **go** to take a holiday this year.

d Are you **plan** to stay at home this evening?

e **Did** you rather go to a different restaurant?

f We are planning **invite** at least fifty people to the party.

g Are you going **come** out with us this evening?

h I **had** like to say something, please.

▶ **Need to check? Language summary A, page 151.**

2 *will/won't* ☐

Make the sentences refer to the future by using the correct form of *will* or *won't*.

a It's difficult to find a parking space.

b She isn't at home on Tuesday.

c Is your cousin at home?

d Can you find your way without a map?

e The last bus has gone: we must walk.

▶ **Need to check? Language summary B, page 152.**

3 Holidays ☐

Match words from A with words from B to make phrases connected with holidays.

A	B
a to book	catering
b go on	a cruise
c night	life
d sight	online
e self-	pool
f swimming	seeing

▶ **Need to check? Vocabulary, page 54.**

4 Holidays ☐

Correct the words in B which are not spelt correctly.

A	B
a fly	f l i h g t
b sun	s u n s h i n e
c delay	d e l a i d
d accommodate	a c c o m o d a t i o n
e crowd	c r o w d e d
f peace	p e a c e f u l l
g relax	r e l a x e i n g

▶ **Need to check? Vocabulary, page 54.**

5 Social chit-chat ☐

Put the words in the correct order to make questions.

a Australia / first / in / time / Is / this / your ?

b better / feeling / Is / now / she ?

c you / holiday / on / here / Are ?

d a / Did / good / have / weekend / you ?

e any / for / got / Have / plans / today / you ?

f the / see / Saturday / you / on / football / Did ?

g day, / isn't / Nice / it ?

h you / weather / nice / get / Did ?

▶ **Need to check? Real life, page 57.**

6 Write a postcard ☐

Choose the correct alternative.

a Hi Dave! Here / There / Where we are in Greece – and the weather's great!

b We're being / living / staying in a five-star hotel.

c We'll tell you all about it when we get at home / home / to home.

d It has / It's / There's lovely and sunny here – everything's perfect!

e Bye at / for / from now!

▶ **Need to check? Writing, page 60.**

Pronunciation spot

The /ŋ/ and /n/ sounds

1 **T6.11** These two sounds often come at the end of words. The letters 'ng' at the end of a word are pronounced /ŋ/, and the letter 'n' is pronounced /n/.

2 **T6.12** Listen to the words below. Notice how the ending of each word is pronounced.

a been / being

b sun / sung

c thin / thing

d ban / bang

e win / wing

f ran / rang

3 **T6.13** Now listen to the same words in a different order. Write down the words you hear.

4 Practise saying the words, paying attention to the /ŋ/ and /n/ sounds.

REMEMBER!

Look back at the areas you have practised. Tick the ones you feel confident about. Now try the MINI-CHECK on page 159 to check what you know!

Ambitions and dreams

▶ Present perfect and Past simple with *for*
▶ Present perfect and Past simple with other time words
▶ Vocabulary: Ambitions and dreams
▶ Listening: Before they were famous
▶ Pronunciation: *for*
▶ Reading and speaking: *An interview with Ewan McGregor*
▶ Task: Talk about your dreams, ambitions and achievements
▶ Wordspot: *for*

Vocabulary and speaking
Ambitions and dreams

1 What were your ambitions when you were younger? Would you still like to do these things now? Were your ambitions realistic?

Example:
I wanted to be a professional footballer!

2 **MD** Match the verbs in A to the phrases in B to make expressions to do with ambitions.

A	B
1 learn	abroad
2 become	children
3 earn	famous
4 start	a house or flat
5 go	how to drive
6 get	married
7 buy	€1 million
8 appear on	a novel
9 go to	television
10 write	the world
11 go round	university
12 have	your own business

3 Make three lists of ambitions.

- Things that most people do.
- Things that very few people do.
- Things that you think are easy/difficult to do.

Listening
Before they were famous

1 How many people in the photos on page 63 do you recognise? Why are they famous?

2 Look at the Celebrity Fact File on page 141. How many were you right about?

3 a **MD** Look at the list of what these people were – or wanted to be – before they were famous.

bellman   child actor/actress   footballer
gymnast   priest   teacher

b **T7.1** Listen to the extract from the radio programme *Before They Were Famous*. Match the job to the person.

Tom Hanks

Catherine Zeta-Jones

Colin Farrell

Keanu Reeves

Renée Zellweger

Kate Winslet

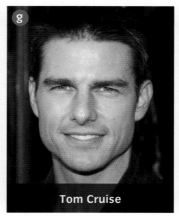
Tom Cruise

Sting

4 Look at the phrases from the tapescript. Put the verbs in brackets into the Past simple. Who does each sentence refer to?

a He _____ (teach) at a primary school …

b He _____ (spend) a year training to become a priest …

c She _____ (make) her first TV appearance at the age of eleven …

d He _____ (drop) out of high school at age of seventeen …

e His dad _____ (laugh) when he told him his plans …

f He _____ (work) in the Hilton Hotel in Los Angeles.

g She _____ (dream) of fame as an international gymnast …

h She _____ (ask) if she could miss school exams to appear in the theatre …

5 Have you ever done a holiday or temporary job? What was it like?

Language focus 1
Present perfect and Past simple with *for*

1 **a** Compare the two sentences below.

1 Sting has been a famous pop star for over twenty years.
2 Before he became famous, he was a teacher at a primary school for several years.

b Which action is finished? Which one continues up to the present?

2 Which tense is used in Sentence 1? Which tense is used in Sentence 2?

Grammar

1 Tick (✓) the correct way to complete each sentence.
  a I've lived in Australia for two years
    • and I'm very happy here.
    • as a child.
  b I was in Australia for two years
    • and I'm very happy here.
    • as a child.

2 What are the Past simple and Present perfect forms of these verbs?
  a **regular:** work   _____
  b **irregular:** know   _____

3 Write the sentence below in the negative and in the question form.
  You've known him for a long time.

► Read Language summaries A and B on page 152.

Practice

1 Use **eight** of these ideas to make true sentences about yourself / people you know.

Examples:
I've had my mobile phone for three months.
My father has worked as an engineer for more than twenty years.

a I have had / had my ... for ...
b I've been / was a ... for ...
c I have been / was at ... (my school) for ... years.
d Before that I have been / was at ...
e I have lived / lived in ... for ...
f I have known / knew ... for ...
g My grandparents have lived / lived in ... for ... years.
h My father / mother has worked / worked as a ... for ... years.
i ... (your teacher's name) has been / was our teacher for ...

Pronunciation

1 **T7.2** Listen and write down the **ten** sentences you hear. Notice the pronunciation of *for* in each sentence.

2 Listen again and practise saying the sentences.

---

2 Look at the list of irregular verbs on page 157. Find:

a **six** verbs that are the same in all forms.
 cost – cost – cost
b **twelve** verbs that have the same past tense and past participle.
 buy – bought – bought
c **two** verbs that are only different in the past tense.
 run – ran – run
d **twelve** verbs that are different in all three forms.
 break – broke – broken

3 Underline all the past tense forms in the tapescript of *Before They Were Famous* on page 167. Do you know the past participle of each verb? Use the verb table on page 157 if you are not sure.

Language focus 2
Present perfect and Past simple with other time words

1 Robbie left school in 1995. He is remembering his old school friends. Complete the sentences using the verbs below.

> decided didn't enjoy didn't go had
> liked spent studied wanted was went

Ameet was always interested in business – he always (1) _____ lots of brilliant ideas for making money and his ambition (2) _____ to be a millionaire by the age of twenty-five!
Lucy was a film addict – she sometimes (3) _____ to the cinema four or five times a week. She (4) _____ to become a famous film actress like her heroine, Halle Berry.
Edward was always very quiet, and he (5) _____ out very much – he (6) _____ most of his time at home in his bedroom, playing games on his computer.
Kate (7) _____ for at least three hours every evening – when she was eighteen years old, she (8) _____ to become an ecologist and help save the planet.
Hannah (9) _____ school at all – for some reason, the only subject she (10) _____ was geography!

2 **T7.3** Listen and check your answers.

3 Robbie contacted his old friends through the *Old Friends* website. What do you think they are doing now? Read the text opposite and find out.

During the last ten years, **Ameet** has had ten different jobs: he has worked in the import–export business, he has been an estate agent, and now he has just started his own company which sells mobile phones – but he hasn't made a million yet.

Edward has moved to the United States, where he now works designing computer games. His most popular game – *Death Trap* – has already sold over ten million copies, and has made him very rich! He isn't married, and in fact he's never had a girlfriend, and he still spends most of his time playing computer games in his bedroom.

Lucy is an actress and a part-time waitress. In the last few years, she's appeared in several plays and a couple of TV commercials – but there's been no call from Hollywood yet!

Since leaving university with a brilliant degree, **Kate** has worked for Greenpeace and other similar organisations, first as a volunteer and now as a manager. She's just had her first baby.

In the last ten years, **Hannah** has been married three times, and has lived in Italy, Egypt, France and Australia. At present, she is running a small restaurant and bar on the Greek island of Kos with her third husband, Nikos.

4 Work in pairs and answer the following questions.

a Say **two** things that each person has/hasn't done.

b Whose experiences in the last few years are:
- the most surprising?
- the most interesting?

Grammar

1 Underline all the examples of the Past simple in exercise 1 and all the examples of the Present perfect in exercise 3. Which tense refers to:
- a past time that is finished?
- a period of time that continues to the present?

2 Look at the time words in the box. Which time words can you use with each of the phrases below?

> already   five years ago   in 2002   just   last year
> never   when I was six years old   yet

a I saw him …   b I've seen … him   c I haven't seen him …

▶ Read Language summary C on page 152.

Practice

1 a Use the ideas below to make sentences in the Present perfect.

Example:
just / I go / the hairdresser's / to
I've just been to the hairdresser's.

1 not / I / yet / finish / school
2 just / lunch / I / have
3 I / on holiday / already / go / this year
4 an arm / or a leg / never / I / break
5 I / go / yet / this year / not / to the dentist's
6 I / do / anything exciting / not / this week
7 I / anyone famous / never / meet
8 I / on a plane / this year / travel / not
9 not / I / do / any sport / this week
10 I / never / anything / steal

b Which of the sentences are true for you? Compare your answers with a partner.

> 'I haven't done any sport this week.' False.

> I've played football twice. How about you?

2 Work in pairs and ask and answer the following questions. In the last five/ten years:

a which cities / foreign countries have you visited?
b how many times have you changed school/job?
c how many times have you moved house?
d which important skills have you learnt?
e which new sports or interests have you taken up?
f what other important things have happened to you?

> I haven't moved house.

3 Think of a group of people that you knew five/ten years ago (for example, schoolmates, colleagues, neighbours). Write a paragraph about what has happened to them.

Reading and speaking

Ewan McGregor was born in Scotland in 1971.
He left school to work in the theatre before attending drama school in London. He is best known for his starring roles in films such as *Trainspotting*, *Moulin Rouge* and *Star Wars*.
He has also worked in the theatre. He is married with two children.

1 **MD** Here are some of the questions members of the audience asked when Ewan made a public appearance at the National Film Theatre, London.

a   Would you like to do more theatre?
b   What film have you enjoyed acting in the most, and why?
c   What do you look for in a script?
d   How do you manage work and fatherhood?
e   Which actor has inspired you most and why?
f   Which actor would you most like to work with and why?
g   What's the best advice you can give to an actor?

2 Look at the answers opposite. They are **not** in the same order as the questions. Write the number of the answer next to the appropriate question.

3 Read the sentences below about Ewan McGregor and write *True* or *False*. Give reasons for your answers.

a   He doesn't enjoy working in the theatre any more.
b   He has been very happy with all his films.
c   He has already worked with Jodie Foster.
d   He feels that Jodie Foster inspired him more than any other actor.
e   His family went with him when he worked in Los Angeles.
f   His daughter was very happy in Los Angeles.
g   He enjoyed all his classes at drama school.

An interview with Ewan McGregor

1
Yes … I trained in the theatre and I love the theatre … yes, I'd like to do more …

2
I absolutely love what I do … and I've got a brilliantly supportive wife and two beautiful girls … my daughter, Clara, is six and at school … when we went to Los Angeles, we took her out of school and it was difficult because she missed her friends, and you can't do anything about that. I feel it's important to be together, so we do the best we can.

3
The only thing you're looking for is a story … and character …

4
It's really difficult, they all do …

5
I've really enjoyed them all. The film I like the best is always the one I'm working on now or the next … in terms of film-making at its best … it would be *Trainspotting* … it was some of the most exciting work I've ever done.

6
You can't be good at all of it … I hated mime classes at drama school … but I'd not shut down on anything … you should just go for it …

7
I might be doing a film with Jodie Foster next year. Imagine that! I hope she's going to direct me and I really respect her work. It's unbelievable.

4 Imagine you are interviewing a famous film star. Make a list of questions you would ask him/her. What answers do you think he/she would give?

5 Act/Write out the interview.

NORTHERN IRELAND
Belfast

REPUBLIC OF IRELAND
Dublin

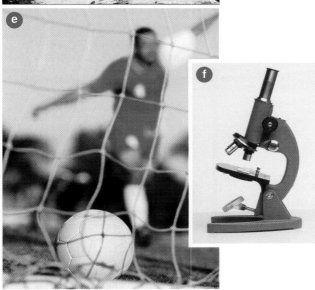

Task: speaking

1 Make a list of **four** or **five** ambitions/dreams/achievements that you have in your life. These could be connected with the following things.

- job/school
- places you'd like to live in / visit
- something you'd like to own (a car, a house)
- money
- someone you'd like to meet / have met
- something you'd like to discover or invent
- marriage/children
- a sporting dream/achievement
- something you have learnt / would like to learn

2 Spend a few minutes thinking about what you would like to say about each thing.

▶ Useful language a and b

3 Work in groups of three or four. Tell each other your ambitions.

- Who has the most interesting or unusual ambition?
- Which people have the same ambition?

Task: Talk about your dreams, ambitions and achievements

Preparation: listening

1 Match the words to the definitions below.

an achievement	something you would like to do, but probably won't
an ambition	something you have done which you are proud of
a dream	something you want to do one day

2 **T7.4** Listen to **five** people talking about their ambitions/dreams, or about their biggest achievement. Which picture(s) belong with each person?

- Bill
- Ralph
- Deb
- Ian
- Swati

3 Listen again and make some notes about each person's ambition/dreams and achievements.

Useful language

a Discussing your ambitions

One/Another thing I'd like to do one day is …

I've always wanted to …

It's always been my dream to …

One thing I'd (also) love to do is …

I'd also like to …

b Discussing your achievements

One thing I've done that I'm very proud of is …

My greatest achievement was when I …

Wordspot
for

1 Match the phrases/sentences in A with the phrases/sentences in B.

A

a How long have you been in London?

b Are you **waiting for** someone?

c What do you want **for your birthday**?

d I'm **looking for** somewhere to live.

e It's one o'clock.

f Eating so many chips and burgers

g The bus didn't arrive so

h 'This coffee's cold.' 'Why don't you

i (Phone rings) 'Hello? Just a moment.

j It's a beautiful morning.

k What's **for dinner**?

l Eating vegetables and fruit

B

ask for another one?'

Chicken and chips!

For about **three months**.

Time for lunch!

is really **bad for you**.

is **good for you**.

I was **late for** class.

Peter? **It's for you**!'

Let's **go for a walk**!

Yes, I am. My brother will be here soon.

Do you know of any apartments to rent?

Well, there's a new computer game I'd like.

2 [T7.5] Listen and check your answers.

3 Add the phrases with *for* to the correct part of the diagram.

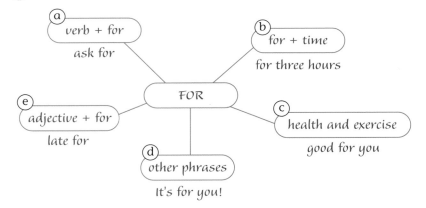

4 a [T7.6] Listen and write down **eight** questions.

b Look at the tapescript on page 168 to check. Then work in pairs and ask and answer the questions.

Learning irregular past tenses and past participles.

There are many irregular verbs in English. The most important ones are shown in the table on page 157. Here are some ideas for helping you remember them.

● Go through the list and highlight them in different colours. Test yourself / each other **only** on the verbs you know already and then on the verbs you're not sure about.

buy	bought	bought
fly	flew	flown
draw	drew	drawn

☐ = *I'm sure I know this verb.*
☐ = *I'm not sure I know this verb.*
☐ = *I don't know this verb.*

● Put the verbs into groups according to their sounds. How many groups can you find?

lose   lost   lost
shoot   shot   shot

● Every time you read something in English, underline all the irregular verbs. Then test yourself on the past tenses and past participles. Use the verb table on page 157 or your mini-dictionary to check.

I've really enjoyed them all. The film I like the best is always the one I'm working on now or the next … in terms of film-making at its best … it would be *Trainspotting* … it was some of the most exciting work I've ever done.

● Make a poster for your classroom wall: arrange the irregular verbs in the way **you** think makes them easy to remember.

● Try to learn four or five new irregular verbs every day. Put them on a piece of card and check them at the end of the week.

PRACTISE...

1 Present perfect: irregular verbs ☐

Here are the irregular verbs from the tapescript of *Before They Were Famous*. Write the Past simple form and past participle for each one.

a become   e know   i take

b can   f make   j teach

c dream   g say   k tell

d have   h spend

▶ Need to check? Irregular verbs table, page 157.

2 Present perfect or Past simple? ☐

Choose the correct alternative.

a I have stayed / stayed with my grandparents a lot when I was younger.

b The couple next door have lived / lived there for twenty-five years: I'm sure they'll never move.

c Gordon has started / started his first business in 2001.

d So far this year, we saved / we've saved over €500.

e Before becoming a banker, my brother has studied / studied abroad for several years.

▶ Need to check? Language summaries A and B, page 152.

3 Present perfect and Past simple with time words ☐

Underline the correct position for the words in brackets: (1) or (2).

a Mr Ferris (1) has (2) gone out.   (just)

b The gym opened about (1) a year (2).   (ago)

c Have you (1) been to see *Spiderman* (2)?   (yet)

d I've (1) seen an elephant (2).   (never)

e We (1) have (2) seen this film three times.   (already)

f He came (1) to England (2).   (last year)

▶ Need to check? Language summary C, page 152.

4 Ambitions and dreams ☐

Choose a verb from the box that belongs with all the words in each group.

| become | buy | earn | go | have | learn |
| make | write | | | | |

a _____	a car	a flat	a house
b _____	famous	rich	a singer
c _____	how to drive	French	a language
d _____	abroad	round the world	to university
e _____	a book	an e-mail	a novel
f _____	a film	a lot of money	a mistake
g _____	an ambition	children	an idea
h _____	a lot of money	$1 million	£1,000 a month

▶ Need to check? Vocabulary, page 62.

5 Phrases with *for* ☐

Cross out the word/phrase that does not belong with *for*.

a He asked / He'd like to speak / It's for you.

b Are you thinking / looking / waiting for someone?

c Did you have / What do you want / What's for lunch?

d Do you think that eggs are bad / good / healthy for you?

e I'm going to eat / It's time / We'll be late for breakfast.

f They're too late / Shall we go / They went for a walk.

▶ Need to check? Wordspot, page 68.

Pronunciation spot

The sounds /æ/ and /ʌ/

1 **T7.7** Listen to the following pairs of words. Notice that in these words, the letter 'a' is pronounced /æ/ and the letter 'u' is pronounced /ʌ/.

a cat / cut

b bat / but

c mad / mud

d hat / hut

e cap / cup

2 **T7.8** There are other letters that can be pronounced /ʌ/. Underline all the /æ/ and /ʌ/ sounds in the phrases below. Then listen to check.

a a happy cat

b madly in love

c a bad cut

d her young son

e a black taxi

3 Practise saying the phrases, paying attention to the /æ/ and /ʌ/ sounds.

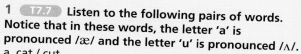

REMEMBER!

Look back at the areas you have practised. Tick the ones you feel confident about. Now try the MINI-CHECK on page 159 to check what you know!

Countries and cultures

▶ Using articles
▶ Quantifiers with countable and uncountable nouns
▶ Vocabulary: Geographical features
▶ Reading: *Where in the world?*
▶ Pronunciation: /ɪ/ and /aɪ/, Polite intonation
▶ Task: Complete a map of New Zealand
▶ Real life: Asking for and giving directions
▶ Writing: Giving written directions

Language focus 1
Using articles

1 Look at the ideas below. Which of them do you think may be true? Which do you think are **not** true?

2 T8.1 Listen to some people who live in these countries giving their opinions. Do they agree or not?

— Just a Myth? —

- **a** English people drink tea every day at five o'clock.

- **b** Italian people eat pasta every day.

- **c** It's always cold in Moscow.

d All Spanish people enjoy bullfighting.

- **e** Japanese people are very polite.

- **f** People in Argentina are crazy about football.

- **g** People in the United States are very keen on fast food.

h People in Australia have a lot of barbecues.

i You often see camels in Arab countries.

j Men in Scotland normally wear kilts.

Grammar

1 Look at the sentences and complete the rules.
   a *English people drink tea every day at five o'clock.*
   b *Italian people eat pasta every day.*

When we talk about people or things in general, we usually use *the* / no article.

With the names of people and countries, we usually use *the* / no article.

2 Which of the following phrases need an article?
   at ___ home   at ___ night   at ___ top
   in ___ afternoon   in ___ south   in ___ world
   on ___ holiday   on ___ left   on ___ coast

▶ Read Language summary A on page 152.

Practice

1 Work in pairs. Make general statements about people in your society, using the ideas below. Use a phrase from b, c and e. Add phrases from a and d if you want.

Example:
Most Spanish people don't drink tea .

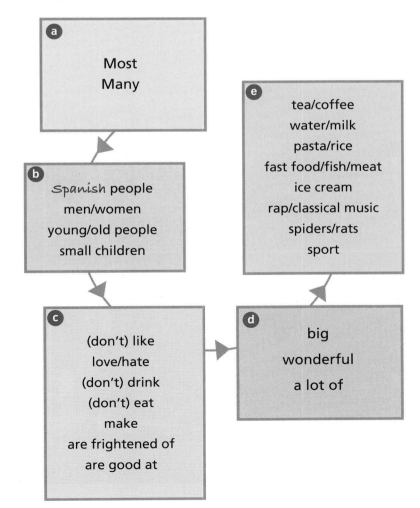

a Most   Many

b Spanish people   men/women   young/old people   small children

c (don't) like   love/hate   (don't) drink   (don't) eat   make   are frightened of   are good at

d big   wonderful   a lot of

e tea/coffee   water/milk   pasta/rice   fast food/fish/meat   ice cream   rap/classical music   spiders/rats   sport

2 **a** Complete the gaps with *the* where necessary. Then mark the sentences *True* or *False*.

1 _____ Asia is bigger than _____ Europe.
2 _____ New York is _____ biggest city in _____ world.
3 _____ Mount Fuji is in _____ Japan. It's _____ highest mountain in _____ world.
4 _____ Queen of England lives in _____ Downing Street.
5 _____ Mediterranean Sea is bigger than _____ Pacific Ocean.
6 _____ Sun is smaller than _____ Moon.
7 _____ Himalayas are in _____ Asia.
8 You can always see _____ Moon in _____ sky at _____ night.
9 _____ Mississippi River is in _____ United States.

b **T8.2** Correct the false sentences. Then listen and check your answers.

3 Complete the sentences about yourself on a piece of paper, using the ideas in brackets. Include articles where necessary. Write your name on the paper.

a I live in … (town/city). It's in … (middle/north/south/east/west) of … (country).
b The continent I would most like to visit is …
c The country I would most like to visit is …
d At 11 a.m. I'm usually … (work/school/university/other).
e At 11 p.m. I'm usually (not) … (home/bed/other).
f I have my English lessons … (morning/afternoon/evening).
g I usually sit … (left/right/middle) of the class.
h My name is … (top/bottom) of this page.

4 Your teacher will give you another student's piece of paper. Read out the sentences, but do not say who wrote them. Can the other students guess who wrote the sentences?

Language focus 2
Quantifiers with countable and uncountable nouns

1 Do you live in a town or city? Which other cities have you visited? Which do you think is 'the world's best city'? Why?

2 Read the extract from a website about 'the world's best city'.

Stuart

The World's Best City?

The Swiss city of Zürich is the best place in the world to live, according to a new survey. The 'quality of life' survey looked at health, education and transport services. It said Zürich is the world's top city for the second year in a row, providing the best quality of life with …

3 **T8.3** Stuart has lived and worked in Zürich for several years. Listen to him talking about life in the city. Which of the topics below does he mention?

- banks
- hotels
- museums
- nightlife
- pollution
- restaurants
- scenery
- shops
- skyscrapers
- traffic

4 **T8.4** Put the words in the correct order to make sentences. Then listen and check.

a really beautiful / around the city / scenery / some / There's
b drive / a few / for / minutes / You
c much / in the centre / traffic / There isn't
d banks / a lot / There are / of
e There are / skyscrapers / enormous / no
f a few years ago / open late / There / many places / weren't
g them all / I don't / enough time / to try / have

Grammar

1 Look at the list of nouns in exercise 3 above. Which are countable and which are uncountable?
  - *Skyscraper* is an example of a countable noun (it has a singular and a plural form).
  - *Traffic* is an example of an uncountable noun (it has no plural form).

2 Look at the pairs of sentences below. Tick (✓) the pairs where the meaning is the same and put a cross (✗) next to the pairs where the meaning is different.
  a *There's **a** bank in the main square.*
    *There are **some** banks in the main square.*

  b *There aren't **any** good restaurants near here.*
    *There are **no** good restaurants near here.*

  c *There are **a few** places to go in the evening.*
    *There are **a lot of** places to go in the evening.*

  d *There's **a lot of** traffic at this time of the morning.*
    *There's **too much** traffic at this time of the morning.*

  e *There aren't **many** parks in the town.*
    *There aren't **any** parks in the town.*

▶ Read Language summary B on page 153.

Practice

1 Choose the best quantifier to complete the sentences.

a Be careful on the road. There's *many / much / a lot of* traffic at this time of day.
b My flat's got a nice view, but there isn't *enough / many / no* space.
c There aren't *many / much / some* young people in our apartment block.
d I can't go out tonight. I haven't got *any / no / many* money.
e The city's mainly modern, but there are *any / much / some* old buildings.
f We're very lucky, there are *a lot of / much / too many* parks where we live.
g There aren't *any / no / much* shops around here.
h There are *no / a few / any* good restaurants, but they're a bit expensive.

2 Imagine you are trying to persuade a foreign visitor that one of these places is 'the world's best city'.

- a town/city you know well
- your town
- your capital city

Use some of the ideas in Language focus 2 exercise 3, or other ideas of your own.

> You should come and visit Dubai. There are a lot of fantastic shops and …

> There isn't much nightlife in my town, but there's some beautiful scenery near there.

> Buenos Aires is great because there are lots of cafés and places to go in the evening.

Vocabulary and reading
Geographical features

1 How good is your geography? Read the questions in blue below. Can you answer the questions without reading the answers?

2 **MD** Read the answers quickly to see if you were right.

Where in the world:

1 **... can you find the Yellow River, the Black Sea and Greenland ... and why do they have those names?**

The Yellow River is the second longest river in China. It carries millions of tons of yellow sand from the deserts of central China, which give the river a yellowish colour. The Black Sea lies between six countries, including Russia, Turkey and Ukraine – but it certainly isn't black! The name probably comes from the black clouds which can cause storms in the area. And Greenland – the world's largest island apart from Australia – is more white than green (85% is permanently covered in snow and ice). One idea is that the first people who arrived there saw it in spring.

2 **... can you find a lake where the water is salty?**

The Dead Sea is not really a sea, but a lake. Water comes into it from the River Jordan, but because the Dead Sea is lower than the land around it, it cannot flow out. The hot desert sun evaporates the water as quickly as it flows in, leaving salt and other minerals. As a result, the Dead Sea is seven times saltier than the sea, and people can easily float on it!

3 **... can you find the country with the world's longest coastline?**

Canada has the world's longest coastline – just over 240,000 km (this is nearly five times longer than the next country, Indonesia). As a single line, the coastline would go round the Earth six times!

4 **... is the country with the most extreme climate?**

Two of the hottest and coldest temperatures ever recorded were in the same country – Argentina. A temperature of 49°C was recorded in the town of Rivadavia on 11th December 1905 and -33°C in Sarmiento (only 115 km away) in June 1907 – that's a difference of 82°C!

5 **... is the world's longest mountain range?**

In South America, the Andes stretch more than 7,000 km from Lake Maracaibo in the north to Tierra del Fuego in the south – the whole length of the continent and a distance greater than New York to London. In the Andes you can also find the world's highest volcano (Nevado Ojos del Salado on the border between Chile and Argentina) and the world's highest lake (Lake Titicaca).

3 Find geographical words in the text to complete the puzzle below. What is the missing word going down? Check your answers on page 147.

a   water which is frozen (paragraph 1)
b   the dividing line between two countries (paragraph 5)
c   an area of water surrounded by land (paragraph 2)
d   a very dry place where there is very little rain (paragraph 7)
e   strong wind and rain (paragraph 1)
f   an area of land surrounded by water (paragraph 1)
g   the type of weather found in a particular place (paragraph 4)
h   a man-made river (paragraph 6)
i   a stretch of water which goes to the sea (paragraph 1)

a				C			
b							
c				A			
d							
e				T			
f							
g				I			
h							
i				E			

6 ... can you find 150 canals – but no cars and no roads?

In the city of Venice in the north-east of Italy. No cars are allowed into this historic city. The only way to get around is on foot, by boat ... or water taxi. It's famous for its historic palaces, churches and art galleries.

7 ... can you find the world's driest desert?

In most of the Atacama Desert in northern Chile, it rains regularly – between two and four times a century! In parts of the desert, it has never rained as far as we know!

Pronunciation

1 **T8.5** Listen to how the letter 'i' is pronounced in the words below.
river   China
/ɪ/   /aɪ/

2 Look at the list of words below. How is the letter 'i' pronounced: /ɪ/ or /aɪ/?

a mineral   e fill   h size
b white   f coastline   i ice
c climate   g single   j historical
d island

3 **T8.6** Listen and check. Then listen again and practise saying the words.

Task: Complete a map of New Zealand
Preparation: listening

New Zealand Quiz

1 New Zealand is:
a in the Atlantic Ocean.
b in the Mediterranean Sea.
c in the Pacific Ocean.

2 The nearest country is:
a Australia.
b Austria.
c Great Britain.

3 There are two islands. Together they are about the same size as:
a Australia.
b Great Britain.
c Canada.

4 How many official languages are there?
a one   b two   c three

5 Which of these things is New Zealand famous for?
a scenery   e The *Lord of the Rings*
b beaches   f mountains
c fjords   g glaciers
d volcanoes   h sheep

Task: speaking

Work in pairs, Student A and Student B. You are going to find out more about New Zealand.

Student A: Look at the map of New Zealand on page 142 and follow the instructions.

Student B: Look at the map of New Zealand on page 144 and follow the instructions.

▶ Useful language a and b

Useful language

a Asking about places
Where is … ?
Why is it important?

b Explaining where places are / why they are important
It's in the north/south/east/west of the …
It's on/off the east/west coast.
It's the highest/biggest …
It's a good place for …

1 How much do you know about New Zealand? Can you answer any of the questions above?

2 **T8.7** Listen to John talking about New Zealand. Underline the correct answers above.

Real life
Asking for and giving directions

1 **T8.8** You will hear **three** dialogues where people are asking for directions.

For each dialogue, write down:
- the name of the place they are looking for.
- how they are going to get there (by car, bus, etc.).

2 **a** Here are four ways of asking for directions. Complete the gaps in the sentences.

1 Can you _____ me? I'm _____ for Church Street.
2 Do you _____ where Church Street _____ ?
3 _____ you _____ me some directions?
4 Excuse me, how _____ we _____ to Central Station, please?

b **T8.9** Listen and check your answers.

Pronunciation

T8.9 Listen again and practise saying the sentences. Notice the polite intonation.

3 Match the sentences in the box to the pictures below.

Go down to the end of the road.	It's the second right.
Go past the cinema.	Turn left at the traffic lights.
It's on the corner.	Cross the road.
Go straight on at the lights.	It's on your left.
Take the next right.	It's on the other side of the road.

4 Look at the tapescript on page 169. Underline any other phrases you think are useful when you are asking for / giving directions.

5 Work in pairs, Student A and Student B. You are asking for and giving directions. Decide whether you are:
- on a mobile phone.
- in the street.
- in a car.

Student A: Look at the map on page 143. Find the station. Ask for directions to:
- a bank.
- a book shop.
- a car park.
- the Odeon Cinema.
- Rosehill Park.
- Fast Save Supermarket.

Then answer Student B's questions.

Student B: Look at the map on page 146. Find the station. Give Student A directions to the places he/she asks for. Then ask for directions to:
- a garage.
- a good Italian restaurant.
- The Corndale Shopping Centre.
- a good Chinese restaurant.
- Jay's Coffee House.
- the Plaza Hotel.

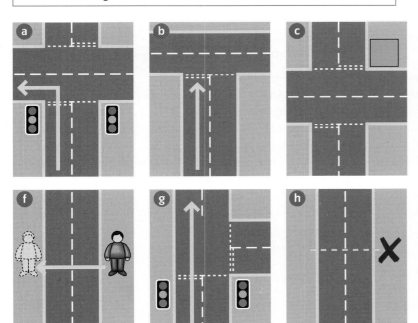

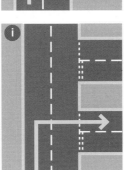
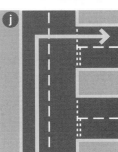

Writing
Giving written directions

1 Patrick has invited a number of friends to his 21st birthday party at his parents' home in Colby, a town outside London. Read the invitation, and the directions which he sent to his guests. Complete the gaps with words/phrases from the box.

> as far as by cross from get lost get off
> keep walking on your outside until you will see your

2 Match the verbs in A with the words and phrases in B.

	A	B
a	take	at the next stop
b	come	lost
c	cross	the signs for Colby
d	turn	walking
e	keep	left
f	follow	the road
g	get	to a set of traffic lights
h	get off	a 71 bus

3 Write a similar set of directions from where you are now to one of the following places.

- your house
- the nearest station / bus stop / airport
- another place you know well

Think about the different ways people can get there (bus, train, car, etc.).

You are invited to
Patrick's 21st barbecue birthday party
at 18 Trinity Road
on Saturday 21st June 2pm till ...?
Bring a friend and/or something
to throw on the barbecue!
See you there

DIRECTIONS TO 18 TRINITY ROAD

BY TRAIN from London (55 mins)
(1) _____ London (Liverpool Street Station)
take any train going to Norton or Clareton
(2) _____ Colby (it takes about 40 minutes).
From there, follow the directions below.

BY BUS from Colby Station (5-10 mins)
Take a 174 or 78 bus from (3) _____ the
station towards Britsea or New Alford. After about
five minutes, you will pass a hospital on your left.
(4) _____ at the next stop - opposite the
Albert Arms pub. Cross the road, and turn left along
Bowley Road. (5) _____ for about 100 m past
the shops on your right. Trinity Road is the second
road (6) _____ right. Number 18 is about
half way down, on your right opposite a garage.

TO WALK from Colby Station (20 mins)
Leave the station and (7) _____ the road.
Walk along Station Road until you come to a set of
traffic lights. Turn left at the lights, and follow the
road for about 2 km (8) _____ you come to

the Albert Arms pub. Then as above.

BY CAR from London
Leave London by the A22 towards Bambridge. After
about thirty miles, (9) _____ signs for Colby.
Leave the A22, and follow signs into Colby past the big
supermarket on (10) _____ right. When you
see the Albert Arms pub, turn left and then take the
2nd turning on the right.
You can also get here (11) _____ plane, bike,
horse or taxi if you're feeling rich! Don't forget your
mobile and phone 01206 825 759 (or see attached
map!) if you (12) _____ !

See you there!

Patrick

STUDY...

Using the mini-dictionary (3): Additional information

1 The mini-dictionary can help you find out more information about words in a reading text. In the entry below, find:

a information about pronunciation / word stress.

b the definition.

c information about whether the noun is countable or uncountable.

d an example sentence.

> **canal** /kəˈnæl/ *noun* C a long straight passage in the ground that is filled with water, for boats to travel on: *Amsterdam is famous for its canals.* • *the Suez canal.*

2 How many of the questions below can you answer without looking in the mini-dictionary?

a Where is the stress on the word *desert*?

b How do you pronounce the word *caught*?

c Is the word *ice* countable or uncountable?

d What is the adjective from the word *salt*?

3 Check your answers in your mini-dictionary.

Pronunciation spot

The sounds /eɪ/ and /aɪ/

1 T8.10 The sounds /eɪ/ and /aɪ/ are diphthongs: two vowel sounds which are pronounced together. Listen to the sounds.

a /e/   /ɪ/   /eɪ/   wait   late

b /a/   /ɪ/   /aɪ/   white   time

2 Look at the words below. Which have an /eɪ/ sound and which have an /aɪ/ sound?

five way train mobile birthday take right sign plane light

3 T8.11 Listen and check. Practise saying the words, paying attention to the /eɪ/ and /aɪ/ sounds.

PRACTISE...

1 Using articles ☐

Add *the* to the following sentences where necessary.

a I'm usually at _____ home in _____ evening.

b Go past the cinema, and _____ Station Road is on _____ left.

c It's a small town in _____ south of Turkey: it's on _____ coast, so it's very popular with _____ tourists.

d While we were on _____ holiday in _____ Egypt, we decided to go on a cruise along _____ River Nile.

e Is _____ Mont Blanc _____ highest mountain in _____ Europe?

> ▶ **Need to check? See Language summary A, page 152.**

2 Quantifiers with countable and uncountable nouns ☐

Choose the correct alternative.

a There's too much / too many sugar in this coffee.

b A lot of / Much people come here on holiday every year.

c I've got some / any bread if you want to make a sandwich.

d I'm sorry, but there isn't enough / no time for us to stop.

e Would you like some / a few more water?

> ▶ **Need to check? Language summary B, page 153.**

3 Geographical features ☐

Put the letters in bold in the correct order to complete the sentences.

a It was so cold there was **e i c** on the pavement.

b In the town, you can take a boat on one of the lovely **n a l a c s**.

c It's a small town near the **r e b r o d** between Hungary and Austria.

d We drove for several hours across the **s r e d e t**.

e I've always wanted to live on a private **n a l d i s**.

> ▶ **Need to check? Vocabulary, page 74.**

4 Asking for and giving directions ☐

Complete the sentences.

a It's _____ the corner.

b _____ left at the traffic lights.

c Can you _____ me some directions?

d Go straight _____.

e Do you know where the station _____?

> ▶ **Need to check? Real life, page 77.**

5 Giving written directions ☐

Put the words in the correct order to make sentences.

a come / the hospital / Keep / until / to / walking / you

b cross / and / Leave / the road / the station

c about / Follow / metres / the road / 500 / for

d at / off / Get / stop / the bus / the next

> ▶ **Need to check? Writing, page 78.**

REMEMBER!

Look back at the areas you have practised. Tick the ones you feel confident about.
Now try the MINI-CHECK on page 160 to check what you know!

Old and new

- ▶ *may, might, will, definitely*, etc.
- ▶ Present tense after *if, when, before* and other time words
- ▶ **Vocabulary:** Modern and traditional
- ▶ **Pronunciation:** Stress in compound nouns
- ▶ **Reading:** *The 1900 house*
- ▶ **Task:** Facelift!
- ▶ **Wordspot:** *if*

Vocabulary and speaking
Modern and traditional

1 **MD** Match the modern items in A with the more traditional items in B.

A	B
a air conditioning	board games
b booking online	cash
c central heating	washing clothes by hand
d charge and credit cards	street markets
e computer games	a cooker/stove
f a dishwasher	buying a CD or cassette
g downloading sound files	electric fans
h a microwave oven	going to the cinema
i renting a DVD	queuing up for tickets
j sending text messages	sending letters and faxes
k shopping malls	coal fires
l a washing machine	doing the washing-up

2 Choose **four** pairs of items in exercise 1. Say which you prefer and give reasons. Do you ever have problems with these items (modern or traditional)? Explain why.

> ## Pronunciation
>
> **1** **T9.1** Look at the difference in stress between the compound nouns below.
>
> **noun + noun**　　**adjective + noun**
> ●　　　　　　　　　　　　●
> air conditioning　　hot water
>
> **2** **T9.2** Mark the stress on these compound words. Listen and check. Practise saying the words.
>
> computer game　shopping mall　fast food
>
> washing machine　mobile phone　vacuum cleaner
>
> text message　electric fan

Reading and speaking

1 Work in pairs. How important are these things in your life (1 = very important, 5 = not important)?

- the Internet
- hot water
- computer games
- central heating
- a washing machine
- a vacuum cleaner
- the telephone
- a fridge

2 The Bowler family on page 81 took part in a reality TV show where they lived the life of people 100 years ago. What differences do you think they found? Make a list.

Example:
No computer games.

3 **MD** Read the text opposite. How many of the differences on your list are mentioned?

❧ The 1900 House ❧

The Bowler family was one of more than 400 families who applied to *1900 House*, a reality TV show which took a typical family back a hundred years to see how people lived in the days before the Internet, computer games and
5 even electricity.

The Bowler family spent three months in a London home without a telephone, fridge, computers, radio, TV, fast food or central heating. TV cameras recorded their day. The Bowlers wore clothes from 1900, ate only food
10 which was available in England at that time, and cooked their meals on a single stove which also gave them their hot water.

Paul Bowler still went to work every day (dressed in a nineteenth-century uniform), and the children went to
15 school as normal. They changed their clothes on the way to and from school and their classmates didn't know about their unusual home life. Joyce stayed at home, cooking and cleaning like a typical housewife of the time. 'I'm jealous, because if it's 1900 or 2005 my husband
20 gets the better deal,' she said. 'Everything takes three times as long, like the cooking and everything.' The stove took twenty-eight minutes to boil water, and cleaning the house and clothes without a vacuum cleaner or washing machine was a nightmare.
25 So does Joyce think that people's lives were better in the old days?

'I think they had just as many troubles and worries, and I don't think their life was better or worse. There were lots of things back then that I'm happy I don't have
30 to deal with nowadays, but on the other hand life was simpler.'

Eleven-year-old Hilary said, 'We had a lot more time with our family, and it was hard being nice to each other all the time. Having contact with your family all the time
35 is really, really weird.'

What did the Bowler family miss most about modern life while living in the 1900 house?
Paul, 39: 'a hot shower'
Joyce, 44: 'a quick cup of tea from a kettle you could just
40 turn on'
Kathryn, 17: 'telephone, shampoo and hot water'
Hilary, 11: 'computer games, music and normal sounds like the washing machine'
Joseph, 9: 'pizza and the computer'

4 Which member(s) of the family:

a didn't wear 1900 clothes all the time?
b stayed at home all day?
c found it strange being with the family all the time?
d missed talking to his/her friends?
e sees positive things about life in the past?

Explain your answers.

5 Look at the phrases in bold below from the text. Find the best meaning for the word or phrase in bold in the box.

problems	really difficult
has an easier life	strange
people could buy	difficult

a … ate only food which **was available** … at that time … (line 9)
b … my husband **gets the better deal** … (line 19)
c … cleaning the house … without a vacuum cleaner … was **a nightmare**. (line 23)
d … I think they had just as many **troubles** … (line 27)
e … it was **hard** being nice to each other all the time. (line 33)
f Having contact with your family all the time is really, really **weird**. (line 35)

6 Imagine you have to live in a 1900 house. Look again at the list of things that the Bowler family missed about modern life. Which would you miss most? Compare your ideas in groups.

> I couldn't live without my telephone!

Language focus 1
may, *might*, *will*, *definitely*, etc.

1 Here are some of the things that the Bowler family normally do that they didn't do in the 1900 house. Do you think people will still do these in another 100 years' time?

a   talk to friends on the telephone
b   have baths and showers
c   play computer games
d   listen to music
e   eat pizza
f   use the Internet

2 **T9.3** Listen to some predictions people made about these things 100 years from now. Complete the gaps in each sentence. Do you agree with these predictions?

a   People _definitely_ won't use a telephone to talk to their friends.
b   In another 100 years, people will _____ listen to music, just like they do now.
c   In 2100, people _____ won't have baths – only showers.
d   A hundred years from now, people will _____ eat pizza!
e   By that time, there _____ be a new way of listening to music.
f   We _____ use the Internet in a completely different way. To replace schools, for example.

Grammar

1 Put the sentences below in order: 1= most probable to 5 = least probable.
   a   We definitely won't buy a new car. ☐
   b   We'll definitely buy a new car. ☐1☐
   c   We might buy a new car. ☐
   d   We'll probably buy a new car. ☐
   e   We probably won't buy a new car. ☐

2 Do *probably* and *definitely* come before or after *will*? Do *probably* and *definitely* come before or after *won't*?

▶ Read Language summary A on page 153.

Practice

1 **a** Use the prompts below to make sentences. about what you think will happen in the future

1   mobile phones / replace / ordinary phones
    Mobile phones probably won't replace ordinary phones.
2   people / write letters
3   people / spend / less time at home
4   computer games / become / more popular than sport
5   credit cards / replace / cash
6   people / travel / by train
7   people / read / books
8   computers / teach people / languages

b Compare your answers with a partner. Give reasons for your ideas.

> Mobile phones probably won't replace ordinary phones because people will probably have both.

2 **a** Complete the following sentences about yourself.

1   I _might_ live to be 100 years old.
2   I _____ have more than two children.
3   I _____ have grey hair when I'm older.
4   I _____ live in _____ all my life.
5   I _____ learn to speak English as well as my teacher.
6   I _____ visit the United States.
7   I _____ go to live in another country.
8   I _____ get married young.
9   I _____ live in the country when I'm older.
10 I _____ become a millionaire.

b Compare your answers with other students.

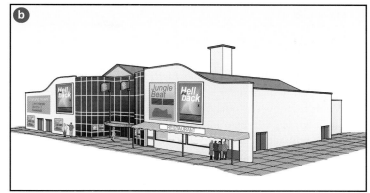

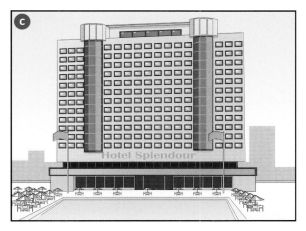

Language focus 2
Present tense after *if, when, before* and other time words

1 An old power station near the centre of town is being demolished. There are four plans to replace it.

2 a **T9.4** Listen to what **four** people say about the plans for a new development. Which plan is each one talking about? Do they think the development is a good or a bad idea?

b Which idea do you like best? Why?

3 **T9.5** Listen and complete the gaps with the correct form of the verbs in brackets.

a If they _____ (build) a new hotel on the site, there _____ (definitely / be) more jobs for local people.

b If they _____ (decide) to put a cinema here, it's _____ (create) very serious parking problems.

c If they _____ (build) new flats, it _____ (help) other businesses in the area.

d The area _____ (change) completely if they _____ (put) a new shopping centre there.

e I hope they ask local people what they want before they _____ (make) a decision.

f They should try to bring more homes to the area as soon as they _____ (can).

g After they _____ (finish) demolishing the old power station, they _____ (wait) for a few months.

h I _____ (be) glad when the work _____ (be) over! The noise is going to be terrible!

Grammar

1 Look at the phrases in bold in the examples below. Are they about the future or about the present?

*If **they build** a new hotel on the site ...*
*I'll be glad **when the work is over** ...*
*... before they **make a decision** ...*

After they finish demolishing the old market ...

2 Which verb form comes after *if, when, before* and *after*?

▶ Read Language summary B on page 153.

83

Practice

1 Choose the best form to complete the sentences below.

a Many small businesses suffer / will suffer if a new supermarket opens / will open near here.

b When the new car park opens / will open, the parking situation in our town is / will be a lot easier.

c I get / will get some advice before I decide / will decide what to do.

d As soon as we hear / will hear what the decision is, we tell / 'll tell you.

e If the number of tourists continues / will continue to grow, the character of our town changes / will change forever.

f Before they start / will start work on restoring the cathedral, they need / will need to raise a lot more money.

g You 'll be / are really happy when you see / will see the plans for the new city square.

h If the local government doesn't give / won't give us money to help with the restoration, the church falls down / will fall down.

2 Work in pairs. Complete the conversations below with your own ideas. Practise reading your conversations aloud.

a A: Oliver, could you do your homework now?
  B: Oh, Mum, I'll do it when …

b A: Are you going anywhere nice this weekend?
  B: We might go for a picnic in the country if …

c A: We haven't got any milk!
  B: Oh no! I'll go and buy some as soon as …

d A: Are you enjoying your new job more now?
  B: No, I hate it! I want to leave as soon as/when …

e A: So when are we going to see each other again?
  B: I don't know – I'm very busy at work at the moment, and I'm going away soon, but I'll phone you when …

f A: Are you going to have a holiday this year?
  B: I hope so, if …

3 **T9.6** Listen and compare your answers with the ones on the recording.

Task: Facelift!
Preparation: reading

Read the description of the Paradiso Coffee Bar and look at the picture on page 85. Make a list of differences between the description and the picture.

Example:
The description says it's crowded, but in the picture there aren't any customers.

Paradiso

Looking for somewhere to relax and meet friends after a long, stressful day? Why not try the Paradiso Coffee Bar? This lively meeting place is always crowded with young, fashionable people who meet for a drink, or just a friendly chat with friends or business colleagues. The surroundings are clean and modern – enjoy the attractive colours, tropical plants and beautiful works of original art.

There is a wide selection of drinks – tea, coffee, alcoholic and non-alcoholic cocktails – and delicious food is available at all times.

So next time you're in town, come to the Paradiso Coffee Bar. Our polite and attentive staff are waiting to serve you!

Task: speaking

1 The owner has given you $500 to improve the Paradiso Coffee Bar. Work in groups and decide what improvements to make. There is a plan of the coffee bar area to help you. Think about the things below.

▶ Useful language a and b

Bar area / Equipment
- How will you change the bar area?
- What food/drinks will you sell? Write a list of ten to twelve items on the menu board.
- What new equipment are you going to buy? Where will you put it?

Decoration
- Are you going to re-paint the walls? What colour?
- What would you like to put on the walls? How many posters/pictures do you think you need and where will you put them?
- Are you going to buy any new plants? Where will you put them?

New furniture
- How many stools/tables/chairs can you buy? Where will you put them?
- Is there anything else you would like to buy?

2 Make a list of ideas in your group. Use the blank plan opposite to show your changes. Then explain what changes you will make to the rest of the class. Which groups had the best ideas?

▶ Useful language c

TO EAT | TO DRINK

sink

kitchen area

counter

Wordspot

if

1 **a** Match the beginnings of the sentences in A to the endings in B.

A	B
1 I don't know	he still remembers me?
2 I'd like a table for two	if I can help you.
3 Do you mind if I	if I were you.
4 We can stop here for lunch	if necessary!
5 I wouldn't buy that	nobody comes to the show?
6 I'll wait here all day	Barbara's arrived yet?
7 I wonder if	she was married.
8 I asked her if	if you like.
9 What if	sit here?
10 Do you know if	if possible.

b **T9.7** Listen and check your answers.

2 Complete the gaps in the diagram below.

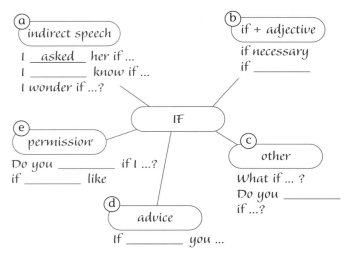

a indirect speech
I __asked__ her if ...
I _____ know if ...
I wonder if ...?

b if + adjective
if necessary
if _____

e permission
Do you _____ if I ...?
if _____ like

IF

c other
What if ... ?
Do you _____ if ...?

d advice
If _____ you ...

3 Work in pairs, Student A and Student B.

Student A: Read the questions and statements on page 143 to Student B.

Student B: Answer Student A, using one of the statements from the box below.

Thanks. I'll see you tomorrow.	Thank you.
I think so – I'll ask him if he's ready.	Yes, I will ... if necessary.
I don't know if he's coming or not.	Sure, go ahead.
No, I wouldn't tell her if I were you.	I'm not sure ... let's ask her.
If possible, yes – I'm hungry.	

STUDY

Guessing meaning from context

1 **Often you may not know the meaning of a particular word, but it is possible to guess the meaning from the other words in the sentence (the context). Look at the examples.**

a *It's cold outside; you'd better put on your **fleece** if you're going out.*

We know *fleece* is a noun because of the word before: *your*. We also know that it is something you *put on* (= an item of clothing) when it's cold.

b *It was a very **dull** day today – let's hope tomorrow is a bit better.*

We know *dull* is an adjective because it comes after the word *very*. We also know that it is something negative because of the second part of the sentence.

2 **Try to guess the meaning of the words in bold by using the context to help you.**

One day, my friend and I went for a bicycle ride in the country. The roads were very **narrow** and we soon got lost – so we were **glad** to see an old man sitting on a **bench** by the road.

'Excuse me. How do we get to Tombridge?' I asked him.

The old man looked **puzzled** and **scratched** his head.

'I'm sorry,' he said 'I don't know where it is.'

After thanking the man, we **carried on** riding until we were so tired we had to stop for a **rest**.

A few minutes later, we were **amazed** to see the man running after us, this time with another old man. I could see he was **exhausted** after running so far.

'This is my brother Jack,' he **panted** 'and he doesn't know either.'

PRACTISE...

1 may, might, will, definitely, etc. ☐

Put the words in the correct order to make sentences.

a arrive / definitely / won't / ten o'clock / before / We

b for / There / not / food / everyone / might / enough / be

c probably / spend / this year / at home / will / Christmas / We

d might / I / the children / later / take / swimming

e not / time / be / There / enough / may

f tomorrow / you / see / won't / I / probably

g The / weather / tomorrow / better / get / may

h definitely / a / will / be / It / game / difficult

▶ **Need to check? Language summary A, page 153.**

2 Present tense after if, when, before and other time words ☐

Choose the correct alternative.

a I tell / 'll tell you if anything exciting happens / will happen.

b I cook / 'll cook the dinner as soon as we get / 'll get home.

c My parents might come / come to visit when they come / will come back from holiday.

d I give / 'll give you my e-mail address before I go / 'll go.

e If she 'll pass / passes all her exams, I 'll be / 'm very surprised.

▶ **Need to check? Language summary B, page 153.**

3 Modern and traditional ☐

Put the letters in bold in the correct order to complete the sentences.

a Can you take your clothes out of the **s n i g w a h h a n c i m e**?

b There isn't enough **t h o t e w a r** for a shower.

c I can't hear. Someone's using the **m u c v a u r a n c l e e**.

d Many people nowadays enjoy playing **p u t e m r o c m e g a s**.

e There's some cold lemonade in the **g e f r i d**.

f The **n e l c a r t h i e g n a t** is off, so it's cold in the house.

g Many people book holidays over the **t I n n t r e e**.

▶ **Need to check? Vocabulary, page 153.**

4 Modern and traditional ☐

Match words from A with words from B to make compound nouns.

	A	B
a	shopping	washer
b	air	oven
c	dish	card
d	board	mall
e	credit	conditioning
f	microwave	game

▶ **Need to check? Vocabulary, page 153.**

5 if ☐

Write if in the appropriate place in each sentence.

a What he can't pay?

b I were you, I'd look for another job.

c Do you know David is coming or not?

d Do you mind I borrow your pen?

e I'll take you to the station you like.

f We'll call the police necessary.

g I wonder that new café is open yet?

h I don't know she wants to see me or not.

i Paul asked me I wanted to see his new motorbike.

j I'd like you to send it to me tomorrow, possible.

▶ **Need to check? Wordspot, page 86.**

Pronunciation spot

The sounds /əʊ/ and /ɒ/

1 (T9.8) **Listen to the words below. Notice the different ways the letter 'o' is pronounced.**
a wo̲n't micr o̲wave do̲n't
b no̲t lo̲t co̲st

2 Look at the words below. Is the letter 'o' pronounced /əʊ/ (as in won't) or /ɒ/ (as in not)?
clothes go home hot long lots mobile
modern old online shopping telephone

3 (T9.9) **Listen and check. Practise saying the words, concentrating on the /əʊ/ and /ɒ/ sounds.**

REMEMBER!

Look back at the areas you have practised. Tick the ones you feel confident about. Now try the MINI-CHECK on page 160 to check what you know!

Take care!

- ▶ *used to*
- ▶ Past continuous
- ▶ **Vocabulary:** Health and accidents
- ▶ **Pronunciation:** *used to*, schwa /ə/
- ▶ **Listening:** Health helpline
- ▶ **Reading:** *Hazardous history*
- ▶ **Task:** Choose the Hero of the Year
- ▶ **Writing:** Time words in narrative

Vocabulary
Health and accidents

1 a Make a list of common health problems.

Example:
a bad cold

b Read the quiz quickly. Which problems from your list are mentioned? Which others are mentioned?

2 **MD** Do the quiz in pairs. Which answers do you think are correct? (More than one answer is possible.)

3 **T10.1** Celia is a nurse in a London hospital. Listen to her answers to the questions in the quiz. Are they the same as yours?

Health Quiz

How much do you know?
What should you do if:

1 you burn yourself on a hot pan?
a Put butter or oil on the burn.
b Put a **plaster** on it.
c Put the burn under cold water.

2 you've got a temperature?
a Stay in bed and **keep warm**.
b Take an aspirin.
c Keep cool and **have a rest**.

3 you're taking a course of antibiotics?
a **Take the pills** at exactly the same time every day.
b Don't stop taking the pills until they are completely finished.
c Never drink alcohol.

4 someone faints?
a **Pour cold water** over their face until they wake up.
b Make sure they are comfortable and wait for them to **come round**.
c **Shake** the person gently until he/she wakes up.

5 you are stung by a bee?
a **Put some ice** on the area of the sting.
b Put a **plaster** on the sting to protect it.
c Phone the doctor if you feel **dizzy** or there is a lot of **swelling**.

6 you develop a rash on your face after eating strawberries?
a Put some cream on your skin.
b Put a plaster on the area with the rash.
c Stop eating strawberries – you may be **allergic** to them.

4 Complete the diagram below with verb + noun/ adjective combinations from the quiz.

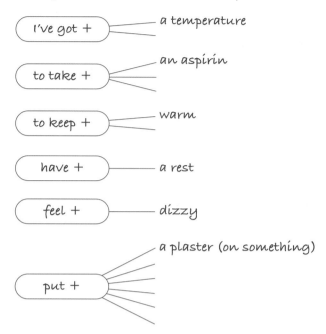

I've got + ——— a temperature

to take + ——— an aspirin

to keep + ——— warm

have + ——— a rest

feel + ——— dizzy

——— a plaster (on something)

put +

Listening and speaking

1 **MD** Look at a page from the Health Helpline website which gives you some questions to think about before you phone for advice.

Call HEALTH HELPLINE ON

0854
7464

Before ringing **HEALTH HELPLINE**, think about these questions. It will save time if you are ready to answer them about yourself (or the person you are phoning about).

▶ What are your symptoms (headache, nausea, sickness, etc.)?

▶ Have you got a temperature?

▶ Are you taking any medicine at the moment?

▶ Do you have any allergies that you know about?

▶ Have you ever had any serious illnesses?

▶ When did you last have something to eat or drink?

PLEASE THINK ABOUT THESE QUESTIONS BEFORE PHONING HEALTH HELPLINE.

2 **T10.2** Listen to someone phoning Health Helpline. Answer the questions below.

a What symptoms does the man have?
b What do you think caused them?
c What advice does the nurse give him?

3 Prepare a similar dialogue to the one on the recording. Choose one of the medical problems in the quiz or invent some of your own. Look at the tapescript on page 170 and underline any useful phrases. Use the diagram below to help you prepare your dialogue.

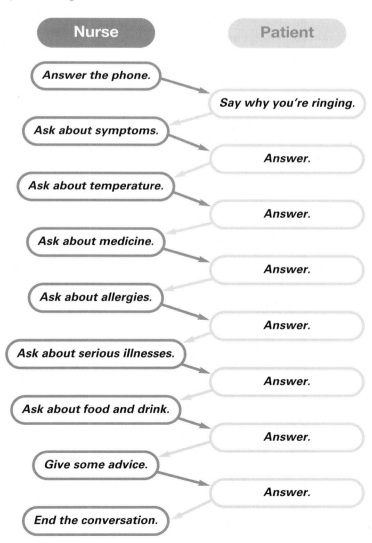

Nurse | **Patient**

Answer the phone.

Say why you're ringing.

Ask about symptoms.

Answer.

Ask about temperature.

Answer.

Ask about medicine.

Answer.

Ask about allergies.

Answer.

Ask about serious illnesses.

Answer.

Ask about food and drink.

Answer.

Give some advice.

Answer.

End the conversation.

Hazardous History

Reading

1 In the past, people didn't live as long as they live today. Think of **three** reasons why.

2 Read the text quickly. Match pictures a–e with paragraphs 1–5.

3 **MD** Check the words in bold, then say if the statements are *True* or *False*.

a   In Japan today the **average life expectancy** is sixty-six.

b   If people **survived childhood**, they often lived another forty or fifty years.

c   20% of women died in **childbirth**.

d   Rich people had good **hygiene**, but many poor people **smelled** and had **lice**.

e   Barbers did many of the **operations** that doctors and dentists do today.

f   People often caught **illnesses** while they were in hospital and died.

4 Underline any information in the text that you already knew. Circle anything that you find surprising. Compare answers with other students.

1 Three centuries ago, people had much shorter lives. In 1700, insurance companies put the average life expectancy of a new-born baby at only fourteen years! The average life expectancy in the world today is sixty-six years, and in some countries it is much higher: in Japan or France, for example, the average is more than eighty. This is mainly because of better diet, better hygiene and better healthcare. Even in the olden days though, it is interesting that if people survived to be an adult they often lived to be sixty or seventy.

* * *

2 Having children was much more dangerous in those days: one in every nine women died in childbirth. Even so, women used to have many more children than they do today: in 1800 the average American family had seven children – today the average is less than two. Perhaps the reason for this was that so many babies died: even a hundred years ago, 20% of children died before they were five.

* * *

3 One reason that there were so many diseases was that people knew much less about hygiene: even rich people didn't use to wash much – many people thought that it was dangerous to take a bath, so they often bathed only once or twice a year. Instead they used perfume to cover body odours. Poor people didn't even have toilets or clean water and most had lice in their hair, bodies, clothes and beds.

* * *

4 There was no toothpaste in those days either: and only rich people used toothbrushes. Of course, toothache was very common, but there were no professional dentists until the middle of the nineteenth century. Before that, if you had toothache you had to go to the barber's. He not only cut hair, but also used to take out teeth and perform other small operations.

* * *

5 And even if you did see a professional doctor, many of their methods seem very strange today. In the eighteenth century, doctors treated almost any illness the same way: by removing blood from the patient – and they often used leeches to help them! Hospitals could also be dangerous places. At the end of the nineteenth century, more than half the patients in hospital died – usually from illnesses they didn't have when they went in!

Language focus 1
used to

Look at these examples from the text. In which is *use* the main verb?

1 Barbers used to take out teeth.
2 People didn't use to wash much.
3 They used perfume to cover body odours.

Grammar

1 Look at examples 1 and 2 again. Choose the correct explanation. We use *used / didn't use to* + verb to talk about:
a Things that happened only once in the past.
b habits (and states) in the past.

2 Find another example of this in the text.

▶ Read Language summary A on page 154.

Practice

1 Match the prompts in A with the phrases in B to make complete sentences with *used to / didn't use to*.

Example:
People didn't use to live as long as they do today.

A	B
a People / not / live	as well as cutting people's hair.
b Families / be	when they had toothache.
c Doctor often / kill	as long as they do today.
d Barbers / pull out teeth	in hospital instead of getting better.
e People not / go to the dentist's	their patients instead of curing them.
f Many people / die	much larger than they are now.
g Many women / die	their teeth very much.
h People / not / brush	baths were dangerous.
i People/ think that	in childbirth.

Pronunciation

1 **T10.3** Listen to the four sentences below. Notice the different pronunciations of *use(d)*.
a Women used to have many more children than they do today.
b Rich people didn't use to wash much.
c They used perfume to cover body odours.
d They didn't use toothpaste.

2 **T10.4** Listen and practise saying the sentences.

2 Complete these sentences about yourself.

a I used to think that …
b I used to be frightened of …
c I used to / I didn't use to like …
d I used to play with …
e I used to spend hours … *-ing*.
f I never used to …

Language focus 2
Past continuous

1 **T10.5** Look at the picture of Frane Selak and listen to Part 1 of his story. How many lucky escapes has he had? Why do you think people say he is 'the world's luckiest/unluckiest man'? (This is a true story!)

2 a **MD** Before you listen to Part 2, check these words/phrases in your mini-dictionary.

> bruises catch fire cuts injuries lose your hair

b **T10.6** Listen to Part 2 of the recording and complete the table with information about Mr Selak's accidents.

	Type of accident (car, train, etc.)	Injuries
1	train	broken arm
2		
3		
4		
5		
6		
7		

Grammar

1 Underline the examples of the Past simple and Past continuous in the sentence below. How do we form the Past continuous?
The train he was travelling on fell into an icy river.

2 Which action started first: travelling on the train, or falling into the river?

3 Which verbs describe the situation in the story? Which verbs describe the main events in the story?

4 Look at this example. Which action happened first? Which action happened second?
... when his car again caught fire and he lost most of his hair.

5 *When* is an example of a time word. Look at the tapescript on page 170 and underline **two** other time words.

▶ Read Language summary B on page 154.

Practice

1 a Complete the sentences with the Past simple or Past continuous of the verbs in brackets.

1 His first escape came when the train he _____ (travel) on _____ (fall) into an icy river.
2 A year later, as he _____ (travel) on a DC-8 aeroplane, a door _____ (fly) open.
3 The bus he _____ (travel) in _____ (leave) the road and _____ (fall) into a river.
4 His car _____ (catch) fire while he _____ (drive) along the motorway.
5 The following year he _____ (drive) in the mountains when he _____ (see) a truck coming straight for him.
6 At the age of seventy-four, he _____ (buy) a lottery ticket for the first time in thirty years.
7 'I feel like I have been re-born. I know someone _____ (watch) me all those years.'

b Listen to Frane Selak's story again or look at the tapescript on page 170 to check your answers.

Pronunciation

1 **T10.7** Listen to the phrases from the recording. Notice the pronunciation of *was* with a schwa /ə/ sound.

2 Look at the tapescript on page 171. Listen again and practise saying the phrases.

2 Look at the pictures of some minor car accidents below. In which picture can you see:

- a traffic jam?
- a fly?
- a telephone pole?
- someone speaking on a mobile phone?
- someone giving a lift to their mother-in-law?

a

b

c

d

3 If you have a car accident, you may have to make an insurance claim. Read what four drivers wrote about their accidents. Match the claims to the pictures.

1

> I was stuck in a traffic jam: the traffic in front of me was moving very slowly, so I decided to have a look to see what was happening in front of me. I didn't know if my car window was up or down. I found it was up when I put my head through it.

2

> I was trying to kill a fly when I drove into a telephone pole. The telephone pole fell down but I think the fly was OK.

3

> The accident happened while I was talking to my girlfriend on my mobile phone. When she said something romantic to me, I lost control.

4

> As I was driving along, I looked at my mother-in-law who was sitting next to me and drove into a tree.

4 **a** Complete the following sentences about yourself using the Past continuous. Compare your answers with a partner.

1 I once had an accident when I …
2 When I left the house today, the sun …
3 I met … when I …
4 At eight o'clock last night, I …
5 At seven o'clock this morning, I …
6 When I arrived for this lesson, our teacher was …

b Close your books. How many of your partner's answers can you remember?

Task: Choose the Hero of the Year

Preparation: reading

1 A newspaper has decided to give a £10,000 first prize for the 'Hero of the Year'. Look at the pictures of the three finalists below. They all rescued someone. What do you think happened?

Kathy Reynolds, 32

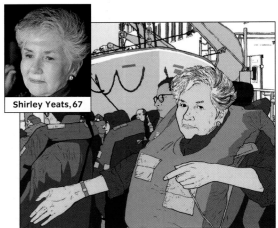

Shirley Yeats, 67

Simon Roland, 10

2 Which questions below can you answer for each story? Use the pictures on the left to help you.

a   What was the age of the finalist?
b   Where did the rescue happen?
c   Who did he/she rescue?
d   Why did these people need help?
e   Why was the 'hero' there and what was he/she doing?
f   What did he/she do to help?
g   Are there any other reasons why he/she was very brave?

3 The pictures a–d on page 95 show what happened to Kathy Reynolds. Put them in the correct order. Read the newspaper story below to check.

Heroine with a cigarette lighter!

Kathy Reynolds, 32, was walking home one afternoon when she stopped to light a cigarette. A car stopped behind her and a man jumped out. To Kathy's horror, the man pulled out a knife and demanded money from an old woman, Eileen Murphy, 73, who was waiting at a bus stop. Kathy – who is only 1.55 m tall – took her cigarette lighter and set fire to the back of the mugger's trousers! The man was so shocked he dropped his knife, and with the help of Mrs Murphy, Kathy knocked the man to the ground, sat on him and tied his arms and legs together with a shoelace! She then called the police using her mobile phone – and moments later the police came to arrest the man!

Task: speaking

1 a Work in two groups, Group A and Group B. Find out what happened to one of the other finalists.

Group A: Look at page 144 (Shirley Yeats).

Group B: Look at page 143 (Simon Roland).

b Work with someone from your own group. Answer the questions in Preparation exercise 2 about your story.

2 Now work with a student from the other group. Ask/Answer the questions.

3 In small groups, discuss who should win the prizes in the competition, and why.

▶ Useful language

1st prize (£10,000) _____
2nd prize (£5,000) _____
3rd prize (£2,000) _____

Useful language

... should get first prize because he/she ...

I think ... was the bravest because ...

He/She was very calm/quick-thinking.

She/He saved ... 's life.

He/She was in danger ...

Writing
Time words in narrative

1 Complete the gaps in the narrative about Shirley Yeats with time phrases from the box.

always	as	as quickly as possible	Immediately
At the age of sixty-seven		Eventually	Later
soon	Then	until	

Shirley Yeats is certainly a very brave woman!
(1) _____ , she decided to go on a cruise round the coast of Malaysia. Everything was fine (2) _____ one day, (3) _____ she was going back to her cabin, she saw smoke coming out of another cabin.
(4) _____ , she phoned the captain from her cabin and told him about the fire.
(5) _____ she went up on deck to see what she could do to help. The fire spread very quickly and (6) _____ it was completely out of control. The captain decided to get all the passengers off the ship (7) _____ .
Many of the other passengers were terrified, but Shirley remained calm. She helped the other passengers to get into the lifeboats and even gave first aid to other passengers.
(8) _____ , all 1,000 passengers were in the lifeboats and not one passenger died in the fire. Shirley was one of the last people to leave the boat. (9) _____ , she told journalists 'I was very frightened but I (10) _____ knew what I had to do. I think all my years as a teacher helped – all that time telling people what to do!'

2 *Either* Write the story of Simon Roland using the pictures on page 143 to help you. Try to use some of the time phrases from the box.

Or Write a story of your own (true or imaginary) about a rescue or an accident. Try to use some of the time phrases from the box.

95

A Past continuous, articles

Complete the gaps in the story below. Either put the verbs in brackets into the Past simple or Past continuous, or put *the* or ø (no article) in front of the noun.

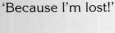

A kind old lady (1) <u>was walking</u> (walk) down some steps on her way to town when she (2) _____ (see) a little boy who (3) _____ (sit) at (4) _____ bottom of the steps. He (5) _____ (cry).

'What is the matter?' she (6) _____ (ask).

He (7) _____ (stop) crying. 'It's my birthday,' he (8) _____ (say), 'and my parents (9) _____ (give) me a new bicycle and some computer games, and this afternoon, we're having a party at (10) _____ home, with (11) _____ ice cream and (12) _____ chocolate biscuits.'

'How strange,' (13) _____ (say) the old lady,' (14) _____ little boys usually like (15) _____ birthday parties and (16) _____ ice cream. Why (17) _____ (cry)?'

'Because I'm lost!'

B Vocabulary: Three things

Work in pairs. The words in the box below are from Modules 6–10. As quickly as possible, find three things:

1 you can **have**.   4 you can **send**.
2 you can **go on**.   5 you can **take**.
3 you can **rent**.

| a cruise   a DVD   a coach tour   pills   a letter   medicine   a 71 bus |
| a fax   a computer game   an accident   a text message   a rest |
| a cycling holiday   accommodation   a serious illness |

C Grammar and listening: Present perfect, future forms, *used to*

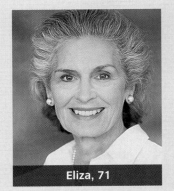

Eliza, 71

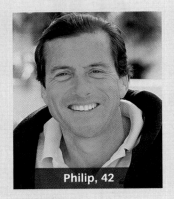

Philip, 42

Carla, 24

1 Look at the three people. Which person do you think:

- used to have more money than he/she has now?
- will probably retire soon?
- would rather spend time with his/her family than go out to work?
- has lived in Los Angeles for nearly forty years?
- has been married four times?
- used to be a famous film star?
- might go abroad next year?
- has already earned over a $1 million?

2 **C1** Listen to the three people talking and see how many of your guesses were correct.

3 Listen again and write down **two** extra pieces of information about each person. Who do you think is:

- the happiest?
- the most ambitious?
- the richest?

D Vocabulary: Revision

Work in pairs. Find words or phrases from Modules 6–10 beginning with the correct letter to fit the definitions (the Module number is in brackets).

1 Which **A** means *to or in another country?* (7) _____
2 Which **B** is the insect which makes honey? (10) _____
3 Which **C** means *full of people?* (6) _____
4 Which **D** is how you feel when your head turns round? (10) _____
5 Which **E** means *after a long time?* (10) _____
6 Which **F** is a cold place for keeping food? (9) _____
7 Which **H** is a person who cuts your hair? (6) _____
8 Which **I** is frozen water you put in a drink? (8) _____
9 Which **L** takes you up and down between floors? (6) _____
10 Which **M** is your wife or husband's mother? (10) _____
11 Which **N** is a bad dream or bad experience? (9) _____
12 Which **O** is the opposite of *indoor?* (6) _____
13 Which **P** is something you put on when you cut yourself? (10) _____
14 Which **Q** means *to wait in a line for something?* (6) _____
15 Which **R** means *to manage* (a business)? (7) _____
16 Which **S** is a very tall office building? (8) _____
17 Which **T** happens when the road is blocked? (10) _____
18 Which **U** means *incredible?* (7) _____
19 Which **V** is someone who offers to do something without being paid? (7) _____
20 Which **W** means very strange? (9) _____

E Speaking: Real life

1 Work in pairs. Choose **one** of the relationships below.

- Two friends meeting in the street
- Strangers in the street
- Neighbours meeting on the stairs
- Work colleagues on a Monday morning
- A travel agent and customer

2 Prepare a short conversation including **two** of the phrases in the box. Act out your conversation for the other students. They must guess what the situation is.

Did you have a good …?	Have you got any plans for …?
We went to …	Excuse me, how can I get to …?
How can I help?	How's your …?
You can't miss it.	We'd like to go to …
Lovely day, isn't it?	How long would you like to …?
How long does it take to …?	Thanks a lot.

The best things in life

- ▶ Gerunds (-*ing* forms) after verbs of liking and disliking
- ▶ *like doing* and *would like to do*
- ▶ Vocabulary: Hobbies and interests
- ▶ Reading: *When an interest becomes an obsession*
- ▶ Pronunciation: *-ing*, Friendly intonation
- ▶ Task: Survey about the most important things in life.
- ▶ Wordspot: *like*

Reading and vocabulary
Hobbies and interests

1 **MD** What are the most popular hobbies and interests in your country? Do you have any special hobbies yourself?

2 In the box below, find:

a **five** things that people **collect**.
b **two** games people **play**.
c **two** things that people might **make**.
d **three** things that people might **go to see**.

> coins a musical trading cards a rock concert
> stamps backgammon jewellery models dolls
> chess memorabilia your favourite football team

3 Read the article *When an Interest becomes an Obsession*. Which hobbies/collections does the article talk about?

When an **Interest** becomes

Whether it's collecting coins, supporting your favourite football team, or just shopping, most people have some kind of interest. But what happens when that interest becomes the most important thing in your life? When does an interest become an obsession?

Take Bob Martin, for example. In 1988, he went to see the musical *Cats* at the New London Theatre. He enjoyed it so much he went to see it again. And again. And again … every week for fourteen years! He travelled 52,000 miles and saw the show 795 times, spending a total of £20,000. 'I don't drink, smoke or run a car, so I could just about afford it,' says the 71-year-old. But sadly Bob is now looking for a new hobby. The show closed last year after a sixteen-year run in London.

For some it's musicals that keep them coming back for more. For others, it's … fast food. Peter Holden, from Washington DC, eats an average of two McDonald's meals a day. He has eaten at more than 11,000 McDonald's (there are 13,500 of them in the whole of the USA) and says, 'I'm a collector of the McDonald's dining experience.' He is 1.9 m tall and weighs 90 kg – he says he doesn't put on weight partly because he is lucky and partly because he doesn't eat the fries.

4 Who does each of these statements refer to? Explain your choice.

a He has the largest collection of memorabilia.
b He now has to find something else to spend his money on.
c He's careful about what he eats.
d His obsession made him into a criminal.
e People come from other countries to see his collection.
f He spent most of his money going to see a show.

5 Which of the obsessions do you find the strangest? Do you know of any other people who have become obsessed in this way?

6 Use the clues to complete the puzzle below with words from the text. Then check your answers on page 147.

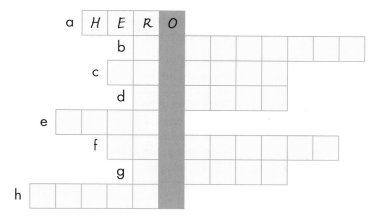

a [H] [E] [R] [O]
b
c
d
e
f
g
h

CLUES

a Someone you really admire is your ...
b If you are so crazy about something you can't think of anything else, you have an ...
c special clothes worn by an actor
d a type of breakfast food
e presents
f wanting or needing something very much
g If you get fatter, you put on ...
h If something is too expensive for you to buy, you can't ... it.

an **Obsession**

Most people collect something at some time in their life, whether it's dolls, trading cards or even stamps, but few take their collections as far as Rodolfo Renato Vazquez, who has the world's largest collection of books, posters and even life-size models related to his heroes, The Beatles. He divides his collection between his apartment and the club he owns in Buenos Aires, Argentina, where he now organises a regular Beatles event which attracts thousands of visitors from all over the world.

But the 6,000 or so items in Rodolfo's collection are nothing compared to the 20,000 items belonging to Jason Joiner – all related to the *Star Wars* films. His collection includes an original Darth Vader costume! But such obsessions can have unfortunate results. John Weintraub became obsessed with collecting plastic figures of US presidents given as free gifts in packets of breakfast cereal. After two years, he had the whole set apart from Thomas Jefferson.

Weintraub was so desperate to get the last one he broke into a factory and opened every box he could find. He was seen by a guard, arrested and sent to prison. 'It's OK though,' he said, 'because at my first prison breakfast I opened the cereal packet ... and out came Jefferson.'

Pronunciation

1 The sound /ŋ/ is usually found in words ending with 'ing'.

spending   looking   coming

T11.1 Underline all the /ŋ/ sounds in the article in exercise 3. Then listen and check.

2 Listen again and practise saying the words.

Language focus 1
Gerunds (-*ing* forms) after verbs of liking and disliking

1 Which of the things in the box do you like? Which do you dislike? Mark each one like this:

5 = I love it/them!   3 = It's OK. / I don't mind it/them.   1 = I hate it/them!

babies buying presents chocolate Christmas computer games dancing dogs hot baths ironing clothes long car journeys receiving flowers snow sports cars sunbathing tattoos watching sport on TV travelling by train

2 **T11.2** Listen to **five** people talking about how they feel about one of the things in exercise 1 and answer the questions for each person. Are any of their opinions surprising?

* What are they talking about?
* Do they like/dislike it?

Grammar

1 Underline the gerunds (-*ing* forms) in the sentences below. Which -*ing* form:
* is the subject of the sentence?
* is the object of the sentence?
* comes after a preposition?
a *I hate buying presents.*
b *Sunbathing is one of my favourite hobbies!*
c *I'm very keen on reading.*

2 Look at the tapescript on page 171. Underline all the phrases used for expressing likes/dislikes. Which form of the verb comes after verbs such as *like, enjoy,* etc?

▶ Read Language summary A on page 154.

Practice

1 Complete the gaps with **one** word only.

a Karen _____ chocolate: she is specially keen _____ white chocolate.
b Dave doesn't _____ buying presents for his family. In fact, he can't _____ it!
c Hazel is crazy _____ watching Formula One on TV, but she doesn't like football or tennis very _____ .
d Simon _____ enjoys sunbathing because he _____ lying down and also because he's _____ on reading.
e Jill hates long car journeys, but she loves _____ by train.

2 Make true sentences about your own likes and dislikes using the words in the box in Language focus 1, exercise 1 and the phrases for likes and dislikes. Compare your opinions with a partner.

3 Make these sentences true, using the -*ing* form.

a I find _cooking_ very relaxing.
b _____ can be stressful.
c I'm (not) very interested in _____ .
d I find _____ quite boring.
e _____ is good fun.
f _____ is bad for you.
g _____ is good for you.
h My friend _____ (name) is crazy about _____ .
i I think _____ is difficult.
j _____ can be very dangerous.

Language focus 2
like doing and *would like to do*

Match the sentences to the pictures.

1 He's crazy about cars.
2 She plans to go to India for her next trip.
3 She really likes being with children.
4 He'd love to own a sports car.
5 She'd like to have lots of children one day.
6 He loves dancing.
7 He hopes to become a professional dancer one day.
8 She really loves travelling.

Grammar

1 Look at sentences 2–8 again. Underline the verbs followed by an *-ing* form, and circle the verbs followed by an infinitive.

2 Look at the sentences and choose the correct alternative to complete the rules.
   a *She likes be**ing** with children.*
   She likes means she enjoys / wants to.
   b *She'd like **to have** lots of children one day.*
   She'd like means she enjoys / wants to.

3 Which form do we use to talk about how we feel about something generally? Which form do we use to talk about something you want to do in the future?

▶ Read Language summary B on page 154.

Practice

1 **a** Choose the correct form to complete the questions.

1 Do / Would you like living / to live abroad one day? In which country?
2 Do / Would you like having / to have a pet? What kind?
3 Do / Would you like to learn / learning any other languages apart from English? Which one(s)?
4 Do / Would you like getting / to get up early? Why (not)?
5 Which city do / would you most like to visit / visiting one day?
6 Do / Would you like listening / to listen to music? What kind?
7 Do / Would you like cooking / to cook? Do you have a speciality? What is it?
8 Which famous person do / would you most like meeting / to meet? Why?

b Ask and answer the questions in pairs.

2 **a** The lines of **two** four-line dialogues have been mixed up. Decide which line belongs to which dialogue and put them in order.

No, I didn't. Do you eat fish?

No, but I'd like to. I've heard it's brilliant. How about going to see it next week?

To be honest, I don't really like action films.

Thanks, I'd love to! Did you know I don't eat meat?

Oh well. Maybe there's something else you'd like to see?

Yes, I love it. That's great. We'll see you on Sunday, then.

Have you been to see *Naked Eye* yet?   *dialogue 2,1*

Would you like to come to our house on Sunday? We're having a barbecue!   *dialogue 1,1*

b **T11.3** Listen and check.

3 Write a similar four-line dialogue. Begin with one of the lines below.

- Would you like to come to …?
- Do you like … *-ing*?
- Have you … yet?

Pronunciation

1 **T11.4** When we make an invitation, it is important to sound friendly. Listen and notice the intonation.

2 Look at the tapescript on page 171. Listen again and practise saying the sentences.

Task: Survey about the most important things in life
Preparation: reading

MD Work individually. Look at the statements opposite that come from a survey about attitudes to life. Tick (✓) the appropriate box to show how much you agree with each statement. Check the meaning of any unknown words and phrases in your mini-dictionary.

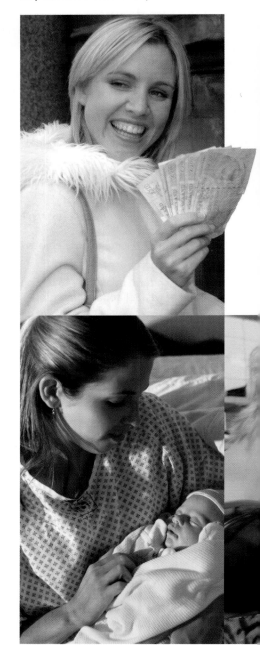

	Agree				Disagree
Having enough money is very important to me.	☐	☐	☐	☐	☐
I would like to be rich, famous or powerful one day.	☐	☐	☐	☐	☐
Having children is more important than having a successful career.	☐	☐	☐	☐	☐
I like spending money more than saving it.	☐	☐	☐	☐	☐
I would rather spend a quiet evening at home than go out to a party.	☐	☐	☐	☐	☐
Money can't buy happiness.	☐	☐	☐	☐	☐
Job satisfaction is more important than a big salary.	☐	☐	☐	☐	☐
Having good friends is more important than having a partner.	☐	☐	☐	☐	☐
I'd like to live or work abroad at some time in my life.	☐	☐	☐	☐	☐

Choose the eight things which are most important for you. Put them in order 1–8.	friends ☐	clothes ☐
	love ☐	car ☐
	family ☐	travel ☐
	money ☐	religion ☐
	good health ☐	sport ☐
	nice home ☐	politics ☐
	school/studies ☐	marriage ☐
	career ☐	other ☐

Task: speaking

1 Work in groups. Compare your answers with the other people in your group and explain why you answered as you did. What similarities and differences do you find?

▶ Useful language a

2 Prepare a short summary of what you found out.

▶ Useful language b

Useful language

a Comparing ideas

Why do you think that ...?

Which do you think is more important, ... or ...?

I agree with you.

For me, ... is more important than ... because ...

b Presenting the results

We all think that ...

Most/All/Some of us think that ...

We didn't agree ...

I was the only one who thought that ...

Wordspot
like

1 a Put the word *like* into the correct place in these sentences.

1   She's such a pretty baby. She looks ^like^ her mother, doesn't she?
2   That sounds David at the door now. I'll go and let him in.
3   I'll cook you a meal if you. How about it?
4   I'd really to meet Gwyneth Paltrow one day. She's such a fantastic actress.
5   What's the weather today?
6   'Just pull the handle and turn.' 'this?'
     'No, the other way.'
7   I've never eaten frogs' legs, but they say they taste chicken.
8   You can sit where you. There are plenty of chairs.
9   I don't feel cooking tonight. Shall we order a pizza?
10   What would everyone to drink?

b T11.5 Listen and check your answers.

2 Complete the diagram with phrases with *like*.

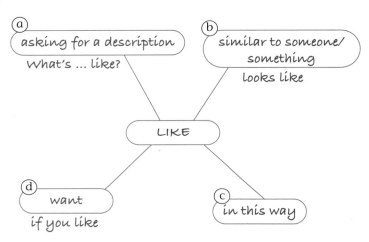

ⓐ asking for a description
What's ... like?

ⓑ similar to someone/ something
looks like

LIKE

ⓓ want
if you like

ⓒ in this way

3 Complete the sentences below using your own ideas.

a   I think ... sounds like ...
b   I'd like to know what the weather's like in ...
     right now.
c   This evening I feel like ...
d   ... tastes a bit like ...
e   Where would you like to ...?
f   I can ... if I like.
g   One person I'd like to meet is ...
h   Of all the people in my family, I look most like ...
i   I can ... where I like.

STUDY

Increasing your vocabulary (2): Remembering new words

1 Here are some ways of remembering new words and phrases. Which of them do you think are useful? Are there any that you think are not useful?

- Don't try and learn too many: it's difficult to remember more than five to eight new words or phrases. Choose the ones which you think are most useful and concentrate on them.

- Test yourself regularly. The Vocabulary sections in the *New Cutting Edge Pre-Intermediate Workbook* will help you do this, as well as the Practise and Remember sections here.

- Keep a vocabulary notebook. When you find a new word, look it up in a dictionary and copy a definition and example sentence into your notebook. Look at your notebook regularly.

- Write some of the new words on a card with a translation, and keep them in a box. Test yourself from time to time by picking cards out of the box and seeing how many you remember.

- Highlight all the words and phrases in the mini-dictionary as you learn them. Read through the mini-dictionary occasionally and see how many you remember.

2 Use one of the techniques above for a week or two. See how many new words you can remember, and which of the techniques you find most useful.

PRACTISE...

1 Verbs of liking and disliking ☐

Do the following sentences mean you like or dislike something? Write *L* for like and *D* for dislike.

a I'm crazy about it.

b I'm keen on it.

c I really enjoy it.

d I can't stand it.

e I hate it.

▶ Need to check? Language summary A, page 154.

2 Gerunds (*-ing* forms) ☐

Correct the sentences by adding *-ing* to **one** verb.

a I really enjoy watch sport on TV.

b Andy can't stand sit at home with nothing to do.

c Go to bed late makes you feel tired the next morning.

d John is crazy about cook Chinese food.

e When she goes away, Anne loves buy presents for all her family.

f I find listen to music helps me relax.

g I don't like listen to other people's conversations on the train!

h My mother hates drive at night.

i Are you keen on play tennis?

▶ Need to check? Language summary A, page 154.

3 *like doing* and *would like to do* ☐

Choose the correct alternative.

a We'd like to have / like having breakfast in our rooms, please.

b Douglas says he likes being / would like to be Prime Minister one day.

c I don't like driving / wouldn't like to drive in the city centre, so I always take the bus to work.

d Do / Would you like to spend Christmas with us this year?

e I like speaking / would like to speak to you for a moment, if that's all right.

f Do / Would you like reading?

g What do / would you like for your birthday?

h I like being / 'd like to be alone sometimes – I can think better!

▶ Need to check? Language summary B, page 154.

4 Hobbies and interests ☐

Cross out the nouns/phrases that do **not** go with the verbs.

a **make**   models / sport / jewellery

b **collect**   stamps / trading cards / chess

c **play**   backgammon / sport / jewellery

d **go to see** a musical / a TV programme / your favourite football team

▶ Need to check? Reading and vocabulary, page 98.

5 When an interest becomes an obsession ☐

Put the letters in bold in the correct order to make words which fit the definitions.

a **o b o s s i n e s**: an unhealthy interest in something

b **f i g s t**: presents

c **t i g w e h**: how heavy you are

d **s e e p t r a d e**: needing something very much

e **r e a c e l**: people eat this for breakfast

f **c l o c t e l**: to own a lot of things of the same type

g **f o r d f a**: have enough money for something

▶ Need to check? Reading and vocabulary, page 98.

6 *like* ☐

Rewrite the sentences, using phrases with *like*.

a I want to go to bed early tonight.
  I feel _____ .

b She looks very similar to her sister.
  She looks _____ .

c Do you want to come to the cinema with us?
  Would _____ ?

d Was the weather good on your holiday?
  What was _____ ?

e I want to talk to you for a moment.
  I'd _____ .

f I can stay in bed all day if I want to.
  I can stay in bed all day _____ .

▶ Need to check? Wordspot, page 104.

Pronunciation spot

The sounds /s/ and /ʃ/

1 T11.6 Listen to the difference between the /s/ and the /ʃ/ sounds in these words.

a   sort / short

b   seat / sheet

c   see / she

2 T11.7 Are the underlined letters pronounced /s/ or /ʃ/? Listen and check.

show   collection   successful   satisfaction

fashion   obsession   concert   chess   cereal

special   receiving   obsessed

REMEMBER!

Look back at the areas you have practised. Tick the ones you feel confident about. Now try the MINI-CHECK on page 160 to check what you know!

Got to have it!

▶ Present simple passive
▶ Past simple passive
▶ Vocabulary: Everyday objects
▶ Reading: *The world's most popular brands*
▶ Pronunciation: Regular past participles, Polite intonation
▶ Task: Decide what you need for a jungle trip
▶ Real life: Making suggestions

Vocabulary
Everyday objects

1 a 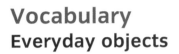 Look at the pictures on page 145. How many of the objects in the box can you find? Which objects can't you find?

keys	credit card	mobile phone
hairbrush	identity card	comb
lipstick	driving licence	plasters
razor	umbrella	sunglasses	torch
toothbrush	towel	shaving foam

b Study the pictures for one minute. Remember as much about the objects as you can.

2 a **T12.1** Listen to **ten** questions and write short answers for each one.

Example:
1 It was black.

b Work in pairs and compare your answers. Then look at the tapescript on page 171 and check with the picture on page 145. How many questions did you answer correctly?

3 a Which of the things in exercise 1 do you keep:

- in your bedroom?
- in the kitchen?
- in the bathroom?
- in your pockets?
- in your handbag?
- in your wallet/purse?

b Which of these things do you always take with you when you go out? Compare your list with a partner.

Reading and vocabulary

1 Which of the brand names and logos in the pictures do you recognise? What products do you think of when you see them?

2 **MD** Read the text about the world's most popular brands. Make a note of:

- where/when each company began.
- what they make.

3 Find the word or phrase in the text which tells you that:

a no other drink is more popular than Coca-Cola.
   best-selling
b Coca-Cola is a non-alcoholic drink.
c Rolex watches show you have a high social position.
d Nokia is the world's number one manufacturer of mobile phones.
e Samsung is a very large company.
f Emil Jallinek was a very rich man.
g there are KFC restaurants in many different countries.
h Colonel Sanders prepared the food at the petrol station himself.

4 Discuss these questions in small groups.

a What do you think of the brands in the text? How often do you use them?
b Which other famous brand names can you think of that are connected with:
   - clothes and sportswear?
   - cars and motorbikes?
   - accessories (bags, shoes, etc.)?
   - perfume?
   Which are your favourites?
c Are there any other brands from your country that are famous? Do you think it's a good idea to buy 'designer labels'? Why (not)?

The World's Most Popular BRANDS

Coca-Cola isn't just a drink, just as a Mercedes isn't just a car ... nowadays you have to be a brand. Here are six of the world's biggest brands and the stories behind them.

1 Coca-Cola
It is the world's number one brand and it is recognised by 94% of the world's population! For many years now, Coca-Cola has been a symbol of American culture. It is also the best-selling soft drink in the world. More than 60,000 products from the Coca-Cola company are drunk around the world every **minute**.

2 Rolex
One hundred years ago, few men wore wristwatches: but the Rolex company – based in Switzerland since 1908 – changed all that. They gave us the first wristwatches to show the date, the first diving watches, the first sports watch, the first watch to show different time zones ... and now Rolex watches (with prices that range from $3,000 to $20,000) are worn as a status symbol all over the world.

3 Nokia
Although most people in consumer surveys guess that Nokia is a Japanese company, it's actually from northern Europe! Originally a paper factory on the banks of the river Nokia in Finland, it became the world's leading mobile phone company in the late 1990s. Their first commercial mobile, the Mobira Talkman, which appeared in 1984, weighed 5 kg. The latest models are a bit lighter, however!

4 Samsung
Samsung (the name means 'three stars') began as a company in 1938. It originally produced noodles and dried fish! However, the company has come a long way since then. Mobile phones, digital cameras, flat-screen TVs, DVD players ... you name it, are all manufactured by this electronics giant from South Korea.

5 Mercedes
The makers of cars driven by the rich and famous, the Mercedes company has its base in Germany. Emil Jallinek, a wealthy banker who bought and loved cars, named the car Mercedes after his nine-year-old daughter. And the famous three-point Mercedes star was designed to symbolise the growth of the business into transport on land, sea and air.

6 KFC
The famous face which is seen at more than 9,000 KFC restaurants worldwide actually belonged to a real person: Colonel Harland Sanders. At different times he was a soldier, an insurance agent, a tyre salesman and worked in his parents' petrol station. When he saw that people were more interested in his home-made food than the petrol he was selling, he decided to open his first restaurant in Utah, USA, in the early 1950s. Colonel Sanders is also remembered for organising the biggest party in history – about 35,000 people attended his seventy-ninth birthday in 1970.

Language focus 1
Present simple passive

Grammar

1 Underline the passive forms in the sentences below.
   a *Colonel Sanders is also remembered for organising the biggest party in history.*
   b *The brand is recognised by 94% of the world's population.*

2 How do we form the Present simple passive?

3 Who or what is the subject of the sentences above?

4 In sentence a, who remembers Colonel Sanders? In sentence b, who recognises the brand?

▶ Read Language summary A on page 155.

Practice

1 Look again at the objects on page 145. Which object do the following sentences refer to?

a It's mainly used by women.
   It's usually sold in chemist's shops.
   It's usually kept in a handbag or purse.
b They're usually made out of plastic.
   They're sometimes kept in people's bathrooms.
   They are used more by men than by women.
c They're accepted all over the world nowadays.
   They're always made out of plastic.
   They're used by millions of people every day to buy things.

2 Write some more sentences about **three** of the other objects on page 145 using the Present simple passive. Give your sentences to another student. Can he/she guess which object they refer to?

Pronunciation

1 Notice that the pronunciation of regular past participles can be:
   a /ɪd/ accepted
   b /d/ recognised
   c /t/ liked

2 Look at the list of regular past participles in the tapescript on page 171. Are they pronounced like a, b or c?

3 **T12.2** Listen and check. Then listen again and practise saying the past participles.

Language focus 2
Past simple passive

1 a Here are three versions of how some everyday objects were invented. Which one do you think is true?

1 The first dark glasses:
   a were made to help pilots flying aeroplanes.
   b were used by blind people.
   c were worn in China by Chinese judges.

2 The first blue jeans:
   a were designed as working clothes by a man called Levi Strauss.
   b were made in China in the 1960s.
   c were worn by US soldiers during World War II.

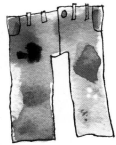

3 The first liquid shampoo:
   a was invented by a Frenchman called Charles Champú.
   b was used in India over two thousand years ago.
   c was developed by a bald man.

4 Chanel's most famous perfume is called No 5 because:
   a No 5 was its inventor's lucky number.
   b it took five years to develop it.
   c it was created in 1905.

b **T12.3** Listen and check your answers.

Grammar

1 Underline the passive forms in the sentences below.
  a *Chanel No 5 was introduced by the French fashion designer Coco Chanel in the 1920s.*
  b *Because she considered the number five to be her lucky number, the perfume was first presented on the 5th of May.*

2 How do we form the Past simple passive?

3 Who introduced Chanel No 5? What is the subject of each sentence?

▶ Read Language summary B on page 155.

Practice

1 Choose the best form (active or passive) to complete the sentences.

a The disposable razor invented / was invented by King Camp Gillette about 100 years ago.

b Hungarian journalist László Biro invented / was invented the world's first ballpoint pen in the 1930s.

c The DVD player is now the world's number one entertainment product. The first one manufactured / was manufactured in 1997.

d Singer Alison Krauss was worn / wore a pair of $2 million shoes at the 2004 Oscar ceremony. The shoes contain more than 500 diamonds and designed / were designed by US designer Stuart Weitzman.

e The world's first robot dog, Sony Corporation's ERS-110, went on sale in 1999. 3,000 sold / were sold in the first twenty minutes!

f In March 2004, 2.1 billion text messages sent / were sent in the UK alone. That's thirty-six text messages for each person!

g In 2003, Google voted / was voted the world's most popular Internet search engine.

h Ingvar Kamrad started / was started the Swedish furniture company IKEA more than fifty years ago. He named / was named the company after his own initials (IK), his parents' home (Elmtaryd = E) and his home village (Agunnaryd = A).

2 a Complete the sentences with the correct active or passive form of the verbs in brackets.

b **T12.4** Listen and check your answers.

Take a look around the room. How many people are wearing Nike? Millions of items of Nike sportswear (1) _____ (sell) every year, and the company is now the world's biggest sportswear manufacturer. The company – whose name (2) _____ (pronounced) Nye-kee – has come a long way from its small origins in the US state of Oregon.
The company (3) _____ (name) after the Greek goddess of victory, and (4) _____ (make) its first shoes back in the 1970s. Nowadays, Nike (5) _____ (know) for its clever advertising campaigns, using the world's best-known sportsmen and women. In the eighties and nineties, basketball legend Michael Jordan (6) _____ (make) a series of adverts for the company and in 1997, golf star Tiger Woods (7) _____ (pay) $40 million to star in another series of adverts.
A sign of the company's fame is that the word (8) _____ (no / appear) on the company's products. The famous Nike tick (9) _____ (recognise) all over the world. It (10) _____ (created) by a designer who (11) _____ (receive) just $35 for the idea!

Task: Decide what you need for a jungle trip

Preparation: reading

1 The TV show *Survival!* is sending a group of people to the island of Bedaira. Each person will be sent to a different part of the island. They need to survive for seventy-two hours without help from the others.

2 Read the fact file about Bedaira.

Bedaira

- Bedaira is a small island covered in tropical rainforest. It is completely uninhabited and can only be reached by helicopter.
- The average daytime temperature is 40°C. At night the temperature is a little cooler.
- It usually rains heavily in the late afternoon, and during the night.
- There are many streams, rivers and small lakes. There are plenty of fish in the rivers, but there are also some dangerous crocodiles.
- There are plenty of coconut trees and other fruit.
- The island is home to thousands of different types of insects (mosquitoes, etc.) plus spiders and snakes which can be a problem at night.

Task: speaking

1  Imagine you are going to take part in *Survival!* You are allowed to take a survival pack containing **twelve** items. Work individually and tick (✓) the items you would like to take with you.

batteries	insect repellent	sunglasses
blanket	knife	sunscreen
bottled water	magnifying glass	tent
clean clothes	matches	toilet paper
compass	mirror	toothbrush
digital camera	mobile phone	torch
energy bars	pencil and paper	umbrella
fishing rod	rope	water purification tablets

2 **a** Work in groups. Each person explains to the rest of the group which twelve items he/she would take and why.

▶ Useful language a

b Try to agree on the best list of twelve items. Explain your group's choice to the rest of the class.

▶ Useful language b

3 **T12.5** Listen to a survival expert talking about the items he thinks you should take. How many of his items are the same as yours?

Useful language

a Discussing what to take

I think it's a good idea to take a … because …

You'll need a … because …

It might rain / be very hot, so you need a …

I'd like to take a/some …

What else?

b Agreeing, disagreeing and making suggestions

How about a …?

You won't need a … because …

How about taking a/some …?

I (don't) think that's a good idea …

Real life
Making suggestions

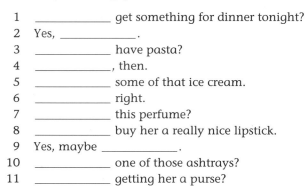

1 **T12.6** Listen to **four** conversations where people are making suggestions. Answer the following questions for each conversation.

- What is the relationship between the two people?
- What (if anything) do they decide to buy?

2 a **T12.6** Listen to the extracts again and complete the gaps in the sentences below.

1 _____ get something for dinner tonight?
2 Yes, _____ .
3 _____ have pasta?
4 _____ , then.
5 _____ some of that ice cream.
6 _____ right.
7 _____ this perfume?
8 _____ buy her a really nice lipstick.
9 Yes, maybe _____ .
10 _____ one of those ashtrays?
11 _____ getting her a purse?

b Look at the dialogues on page 172. Underline the phrases for making suggestions.

> ## Pronunciation
>
> **T12.7** Listen again to the phrases for making and responding to suggestions. Practise saying the phrases, paying attention to the intonation.

3 Choose **one** of the situations below. Then work in pairs and prepare a conversation to act out.

- You are trying to decide what to wear for a special occasion (a wedding, a party, etc.). Your partner makes some suggestions.
- You and your partner are going to cook dinner for some friends. You are trying to decide what to cook.
- Your partner is staying with an English family for a month and wants to take them a present from your country. Make suggestions.

STUDY...

English around you

Here are five ways to learn more English outside the classroom. Which of these do you do already? Are there any others you'd like to try?

- Look for signs in English. These are particularly common in hotels, large shops, railway stations, etc. Do you know what they mean? Can you translate them into your own language?

- Is there an English-language newspaper in your city/country? Buy a copy and see how many words/phrases you recognise.

- Look for websites which have an English version and a version in your own language. Read the English one first, then the one in your own language.

- Look for films/videos/DVDs which have English dialogue and subtitles in your own language. Note down the words/phrases that you recognise.

- Look for song lyrics in English (especially on the Internet). See if you can translate the words of your favourite songs into your own language.

Pronunciation spot

The plural 's': /s/, /z/ or /ɪz/

1 **T12.8** **Listen to the words below. Notice the different pronunciations of the plural form.**
a   pocket / pockets /s/
b   key / keys /z/
c   toothbrush / toothbrushes /ɪz/

2 **T12.9** **Look at the words below. Are the plural forms pronounced /s/, /z/ or /ɪz/? Listen and check.**

blanket   credit card
driving licence   glass   mirror
match   rope   tablet   tent
torch   towel   umbrella

3 **Practise saying the words, paying attention to the pronunciation of the final 's'.**

PRACTISE...

1 Present simple passive ☐

Write sentences in the Present simple passive, using the words in brackets.
a   Thousands of cars _____ every year.   (steal)
b   All the tickets _____ over the Internet.   (sell)
c   A lot of the world's gold _____ in South Africa.   (produce)
d   The rooms _____ every morning.   (clean)
e   Millions of barrels of oil _____ to Europe.   (export)

▶   **Need to check? Language summary A, page 155.**

2 Past simple passive ☐

Complete the sentences in the Past simple passive with the words in the box.

by   were   was   stolen   written

a   The three men _____ arrested at about six o'clock this morning.
b   The car _____ designed by a Korean company.
c   The new shopping centre was built _____ an American company.
d   The painting was _____ during the night.
e   The Harry Potter books were _____ by J K Rowling.

▶   **Need to check? Language summary B, page 155.**

3 Everyday objects ☐

Write the names of the objects next to the pictures.

a      _____

b   _____

c   _____

d   _____

e   _____

▶   **Need to check? Vocabulary, page 106.**

4 Making suggestions ☐

Choose the correct alternative.
a   Let's go / going / to go out for a meal after class.
b   How about play / playing / to play football?
c   Why don't we / we don't / we will stay in tonight?
d   Do / Shall / Would we go out and buy some sandwiches?
e   You could buy / buying / to buy her some sunglasses for her birthday.

▶   **Need to check? Real life, page 112.**

REMEMBER!

Look back at the areas you have practised. Tick the ones you feel confident about.
Now try the MINI-CHECK on page 161 to check what you know!

Choosing the right person

► Present perfect continuous with *how long, for* and *since*
► Present perfect continuous and Present perfect simple
► Vocabulary: Personal characteristics
► Pronunciation: Contracted forms: *'ve*
► Listening: Interview with the manager of Vacation Express
► Wordspot: *how*
► Task: Choose a manager for a pop group
► Writing: Completing an application form

Vocabulary and speaking
Personal characteristics

1 What do the people in the photos do? Would you like to do any of these jobs? Why?

2 **MD** Read the texts below. Check the meaning of the words and phrases in bold in your mini-dictionary. Which of the jobs in exercise 1 are the people talking about? (There is one extra picture.)

1
❝People come to you with all kinds of problems – not just medical ones – so of course you have to be **sympathetic** and a **good listener**. And of course, you need to keep up with all the latest treatments.❞

2
❝It's not enough to be **naturally talented**. You need to be **totally committed** to being the best: nothing else will do. If you are **lazy**, then you'll never reach the top.❞

3
❝You need to be **experienced** in the game: it's your job to make sure that players are **motivated** and to do that you have be **honest** with them.❞

4
❝Obviously, you need to be **imaginative**, but it's not just that. You need to be very **well-organised** with your time, and have a lot of **self-discipline**. Sometimes it's hard to think of ideas … but you have to keep thinking until something comes to you!❞

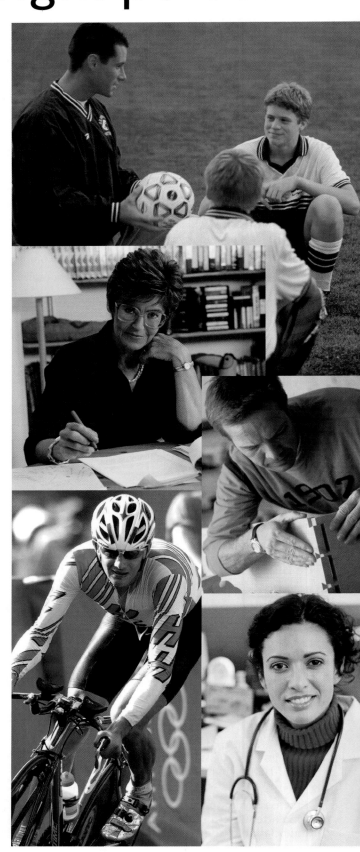

3 a **MD** Use your mini-dictionary to complete the table below.

Verb	Noun	Adjective
imagine		imaginative
organise		organised
	discipline	
		talented
		committed
		lazy
	experience	
		honest
		motivated
		sympathetic

b **T13.1** Listen to the pronunciation of each group of words and mark the stress on each one, as in the example.

4 a Which **three** of the qualities in exercise 2 are most important for a good:

- parent?
- restaurant manager?
- teacher?
- musician?
- lawyer?
- doctor?
- friend?
- language learner?

b Make sentences like this:

> A good parent has to be a good listener because …

> A good teacher has to be imaginative and sympathetic because …

Listening
Interview with the manager of Vacation Express

1 What kinds of jobs can you see in the pictures? Would you like to do any of these jobs? Why (not)?

2 **T13.2** Tanya Hanford runs an employment agency called Vacation Express, which finds summer jobs for people all over the world. Listen to her interview and make notes under these headings.

- Type of people who register
- Reasons for doing this type of work
- Personal qualities they are looking for
- Examples of jobs they are offering at the moment

3 a Choose the correct adjective from the box to make an adjective–noun combination.

big different great new positive special temporary ~~young~~

1 _young_ people
2 a _____ job
3 learn _____ skills
4 a _____ opportunity
5 a _____ attitude
6 a _____ advantage
7 a _____ talent
8 a _____ culture

b Check your answers in the tapescript on pages 172–173.

4 Would you like to do any of the jobs mentioned? Which one(s)? Why?

Language focus 1
Present perfect continuous with *how long*, *for* and *since*

1 Look at the pictures of **four** people who are looking for work with Vacation Express. What kind of work would each of them like to do? Can you think of a suitable job for each of them?

Sandra, 24

'I think I'm very good with children. When I was younger, I used to look after my two little brothers when my parents went out. Then, when I was at university, I earned extra money in the evenings by babysitting … so I've been looking after children since I was about fourteen. I'm twenty-four now, and I'd really like to travel before I settle down.'

Marc, 21

'I got interested in sailing when I was about eleven. My father used to take me sailing most weekends, and that's how I learned the basics … and from then, I just carried on. So I've been sailing for about ten years now … I just love it. It's more than a hobby to me now.'

Yolanda, 21

'Chinese culture fascinates me. I think learning the language is really the best way to find out about a culture, so I started studying Chinese two years ago. It's not an easy language at first, but I think I can make myself understood now. I'd like to spend some time there getting to know the people, and learning more about the place.'

Sanjiv, 28

'I left my job in January last year because I want to be comedian. I've been trying to get work for about a year now. I can sing as well, and play a bit of piano, but it's not easy to find work. Basically, I need to get experience in front of a live audience.'

Grammar

1 Look at the examples of the Present perfect continuous below. How do we form the Present perfect continuous?
 a ***I've been looking*** *after children since I was about fourteen.*
 b ***I've been trying*** *to get work for about a year now.*

2 In sentence a, does she look after children now? When did she start doing this? In sentence b, is he trying to get work now? When did he start doing this?

3 Which of the phrases in the box below go with *for*? Which go with *since*?

forty years   1965   last year   2004   Tuesday
five hours   six o'clock   six months   October

▶ Read Language summary A on page 155.

Practice

1 Answer the questions about the people on page 116, using the word in brackets.

a How long has Sandra been looking after young children? (since) <u>She's been looking after young children since she was about fourteen.</u>

(for)

_____

_____

b How long has Sanjiv been looking for work? (since)

_____

_____

(for)

_____

_____

c How long has Yolanda been studying Chinese? (for)

_____

_____

d How long has Marc been sailing? (since)

_____

_____

Pronunciation

With the Present perfect continuous, we often use contracted forms when we speak.

I/you/we/they have = I've/you've/we've

T13.3 Look at the tapescript on page 173. Listen to the full and contracted forms. Listen again and practise saying the contracted forms.

2 Read the information about Florence Gaulthier.

Florence Gaulthier came to live in England almost five years ago. A year later, her children began school, and Florence started working as a teacher – first as a teacher of French at a secondary school. She is now a full-time yoga teacher. 'I started studying yoga about ten years ago … I enjoyed teaching French, but I wanted a change. I started teaching yoga about a year and a half ago, and I must say I really enjoy it.'

3 **T13.4** Listen to the **four** questions about Florence. Write answers to the questions using *for* and *since*.

4 a Complete the gaps in the sentences below with information about yourself (you can invent information if you want).

1 I came to live in _____ (place) almost _____ ago.
2 _____ years later I _____ .
3 I began _____ing _____ about _____ ago.
4 I've been working as a _____ for _____ .
5 I've been studying _____ since _____ .
6 I've been playing _____ for _____ .
7 I joined _____ _____ years ago.
8 I've been driving since _____ .

b Ask and answer questions about your partner's information.

> How long have you been living in … ?

> Do you enjoy …-ing?

Language focus 2
Present perfect continuous and Present perfect simple

Hopeful pop stars brave the rain

- Hundreds of wannabe pop stars waited patiently in the rain outside London's Wembley Conference Centre yesterday. They were all hoping for the chance to star in a TV talent competition which will see five youngsters chosen to create a new pop group.

- First in the queue was 20-year-old Catherine Hill from Hayes in Kent.

- 'I've been here since midnight,' she said as the doors opened. 'I've got thirty seconds to show what I can do. I know it's going to be worth it.'

- 'I've wanted to be a pop star ever since I was little,' said 18-year-old Anton Yardley from Northampton. 'I've been taking singing and dancing lessons for over a year ... this is my big chance!'

- But judge Davina McAndrew was less optimistic when we spoke to her at the end of the day. 'Occasionally, you see someone who you know is going to be a star. But, to be honest, I haven't seen anything that really excites me today.'

1 Read the text above about the auditions for a TV talent competition. Do you know of similar TV programmes in your country?

2 Mark the following statements *True, False* or *Not sure*.

a   The people waiting outside the Wembley Conference Centre would like to become pop stars.
b   People had to wait for hours in hot, sunny weather.
c   They had less than a minute to show what they could do.
d   Anton Yardley began taking singing and dancing lessons when he was a small child.
e   Davina McAndrew felt she had seen a lot of exciting, talented young people.

Grammar

1 Look at the sentences below and answer the questions.
  a *I've been taking singing and dancing lessons for over a year.*
  b *I've taken singing and dancing lessons for over a year.*
  c *I've liked pop music ever since I was little.*
  d *I've been liking pop music ever since I was little.*

2 What is the form of the verb in sentence a? What is the form of the verb in sentence b?

3 Which of the four sentences is incorrect?

▶ Read Language summary B on page 156.

Practice

1 Look at the questions below. Write a new question for each one to ask one person.

a 1 How many people are learning (French/Spanish/another language)?
   Are you learning French?
  2 Who has been learning French/Spanish, etc., the longest?
   How long have you been learning French?

b 1 How many people own a car?
  2 Who has owned a car the longest?

c 1 How many people ride a scooter/motorbike?
  2 Who has been riding a scooter/motorbike the longest?

d 1 How many people wear glasses/contact lenses?
  2 Who has been wearing glasses/contact lenses the longest?

e 1 How many people own a pet?
  2 Who's had their pet the longest?

f 1 How many people play football/tennis/another sport?
  2 Who has been playing football/tennis, etc., the longest?

g 1 How many people play the guitar/the piano/another musical instrument?
  2 Who has been playing the guitar/the piano, etc., the longest?

h 1 How many people like football?
  2 Who has liked football the longest?

2 Choose **one** of the questions in exercise 1. Ask the question to as many students as possible. Then tell the class what you found out.

> Four people in the class are learning French.

> Carolina has been learning French the longest – she's been learning for two years.

Wordspot
how

1 **a** Complete the questions with *how* and a word from the box.

about   are   do (×2)   ~~far~~   fast   high   long   much   tall

1 A: How ___far___ is your house from the city centre?
  B: About 3 km.
2 A: How _____ coming to my house for lunch on Saturday?
  B: Sorry, I'm away this weekend.
3 A: How _____ did those earrings cost?
  B: I don't know. I didn't pay for them.
4 A: How _____ you spell your family name?
  B: It's H-E-R-N-A-N-D-E-Z.
5 A: How _____ has Stephanie been working here?
  B: Just over a month.
6 A: How _____ was he driving when he crashed his car?
  B: Only about fifty kilometres an hour.
7 A: How _____ you feeling now?
  B: Much better, thanks.
8 A: How _____ are you?
  B: I'm about 1 m 80.
9 A: Thomas, I'd like you to meet my father.
  B: How _____ you do, Mr Harvey. It's nice to meet you.
10 A: How _____ is this building?
   B: Over 100 m.

b **T13.5** Listen and check your answers.

2 Complete the diagram with phrases with *how* from exercise 1.

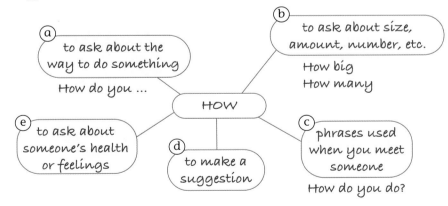

a to ask about the way to do something — *How do you …*

b to ask about size, amount, number, etc. — *How big / How many*

c phrases used when you meet someone — *How do you do?*

d to make a suggestion

e to ask about someone's health or feelings

HOW

3 **a** Work in pairs, Student A and Student B. Complete the questions using a phrase with *how*.

Student A: Look at the card on page 145.

Student B: Look at the card on page 146.

b Read the questions and three possible answers to your partner. He/She must guess the correct answer.

Task: Choose a manager for a pop group
Preparation: reading

1 Read about the group SPOTS!

SPOTS! – Jacqui, Zoë, Chris, Justin and Heather – are one of the most popular pop groups in the country right now. They became famous after winning the TV show *Star Search* last year. Since then, they have had many TV appearances, three hit singles and a hit album, *Spots Alive!* However, their manager, Des Conley, has decided to quit his job and start a new life as a TV presenter.

2 There are **four** candidates to replace Des Conley. Read about **two** of the candidates below. Complete the table with the facts about each person.

ANITA ROBSON (45)

Anita has been in show business all her life. As a child, she was the star in TV soap opera *On Top of the Hill*. At the age of sixteen, she began a musical career and she had several hit singles in the 1980s. Since then, she has been working mainly in the theatre and on TV. She has been married to millionaire rock guitarist Bob Marshall for ten years. Although she hasn't worked in the pop world for some years, she promises, 'My experience and my husband's money will keep SPOTS! at number one.'

JACK MARKUS (28)

Jack organised his first school concert at the age of ten, and managed his first group at the age of eighteen. In the 1990s, he was manager of the world-famous boy band Twizzle until they had serious financial problems. He came out of prison a year ago. Since then, he has been working as a car salesman. 'Now I've lost all my money, I've changed as a person. I have all the experience you could ask for. With me, SPOTS! could be even bigger than The Beatles, Abba and Elvis.'

	Good points	Bad points
Anita Robson		
Jack Markus		
Roland Bunting		
Simona Callas		

Task: speaking

1 You are going to find out about **two** other people who want to become manager of SPOTS! Work in pairs, Student A and Student B.

Student A: Read the information about Roland Bunting on page 147.

Student B: Read the information about Simona Callas on page 146.

2 Ask your partner questions to complete the missing information in the table. First, spend a few minutes thinking about the questions you are going to ask.

3 Put the candidates in order 1–4 (1 = the best, 4 = the worst). Think about how you made your choice and how you will persuade the others to agree with you.

▶ Useful language a and b

4 Compare your ideas in groups of three or four. Do the others agree or not? Then compare your ideas with the class.

▶ Useful language c

Useful language

a Saying who you prefer

I think ... will the best manager because ...

I prefer ... because ...

b Explaining your choice

... he/she has a lot of / no experience of ...

... he/she knows more about ...

... he/she could ...

c Agreeing and disagreeing

I agree.

I don't agree.

Yes, but what about ...?

Writing
Completing an application form

1 Ela is a student from Poland. She wrote an e-mail to Vacation Express. They sent her an application form to complete. Work in pairs.

Student A: Read her e-mail below.

Student B: Ask questions to complete the form on page 122.

What's her date of birth?

The twelfth of the seventh eighty-three.

2 Work in pairs and ask and answer questions about yourselves. Student A asks questions to complete the application form about Student B.

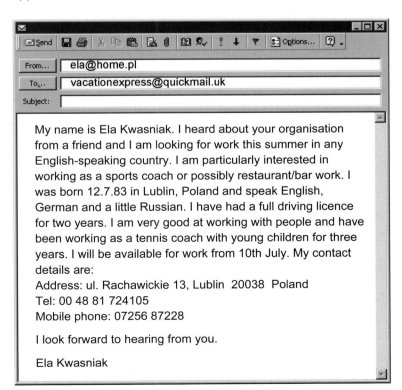

From... ela@home.pl

To... vacationexpress@quickmail.uk

Subject:

My name is Ela Kwasniak. I heard about your organisation from a friend and I am looking for work this summer in any English-speaking country. I am particularly interested in working as a sports coach or possibly restaurant/bar work. I was born 12.7.83 in Lublin, Poland and speak English, German and a little Russian. I have had a full driving licence for two years. I am very good at working with people and have been working as a tennis coach with young children for three years. I will be available for work from 10th July. My contact details are:
Address: ul. Rachawickie 13, Lublin 20038 Poland
Tel: 00 48 81 724105
Mobile phone: 07256 87228

I look forward to hearing from you.

Ela Kwasniak

VACATION EXPRESS

Please complete the entire application. Remember to tick the job you are applying for.

Mail this application to Vacation Express, PO Box 99, Lichton, LI2 8FH UK.

NAME: (First) _____

(Last) _____

SEX: MALE/FEMALE

DATE OF BIRTH: _____ (Month/Day/Year)

ADDRESS: _____

Post Code: _____ City: _____

Country: _____

TELEPHONE: (please include country/city code)

Home _____ Work _____

Mobile _____

E-MAIL: _____

DO YOU HAVE A VALID DRIVER'S LICENCE? YES/NO

LANGUAGES SPOKEN: _____

PRESENT OCCUPATION/STUDIES: _____

_____

WHICH OF THESE WORK AREAS MOST INTERESTS YOU?

Hotel / Restaurant ☐   Child Care ☐   Tour Guide ☐

Sports Instructor ☐   Activity Leader ☐

DESCRIBE ANY SPECIAL QUALIFICATIONS OR WORK EXPERIENCE YOU HAVE.

_____

_____

_____

_____

_____

HOW DID YOU HEAR ABOUT VACATION EXPRESS?

Newspaper ☐   Website ☐   Personal Recommendation ☐   Other ☐

I certify that the statements on this application are true and complete to the best of my knowledge.

SIGNATURE OF APPLICANT: _____

DATE: _____

3 Work in pairs and role play an interview for a job with Vacation Express. Take it in turns to be the interviewer and the applicant.

Revising effectively

Here are some suggestions about how to revise what you have learned in *New Cutting Edge Pre-Intermediate*. Try as many of these techniques as you can. Spend thirty minutes to an hour on each one.

Revision table

Don't leave all your revision to the last minute, and don't try to do too much at once. An hour a day for ten days is much more effective than ten hours in one day. Make a list of the areas you need to revise, and make a timetable. Cross out each point when you feel confident about it.

Contents page

Look at the contents pages (pages 2–5). How many of the grammar and vocabulary points do you feel confident about? Use a highlighter pen to mark the areas you still need to work on.

Workbook

Look at the Workbook, paying particular attention to the on Grammar and Vocabulary sections. Re-read the exercises you've already done and look carefully at any questions you got wrong.

Using the mini-dictionary to revise vocabulary

Look at the words in your mini-dictionary. Re-read the definitions and example sentences. They will help you remember the word.

Grammar

Look back at the Grammar sections in the Students' Book. Can you answer the questions? If not, look at the Language summary at the back of the book. Then look at the exercises in the Workbook for each language point.

Reading texts

Re-read as many of the reading texts as you can. They contain a lot of useful grammar and vocabulary. How much of the text do you remember? When you've read the text, close the book and write down words and phrases you think are useful.

PRACTISE...

1 Present perfect continuous with *how long*, *for* and *since* ☐

Complete the sentences below with *how long*, *for* or *since*

a _____ have you been waiting here?

b I've been studying English _____ three years.

c We've been coming here on holiday _____ 1998.

d Adrian has been looking for a new flat _____ October.

e He's been driving _____ about a year.

f _____ have you been sitting there?

▶ **Need to check? Language summary A, page 155.**

2 Present perfect simple and Present perfect continuous ☐

Which of the sentences below can be changed into the Present perfect continuous?

a How long have you known Steve?

b I've played tennis for many years.

c I've never liked romantic films.

d It's rained since six o'clock this morning.

e We've waited for nearly an hour.

▶ **Need to check? Language summary B, page 155.**

3 Personal characteristics ☐

Put the letters in bold in the correct order to make words which fit the definitions.

a **t i m m t e d o c**: ready to work hard at something

b **n e e c p i x e d e r**: good at something because you have done it before

c **n o t s h e**: not likely to steal or lie

d **z l a y**: not ready to work hard

e **i v i e t m a n g a i**: good at original pictures or ideas

f **d o v e m i t a t**: having a strong reason for doing something

g **p a t m y t i c s e h**: kind and understanding about other people's problems

▶ **Need to check? Vocabulary, page 114.**

4 Adjective-noun combinations ☐

Complete the sentences with the nouns in the box.

advantage   attitude   opportunity   skills   talent

a It's important to have a positive _____ and do your best at all times.

b From an early age, Lisa had a great _____ as a singer.

c I'm trying to improve my computer _____ by doing a course.

d The fact that he speaks English gives him a big _____.

e It is a very good _____ for you to show everyone what you can do.

▶ **Need to check? Listening, page 115.**

5 *how* ☐

Add one word to complete the questions with *how*.

a 'How was he driving?'
'140 km an hour.'

b How does this cost?

c How you spell your surname?

d 'How is Paul?'
'I'm 80.'

e 'How is it from here to the town centre?'
'About three km.'

f It's very nice to meet you. How do do?

g 'How you feeling now?'
'Much better, thanks.'

h How another cup of tea?

i How did you have to wait?

▶ **Need to check? Wordspot, page 119.**

Pronunciation spot

The /h/ sound

1 All the words below begin with the letter 'h', but in two of them it is not pronounced. Which ones?

hungry	heart
holiday	hot
headache	half
how	honest
hate	home
hour	homework

2 **T13.6** Listen and check. Practise saying the words, paying attention to the /h/ sound.

REMEMBER!

Look back at the areas you have practised. Tick the ones you feel confident about. Now try the MINI-CHECK on page 160 to check what you know!

Money, money, money

▶ **Past perfect**
▶ **Past time words:** *already, just* and *never … before*
▶ **Vocabulary:** Money
▶ **Reading:** Money facts
▶ **Pronunciation:** Large numbers, Polite intonation
▶ **Task:** Tell a story from pictures
▶ **Wordspot:** *make*
▶ **Real life:** Dealing with money

Vocabulary and speaking
Money

1 Look at the pictures. Which of the following can you see?

bank notes   cashpoint machine   change   coins
foreign currency   purse   wallet

2 **MD** Answer the questions below with a partner. Check the meaning of the phrases in bold in your mini-dictionary if necessary.

a   Have you ever:

- **won** any money (in a competition/lottery, etc.)?
- **lost** a large amount of money (in the street, etc.)?
- **earned** a lot of money?
- **spent** a lot of money **on** a Christmas or birthday present?
- **saved up** to buy something special and then thought it was **a waste of money**?

b   Do you never/sometimes/often:

- **lend** money **to** other people?
- **borrow** money **from** members of your family?
- forget to **pay back** money which you have borrowed?
- dream about buying things you really **can't afford**?

c   Who pays each of these? Who receives the money?

- pocket money
- a fine
- a salary
- a tip

3 a **Complete the sentences below with information which is true for you, or someone you know.**

1   I usually carry my money in my _____ .
2   In my country, it's (not) normal to give a _____ when you go to a restaurant.
3   I would never lend money to _____ because he/she would never pay it _____ .
4   I would never borrow money from _____ .
5   The name of the currency in my country is _____ . The most valuable coin is _____ and the smallest bank note is _____ .
6   I find it easy / difficult / impossible to save up.
7   I'd like to buy a(n) _____ , but I can't afford one.
8   The person in my family who earns the most money is _____ .
9   In my country, you can be given a _____ for parking or speeding offences.
10 I think _____ is a waste of money.
11 I often / sometimes / never use a cashpoint machine to get money.
12 When I was younger, I received _____ a week / month as pocket money.

b   **Compare your answers with a partner.**

Reading

1 Read the text below and complete the gaps with a number from the box.

> 2 17th ~~25~~ 34 100 150 1,000 1929 2002
> 100,000,000,000,000,000,000

Money Facts

○ More than (1) ___25___ countries use dollars as their currency – including Canada, New Zealand and Australia.

○ If you toss a coin, there are (2) _____ possible results: 'heads' or 'tails'. But if you toss a coin 10,000 times, there will be more 'heads' than 'tails'. This is because the picture of the head weighs more, so it ends up on the bottom.

○ There are about 450 dollar billionaires in the world. About (3) _____ of them live in the United States.

○ The world's highest denomination note was the (4) _____ Pengo note, issued in Hungary in 1946. It was worth about $0.20.

○ In (5) _____ century Sweden, the ten-daler coin weighed 19.71 kg.

○ On 1 January (6) _____, 15 billion euro banknotes and 50 billion euro coins came into circulation. Put end to end, the notes would reach to the Moon and back two and a half times.

○ The world's smallest bank note came from Romania. The ten-bani note was (7) _____ mm x 45 mm – the same size as a postage stamp.

○ The heads on US dollar bills have not changed since (8) _____.

○ In Australia, the $5, $10, $20, $50 and (9) $_____ notes are all made of polymer – a type of plastic.

2 Check your answers on page 142. Which facts do you find most surprising? Did you know any of them already?

Pronunciation

1 **T14.1** Listen and write down the numbers you hear.

2 Check your answers in the tapescript on page 173.
Notice that we say:
Two **thousand** pounds (not two ~~thousands~~ pounds).
Four hundred **and** fifty (not four hundred fifty).
Nineteen **point** seven (not nineteen ~~comma~~ seven).

3 Practise saying the numbers in the text in Reading exercise 1.

Language focus 1
Past perfect

1 Read the first part of **three** jokes. Which joke goes with the picture?

① The boss of a company called one of his employees into his office. The young man – who had only worked for the company for a few weeks – sat down nervously.
'When you started working here a month ago, your salary was $50,000,' said the boss. 'Two weeks later, I doubled your salary to $100,000. Now I'm going to pay you $250,000 a year. What do you say to that?'
'_____,' said the young man.

② The American comedian Jack Benny was famous for being mean.One day he had been to the bank and he was on his way home, when a robber appeared and pointed a gun at him
'Your money or your life,' hissed the robber.
There was a long silence.
'What's the matter with you? said the robber. 'I said your money or your life.'
'_____,' said the old man.

③ Someone asked a millionaire how he had become so rich.
'As a young man, I was very poor,' he said. 'I spent my last $100 on an old second-hand car. I spent the next week cleaning and repairing it. Then I sold the car for $200. With the $200, I bought two second-hand cars. I spent the next two weeks cleaning and repairing them. Then I sold them for $400. It wasn't much, but I had made a profit of $200.'
'What then?'
'My wife's father_____,' he replied.

2 **T14.2** Listen and write in the last line of each joke. Which do you think is the funniest?

Grammar

1 Look at the sentence below. Which verb is in the Past simple? Which is in the Past perfect?
*He **had been** to the bank and he **was** on his way home.*

2 Which action happened first: going to the bank or going home?

3 Look again at the jokes in exercise 1. How many other examples of the Past perfect can you find?

▶ Read Language summary A on page 156.

Practice

1 Match the beginnings of the sentences in A with the endings in B. Put the verbs into the Past perfect.

A
a She couldn't afford the shoes because
b By the time George retired,
c Hilda and Jerry bought a new car
d Michael was in a panic because
e When Grandma died, nobody knew that

B
1 with the money they (win) in a competition.
2 he (lost) his wallet.
3 she (spend) all her money on presents for her family.
4 she (save up) thousands of pounds in a box.
5 he (earn) enough money to buy a holiday home.

2 **a** Complete the gaps with verbs from the box.

died	discovered	had	had arrested
had arrived	had bought	had made	
had sold	~~sent~~	thought	tried	was

When, in 1926, a US court (1) ___sent___ a man called Arthur Ferguson to prison for five years, it (2) _____ the end of an amazing criminal career. The police (3) _____ him several months earlier as he (4) _____ to sell the Statue of Liberty to an Australian tourist. After the arrest, the police soon (5) _____ that Ferguson (6) _____ money by selling famous buildings several times before.

Ferguson (7) _____ in the United States from Scotland the previous year. Soon after his arrival, he sold a luxurious house in Washington to a rich Texas farmer. But for the farmer, this wasn't an ordinary house: he (8) _____ that he (9) _____ the White House – the home of US Presidents for 150 years!

Before coming to America, Ferguson (10) _____ Buckingham Palace, home of the English royal family, for £2,000, Big Ben for £1,000 and Nelson's Column for £6,000 – all to rich Americans who perhaps (11) _____ more money than intelligence. Ferguson (12) _____ in 1938.

b **T14.3** Listen and check your answers.

Language focus 2
Past time words

1 Read the newspaper stories about how people got money – or lost it – in unusual ways. Match a headline to each newspaper story (there is one extra headline).

a EASY COME … EASY GO

b Why the Internet is bad for you

c THE MOST GENEROUS MAN IN THE WORLD

d Love wins in the end

1 A Swiss man was amazed to see an extra £100,000 in his bank account one day. He started spending the money immediately, organising expensive parties for his friends and buying things he'd never been able to afford before. When the bank noticed its mistake – the money actually belonged to a much richer man with the same name – he had already spent £85,000. A court ruled that the money wasn't his, and that he would have to repay the full amount.

2 As he arrived at the restaurant where he planned to give his girlfriend a wonderful surprise, Eric Culbertson checked in his pocket … and realised that he had left the $10,000 engagement ring he had just bought in a taxi! He had saved up for a year to buy the ring. The next day, Culbertson bought another ring for just $25 and asked his girlfriend to marry him. She said yes.

3 A man in Germany had a horrible surprise when he checked his e-mail one morning. Thomas Vogel, aged 22, found he had bought items worth nearly £1 million from an Internet auction company. Thomas Vogel, who makes his living by gardening and planting trees, says he had never heard of the company before and knew nothing about the £800,000 house, £100,000 car and £25,000 small aeroplane he had just bought. The Internet company insisted that he paid for the items, however, as the bids were made in his name. 'I don't know what I'm going to do or how I'm going to pay,' he said. 'I can't plant that many trees.'

Grammar

Look at the examples below. Underline the phrases that mean the same as the word(s) in bold.

1 *… the $10,000 engagement ring he had **just** bought.*
   a a long time before
   b a short time before

2 *When the bank noticed its mistake, he had **already** spent $85,000.*
   a after that time   b before that time

3 *… he'd **never** heard of the company **before**.*
   a he had heard of the company in the past
   b it was the first time he'd heard of the company

► Read Language summary B on page 156.

Practice

Choose the correct time words to complete the sentences.

a Although he had already / before / never spent most of the money, the Swiss man had pay it all back to the bank.

b He'd already / before / never had so much money already / before / never, so it was a new experience for him.

c Eric Culbertson had before / never / just arrived in the restaurant when he realised he'd lost the engagement ring.

d He ran outside to look for the taxi, but it had already / before / never left.

e He had already / never / just asked anyone to marry him before, so he was probably a little nervous.

f Thomas Vogel had already / just / never bought anything over the Internet already / before / just.

g The e-mail told Mr Vogel that he had before / just / never bought nearly £1 million worth of items.

h The Internet company said that they had already / just / never known a mistake like this already / before / just.

Task: Tell a story from pictures
Preparation: vocabulary

The pictures below tell a true story. Match the phrases to the pictures.

1 'Don't worry, darling. Money isn't important ... love is the most important thing.'
2 'Yes! I've won!'
3 a hole in the floorboards
4 inside an envelope
5 tearing up money
6 playing with a coin
7 'But you said money isn't important ...'

a week later ...

Task: speaking

1 What do you think the story is? Spend a few minutes planning how to tell the story, using the phrases and pictures on page 128 to help you.

► Useful language a

2 Practise telling the story in pairs.

3 **T14.4** Listen to the version of the story told by the father. There are **five** differences from the version in the pictures. Make a note of the differences you hear.

4 Work in groups and make a list of the differences you found. Compare your answers with the class.

► Useful language b

Useful language

a Telling the story

One day, a little boy was …

His father / The little boy said …

A few days later …

He was horrified/delighted …

b Finding the differences

We've got …

The first one is …

Another thing that's different is …

In the first story …, but in the second story …

Wordspot
make

1 **T14.5** Complete the gaps in the sentences with words from the box. Then listen and check your answers.

> a cup of tea   a mess   a phone call   angry   cry   dinner
> feel   friends   noise   profit

a   Wait a minute – I need to make _____ before we go out. Have you got Ana's number?

b   His new Internet company, Opportunities.com, made a big _____ in its first year.

c   Are you hungry? I'll start making _____ if you want.

d   Stella's already made lots of _____ at her new school. She's very happy there.

e   That new washing machine is making a very strange _____ .

f   You look really tired. Sit down and I'll make you _____ .

g   Our Maths teacher is really horrible – she nearly made Lucy _____ the other day.

h   Andrew really makes me _____ . Why is he always, always late!!

i   You can only use this room if you promise not to make _____ .

j   I hate flying. It makes me _____ really ill.

2 Complete the diagram with phrases with *make* from exercise 1.

(a) produce something
make a sandwich/breakfast/lunch

(b) make money
He makes $5,000 a month. The company made a loss last year.

MAKE

cause something

(e) other phrases
make a mistake/speech/decision/bed

(d) make + verb
She made us wait.
He makes me laugh.

(c) make + adjective
It makes me happy/sad.

3 Discuss with a partner. Think of **two**:

• things that make you angry.
• things that make a lot of noise.
• reasons why people make speeches.
• things that are made in Scotland.
• things that you can make with eggs.
• mistakes that you often make in English.

Real life
Dealing with money

1 Where are the people in the pictures? In which of these situations would you:

a   change money?
b   pay by credit card?
c   ask about the exchange rate?
d   leave a tip?
e   ask how much something costs?
f   ask if service is included?
g   open a bank account?
h   pay commission?

2 **T14.6** You will hear **four** conversations. Match the conversations with the pictures above.

3 Listen to the conversations again and complete the information below.

a   The woman wants to change $ _____ into pesos. The exchange rate is _____ to the dollar. She receives _____ .
b   The woman would like to buy some earrings. The larger ones cost _____ , and the smaller ones cost _____ .
c   In order open a bank account, the young man needs to bring his _____ and a _____ from his _____ .
d   To drink, the two young women had one _____ and a _____ . They also ordered a club sandwich and a _____ . This all cost _____ , and they decided to leave _____ as a tip.

4 **a** Look at these sentences. In each case cross out the incorrect/unnecessary word.

1   What's the exchange rate for ~~the~~ US dollars?
2   I'd like to change this into pesos, please. It's 200 of American dollars.
3   Excuse me. How much are these earrings cost?
4   OK, I'll take this one pair.
5   Can I pay by my credit card?
6   What kind documents do I need?
7   Can we to have the bill, please?
8   Is it service included?
9   Do you think we should to leave a tip?

b **T14.7** Listen and check your answers.

Pronunciation

T14.7 Listen again to the correct sentences from exercise 4. Practise saying them. Pay attention to the polite intonation.

5 **a** Look at the tapescript on page 173. Underline any other useful phrases for dealing with money.

b Look back at the pictures. Invent **three** conversations of your own, using some of the phrases from exercise 4.

STUDY...

Test dos and don'ts

If you have to take a test at the end of your course, these dos and don'ts could help.

Dos

- **Do** make sure you know how much time you have for the whole test. Divide up the time for each section, according to the number of questions.
- **Do** read each question carefully so you know exactly what to do (for example, underline the correct answer, ~~cross out~~ an incorrect answer, write in the correct preposition, etc.).
- **Do** make sure you answer **all** the questions.
- **Do** check **all** your answers before you give in your paper.

Don'ts

- **Don't** spend too much time thinking about an answer. Answer the questions you're sure about first.
- **Don't** keep changing your answer. Leave the answer blank until you make a definite decision, but ...
- **Don't** leave a question without answering it. If you don't know the answer, guess.

Good luck!

Pronunciation spot

Review

1 **Look at the symbols. How many of them can you remember? Find a word for each sound in the list below. Some words contain more than one of the sounds.**

a /w/	f /ŋ/	k /eɪ/
b /v/	g /s/	l /æɪ/
c /θ/	h /ʃh/	m /əʊ/
d /ð/	i /æ/	n /ɒ/
e /n/	j /ʌ/	o /h/

bank   cash   eight   envelope
fine   horrible   money   note
office   ring   sell   them
thousand   tin   wallet

2 **T14.8** **Listen and check. Practise saying the words.**

PRACTISE...

1 Past simple and Past perfect ☐

Choose the correct alternative.

a When I had got / got downstairs the phone had stopped / stopped ringing.
b I had been / was sorry to leave, as I enjoyed / had enjoyed the party very much.
c Silvana had been / was very upset because she had lost / lost her purse.
d It had been / was a very difficult day, so I had gone / went to bed early.

▶ **Need to check? Language summary A, page 156.**

2 Past time words: *already*, *just* and *never ... before* ☐

Put the words brackets in the correct place in the sentence.

a Our friends had left when we arrived at the party.   (already)
b Laura had never eaten Thai food.   (before)
c He had left the bank when the alarm bell rang.   (just)
d She had been married for ten years when she met him.   (already)

▶ **Need to check? Language summary B, page 156.**

3 Money ☐

In the box, find:

1 **four** things you might keep in your wallet or purse.
2 **three** verbs which mean you receive money from other people.
3 words for money you pay:
   - after committing a crime.   • to people who work.   • to a waiter/hairdresser.

> a fine   a tip   bank notes   borrow   change   coins
> earn   foreign currency   salary   spend   win

▶ **Need to check? Vocabulary, page 124.**

4 *make* ☐

Cross out the word or phrase that does not belong with *make* in these sentences.

a Frank really makes me angry / laugh / to laugh.
b Don't worry. I'll make a cup of tea / dinner / the washing up.
c Please don't make a mess / noise / lie.
d It's not always easy to make a bank account / friends / a profit.
e The film really made me cry / to cry / feel sad.

▶ **Need to check? Wordspot, page 129.**

5 Dealing with money ☐

Put the words in the correct order to make sentences.

a Do / should / you / tip / a / think / leave / we ?
b like / this / I'd / into / please / change / euros / to
c the / we / Can / please / have / bill ?
d euros / rate / the / exchange / What's / for ?

▶ **Need to check? Real life, page 130.**

REMEMBER!

> Look back at the areas you have practised. Tick the ones you feel confident about.
> Now try the MINI-CHECK on page 161 to check what you know!

Imagine ...

▶ Conditional sentences with *would*
▶ *will* and *would*
▶ **Pronunciation:** Contractions *'ll* and *'d*
▶ **Reading:** *Imagine: the story of a song*
▶ **Song:** *Imagine*
▶ **Task:** Choose people to start a space colony

Reading

1 Do you have a favourite song? What is the title? Who sang/wrote it? Why do you like it?

2 The pictures all show John Lennon, member of The Beatles and writer of the song *Imagine*. Discuss which of the statements you think are true.

a John Lennon was born in the United States.
b He and Paul McCartney wrote songs for The Beatles.
c He was married to a Japanese woman.
d He wrote *Imagine* with Paul McCartney.
e He lived in New York City for several years.
f He died in London.
g There is a special memorial to John Lennon in Central Park.
h People now pay a lot of money for his possessions.

3 Read the text about Lennon's life to check your answers.

4 Below are the answers to some questions. Write the questions.

a in Liverpool
  Where was John Lennon born?
b 1957
c on an aeroplane
d outside his home
e in Central Park
f *Bohemian Rhapsody*
g £1.6 million
h twelve

IMAGINE
THE STORY OF A SONG

In 1940 John Winston Lennon was born in Liverpool, a city in the north-west of England.

In 1957 Lennon met Paul McCartney and they began writing songs together. They later formed The Beatles, who became one of the most successful groups in pop history during the 1960s.

In 1958 Lennon's mother, Julia, died in a road accident.

In 1969 Lennon married Japanese artist Yoko Ono.

In 1970 The Beatles broke up and Lennon began a solo career, becoming more and more active as a peace campaigner. He wrote the lyrics to *Imagine* on the back of a hotel bill while he was on an aeroplane.

In 1971 Lennon recorded *Imagine*. A pop video showing Lennon performing the song with Yoko at his side was also made, but *Imagine* was not released as a single. In the same year, Lennon went to live in New York City.

In 1980 Lennon was shot dead outside his New York home by an obsessed fan. *Imagine* was released as a single and became a Number One record around the world

In 1984 the 'Imagine' memorial for peace was opened in Central Park, New York, near Lennon's former home. Every year, thousands gather round the memorial on Lennon's birthday (October 9th) to remember Lennon's life and work.

In 1990 on Lennon's 50th birthday, *Imagine* was played simultaneously in 130 countries. Yoko Ono says, 'I would like us to remember and celebrate John's birthday as a day of love because he was a man of love and because love is much needed at this time.'

In 1999 the lyrics to the song were voted the UK's favourite in a BBC poll. The song itself was voted the second favourite song of the millennium (after Queen's *Bohemian Rhapsody*).

Song
Imagine

1 **MD** Mark the pairs of words *S* if they mean the same and *D* if they are different. Can you explain the differences?

a peace / war D
b above us / below us
c it's easy / it isn't hard
d heaven / hell
e heaven / the sky
f to kill / to die
g to imagine / to wonder
h possessions / furniture
i greed / hunger
j to share / to join

2 **T15.1** Listen to the song and complete the gaps.

3 **a** Tick (✓) the things that John Lennon thought were good. Put a cross (✗) next to the things he didn't like.

> brotherhood countries dreamers greed heaven hell
> hunger living for today living in peace possessions

b Which of his ideas do you agree/disagree with? Do you agree with the Internet fan?

In 2000 the Steinway piano Lennon used when he was writing *Imagine* was sold to pop star George Michael for £1.6 million – the highest price ever paid for a piece of pop memorabilia. It is now in a museum in Liverpool, Lennon's home town. The pair of glasses which Lennon wore while he was writing the song were also sold for £6,000.
In 2001 the airport in Liverpool was renamed John Lennon Airport.
In 2004/5 a musical show about John Lennon's life – *Imagine* – opened in New York. Twelve actors played the part of Lennon from his earliest years to his death. The dream of *Imagine* lives on!

What they said about the song:
'I don't know what the music of the future will sound like, but I believe a song like this is one that can be enjoyed by all generations to come.'
Lennon fan on the Internet

'This was the song which John really wanted to communicate to the world. So he really made it very sweet and simple – to get the message across.'   *Yoko Ono*

'It's just a song, man, it doesn't mean anything.'   *John Lennon*

IMAGINE

Imagine there's no (1) _____
(2) _____ if you try
No hell (3) _____
(4) _____ only sky
Imagine all the people
Living for today

Imagine there's no (5) _____
(6) _____ to do
Nothing to kill or (7) _____ for
And no religion too
Imagine all the people
Living life (8) _____

You may say I'm a (9) _____
But I'm not the only one
I hope some day you'll (10) _____ us
And the world will live as one

Imagine no (11) _____
I (12) _____ if you can
No need for (13) _____ or (14) _____
A brotherhood of man
Imagine all the people
(15) _____ all the world

You may say I'm a (16) _____
But I'm not the only one
I hope some day you'll (17) _____ us
And the world will live as one

Language focus 1
Conditional sentences with *would*

Underline the endings to the sentences you think are true. (You can underline both endings if you like.) Compare your answers with a partner.

1 If there were no countries,
- the world would be a better place.
- life wouldn't be so interesting.

2 If people didn't have possessions,
- everyone would be happier.
- life would be much more difficult.

3 If there weren't any wars,
- we would all have a better life.
- people would soon get bored.

4 If everyone lived only for today,
- we would enjoy life a lot more.
- there would be chaos.

Grammar

Look at the sentence below and answer the questions.

if clause	main clause

If there were no countries, the world would be a better place.

a Does this sentence refer to:
 • a real possibility? • an imaginary situation?
b What is the verb form in the *if* clause?
c What is the verb form in the main clause?
d Does the sentence refer to:
 • the past? • the future? • no specific time?

▶ Read Language summary A on page 156.

Practice

1 Choose the correct form of the verb to complete the sentences.

a If there were / would be no countries, there weren't / wouldn't be any governments or laws.
b We didn't need / wouldn't need policemen or prisons if we didn't have / wouldn't have any laws.
c If countries didn't / wouldn't exist, people didn't / wouldn't need passports.
d Perhaps everyone spoke / would speak the same language if there weren't / wouldn't be any countries.
e If there were / would be no possessions, nobody needed / would need money any more.
f If people didn't / wouldn't need to buy things, there weren't / wouldn't be any shops.
g Life would be / was very different if we couldn't / wouldn't be able to go shopping.
h If people didn't / wouldn't own anything, what did / would they give each other as presents?

2 a Read the sentences below.

If I were president of my country, I'd make the weekend four days long.

If we had four-day weekends, people wouldn't have enough to do.

If people didn't have enough to do, everyone would get very bored.

If everyone was very bored, they might start thinking about politics.

If people started thinking about politics, they might look for a new president.

b Make another 'chain' of conditional sentences like the one above. On a piece of paper, begin with **one** of these ideas:

- If all the world spoke one language, …
- If everyone had the same amount of money, …
- If I could be another person for one day, …
- If I had all the money in the world, …
- If I could change one thing in my country, …

c Hand your paper to another pair to write the next sentence. They hand the paper to the next pair. Continue until you have **five** sentences.

Language focus 2
will and *would*

1 Which of these things do you think are possible? Compare your ideas with a partner.

- The Earth will become too crowded and polluted for us all to live on.
- Human beings will start a new society in space.
- People will decide to live on the Moon rather than on Earth.

2 Read the extract from a web page. Would you ever volunteer for a space mission like this? Why / Why not?

> Humans could be living on the Moon in just twenty years, says scientist. James Davies of the United Space Agency says, 'Soon scientists will be able to build somewhere for visiting astronauts to live.' Mr Davies says governments as well as scientists have to make it possible to live on the Moon.

3 **T15.2** Listen to some young people talking about living in space. Complete the missing phrases using the verb in brackets.

a

'If we _____ (continue) to pollute the Earth, humanity _____ (survive). Maybe living in space is one answer.'
Nadine, Australia

b

'I _____ (go) there on holiday if I _____ (have) the chance, but I don't think I'd live there … I _____ (miss) all my friends on Earth too much.'
Amy, Berkshire

c

'If I _____ (get) the chance, I _____ (go) and live on Saturn, because it's got rings round it and it looks much nicer than the other planets.'
Sinead, Ireland

Grammar

Look at the sentences below and answer the questions.
If I got the chance, I'd go and live on Saturn.
If we continue to pollute the Earth, humanity won't survive.
a Which sentence is about something that might really happen?
b Which sentence is about an imaginary situation?
c What are the verb forms in the *if* clause of each sentence?
d What are the verb forms in the main clause of each sentence?

▶ Read Language summary B on page 156.

Practice

Complete the sentences below with your own ideas using *will* or *would*. Compare your answers with a partner.

1 If I learn to speak English well, …
2 If I could live anywhere in the world, …
3 If I have time this week, …
4 If I could change places with a celebrity, …
5 If I go out tonight, …
6 If I were invisible, …
7 If I'm up early tomorrow, …
8 If I could live my life again, …
9 If I live to be eighty years old, …
10 If I were the richest person in the world, …

Pronunciation

1 **T15.3** Listen and write the sentences you hear. Notice the pronunciation of *'ll* and *'d*.

2 Look at the tapescript on page 174 to check. Listen again and practise saying the sentences.

Task: Choose people to start a space colony

Preparation: reading

1 Look at the picture. Imagine you had to survive on a space colony. Add to the lists of things you would need, and the kind of people you would need to have with you.

Things you would need	People you would take with you
air space suit	a doctor an expert on …

2 **MD** Read about the new planet Hero and answer the questions. Compare your answers with a partner.

a   Why do scientists think that humans will be able to live on Hero?

b   Is there any alien life on Hero?

c   How many people will they send to Hero, and why?

d   When will these people come back to Earth?

e   Will other people join the space colony later?

f   What will the volunteers take with them?

g   How long will it take to travel to Hero?

h   How many people have volunteered to go?

3 Read about the ten candidates. Decide which **six** candidates you want to take. Underline the reasons that make them suitable to travel and put a line through any things that make them unsuitable.

THE NEW PLANET HERO

Scientists have discovered a new planet, Hero. They are very confident that human beings will be able to live there as it has plenty of water, light and oxygen, and the temperature and air are all very similar to those on Earth. They have done tests and know that plants can grow there. They have not found any alien life there, though they cannot be sure it doesn't exist.

They have decided to send a spaceship of people to Hero from Earth to start a space colony, and a new human society. But the spaceship can only carry six people: any volunteers with children will have to leave them behind. These people will have to stay on Hero for the rest of their lives. No one else will be able to join the space colony for at least a hundred years. They will take enough food tablets for five years, together with four guns to protect themselves, and blankets, space-tents, etc. The spaceship will be controlled from Earth, so there will not be a pilot. The journey to Hero will last about ten weeks.

The organisers have asked for volunteers, but only ten people have come forward.

The spaceship must leave in ten days' time, so there is no time to find new volunteers.

Name
Natalya B (female)
Jack G (male)
Renato B. (male)
Claudette P (female)
Brandon P (male)
Gheeta S (female)
Yong (male)
Luciana D (female)
Chan (male)
Lourdes L (female)

Age, Nationality, No. of children	Occupation	Health
38, Russian No children.	University lecturer (Mathematics).	Very good.
42, US Divorced, no children.	Engineer.	Was treated for cancer two years ago.
76, Italian 7 children.	Retired doctor. Has worked all over the world.	OK. Has some difficulty walking without help.
22, US 6 months pregnant.	Factory worker. Married to Brandon P (see below).	Heavy smoker.
25, US Wife pregnant (see above).	Unemployed. 1 year in prison for violent crime. Married to Claudette P (see above).	Excellent. Very fit.
29, Indian Single, no children.	Nurse.	Suffers from depression.
56, Korean Widower, 1 child.	Has worked as an international lawyer.	Good.
17, Brazilian. Unmarried, no children.	Wants to be a pop singer when she's older.	Excellent.
31, Hong Kong Chinese Divorced, 3 children.	Policeman.	Very good.
43, Spanish 1 child.	Agricultural scientist.	History of health problems, but these now appear to be finished.

Task: speaking

1 Work in pairs. Discuss who you think are the **six** best candidates and why.

▶ Useful language a

2 Work in groups and compare your answers and reasons. Try to agree on the **six** best people to take.

▶ Useful language a and b

Useful language

a Explaining why people are suitable

He/She would be suitable because …

He/She knows a lot about …

He/She has a lot of experience of …

He/She can have children …

We need someone who can …

He/She could …

b Explaining why people are not suitable

There might be problems with …

He/She's too old to… / too young to …

If … happened, perhaps he/she would …

3 Compare your answers with the class.

4 Do you think there will be ever a space mission like this? Why / Why not? Would you volunteer? Why / Why not?

Optional writing

You are one of the people travelling to Hero. You have just landed on the new planet. Write a message to a friend back on Earth. Write about:

- the planet.
- the journey there.
- the other people you are with and what you think of them.
- how you feel at the moment.
- what you want to say to your friends and family back on Earth.

A Present perfect simple and Present perfect continuous, Past simple and Past perfect

Underline the correct verb form in the article below.

....

Man, 56, to take school exams for 38th time

....

Have you ever (1) been failing / failed a school exam? If so, you must feel some sympathy for Shivdan Yadav, from the Indian province of Rajasthan. He (2) has been trying / is trying to pass his school exams for thirty-eight years, but he still (3) hasn't been having / hasn't had any success.

At the age of eighteen, Shivdan (4) has taken / took his school leaving exams for the first time and, unfortunately, he (5) failed / has failed. At that time, he (6) has been / had been engaged to a local girl for several months. As Shivdan (7) had previously said / has previously said that he would only marry when he (8) passed / passes his exams, her father (9) agreed / had agreed to postpone the wedding. But three years later, he still (10) didn't pass / hadn't passed. His girlfriend (11) had become / has become his ex-girlfriend, so his fiancé's parents (12) decided / have decided to look for another husband for their daughter.

Since then, Shivdan (13) has been studying / is studying hard, his ex-fiancé (14) has become / has been becoming a grandmother … and Shivdan (15) has been staying / has stayed single.

B Vocabulary: Connections

Work in small groups. Take it in turns to choose a word or phrase from each box and explain the connection between them.

Example:
ambition / pop star
When I was younger, it was my ambition to be a pop star.

ambition	imagine	obsessed with
can't afford	lipstick	save up
coins	look like	sunglasses
comb	makes me laugh	used to
if I could	mirror	would like to

credit card	live abroad	pop star
dolls	metal	status symbol
handbag	mobile phone	successful
heaven	motivated	waiter
jungle	put on weight	a waste of money

If the other students think your explanation is convincing, you win a point. You can use each word or phrase as many times as you like.

C Speaking: Real life

Work in pairs, Student A and Student B. Act out the following situations.

1

STUDENT A
A friend from another country is coming to stay in your city for a few days. You are not sure about the best places to go / things to see. Ask Student B for some suggestions.

STUDENT B
Give Student A some suggestions about the best things to do / places to go with a visitor from another country.

2

STUDENT A
You are waiting for an aeroplane with nothing to do. Start a conversation with Student B and try to find as many things in common as possible.

STUDENT B
You are waiting for an aeroplane and Student A is going to start talking to you. When you have found six things in common, invite him/her to come and have a cup of coffee with you.

3

STUDENT A
You are in a street market and you have seen a ring that you like at a jewellery stall. Ask about the ring (from? made of? price?) and decide whether you want to buy it.

STUDENT B
You have a stall in a street market where you sell home-made jewellery. Answer Student A's questions about something you are selling.

D Passives

Complete the gaps with the correct passive form of the verbs in brackets.

THE WORLD'S FAVOURITE DESSERT

Ice cream is definitely the world's favourite dessert. In Europe alone, about €11 billion a year (1) _____ (spend) on ice cream.

More ice cream (2) _____ (eat) per person in Australia than any other country: 16.6 litres per year.

A form of ice cream (3) _____ (eat) in China, about 4,000 years ago. It (4) _____ (make) of milk, rice, fruit and a secret ingredient … snow!

Ice cream (5) _____ (bring) to Europe in the sixteenth century, but at that time only the super-rich could afford it. When the Italian princess Catherine de Medici married the future King Henry II of France in 1533, a different variety of ice cream (6) _____ (serve) every day for a month!

The first ice cream cone (7) _____ (made) in New York City on September 22nd, 1886. The maker, Italo Marchiony, (8) _____ (give) a patent on his cone in 1903.

The world's most popular flavour is vanilla, which (9) _____ (produce) from vanilla beans. 80% of the world's vanilla beans (10) _____ (grow) on the island of Madagascar, off the east coast of Africa. More ice cream (11) _____ (sell) on a Sunday than on any other day of the week.

E Speaking and listening

1 Work in pairs. The sentences below come from different conversations. Read them and decide:

- who the speakers are.
- where they are.
- what the situation is.

a   Yes, all the rooms are cleaned every morning, madam.
b   I wouldn't go there again if you gave me £10,000.
c   I saw that someone had broken the kitchen window.
d   I've been working on it all day, but I haven't finished it yet.

2 Choose a sentence and make it into a conversation. Act it out for the other students like this.

> How much is a double room?

> €125, including breakfast.

> I see … and are the rooms cleaned every day?

> Yes, all the bedrooms are cleaned every morning, madam.

> Good, well I'll …

3 [C1] Listen to the conversations. What were the similarities/differences with the conversations you invented?

Module 2: Practice, exercise 3, page 17

Answers to Important Firsts Quiz

1 In September 1910, Alice Stebbins Wells became the first female police officer in the world when she joined the Police Department in her home town of Los Angeles, California.

2 The first 100% computer-generated movie, *Toy Story*, appeared in 1995. *Toy Story II* came next in the year 2000.

3 The first space flight took place in 1951 when four monkeys called Albert I, Albert II, Albert III and Albert IV flew into space from White Sands, New Mexico, USA. All four returned safely.

4 The world's first traffic lights started operating in 1928 in Melbourne, Australia.

5 The Tamagotchi, which became popular around the world in the mid-1990s, came originally from Japan.

6 The first man to walk on the moon was Neil Armstrong.

7 The first McDonald's restaurants opened in the United States, but they didn't arrive in Europe until the 1970s. The first European McDonalds opened in Munich, Germany, in 1971.

8 The first World Cup Finals of the 21st century took place in Japan and Korea in the summer of 2002. Brazil played Germany in the final, and won the match 2–0.

Module 5: Preparation, exercise 2, page 48

Group A

Module 1: Practice, exercise 2, page 12

Group B

HOW HEALTHY ARE YOU?

1 How many hours' sleep _____ normally have?

2 _____ normally sleep well or _____ often awake in the middle of the night?

3 _____ usually have a good breakfast in the morning?

4 How many cups of coffee _____ normally drink every day?

5 _____ smoke? If yes, _____ a heavy smoker?

6 How often _____ drink alcohol?

7 _____ play sport regularly?

8 In your own opinion, _____ very fit and healthy, OK or unfit?

Module 4: Wordspot, exercise 4, page 37

Write your answers to the following questions.

1 Did you do anything interesting the day before yesterday?
2 Do you know anyone who sometimes stays in bed all day?
3 Tell me three things you do every day.
4 When was the last time you had a day off school/college/work?
5 What are you doing the day after tomorrow?
6 Where's a good place to go for a day out near your town?
7 Do you think you'll visit New York one day?
8 If something happened 'the other day', did it happen a long time ago?
9 If someone says, 'Have a good day' what should you answer?
10 Tell me something you do twice a day.
11 How many days a week do you study English?
12 Was yesterday a good day or a bad day? Why?

ACTIVITIES

Module 2: Task 2, page 21

1 a You are going to tell the story of the first time Jayne met her boyfriend. Look at the pictures below.

b Say what is happening in each picture. Match the phrases in the box to the pictures.

a sandwich shop	go out for a pizza	smile at someone
to cut yourself	blood everywhere	get on well
order a sandwich	make a sandwich	

2 Tell the story of how Jayne met her boyfriend. Begin like this:

This is the story of how Jayne met her boyfriend for the first time. One day ...

▶ Useful language b

Useful language

b Telling Jayne's story

This happened ... ago.

One day Jayne ...

He/She noticed that ...

She was absolutely shocked/horrified when she saw that ...

He/She felt very ...

Later on he ...

After that they ...

Module 7: Listening, exercise 2, page 62

Celebrity Fact File

Kate Winslet: British actress, star of *Titanic*.

Catherine Zeta-Jones: Welsh actress, singer and dancer. Married to actor Michael Douglas.

Colin Farrell: Irish actor, star of several Hollywood films.

Renée Zellweger: American actress famous for *Bridget Jones* films.

Tom Cruise: American actor, formerly married to Nicole Kidman.

Sting: British musician and singer. Began his solo career in the 1980s

Keanu Reeves: Actor who was born in Lebanon and grew up in Canada. Star of the *Matrix* trilogy.

Tom Hanks: American actor. Has won Academy Awards for *Forrest Gump* and *Saving Private Ryan*.

Module 8: Task, page 76

Student A

1 Look at the map below. It has information about North Island. Student B has a map with information about South Island. Find out where the following places are and why they are important. Mark them on your map.

- Southern Alps
- Christchurch
- Stewart Island
- Mount Cook
- Cook Strait
- Lake Wanaka

2 Now answer Student B's questions.

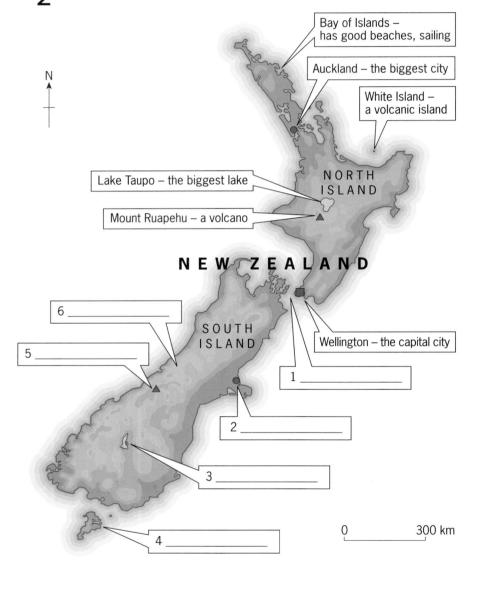

Bay of Islands – has good beaches, sailing

Auckland – the biggest city

White Island – a volcanic island

NORTH ISLAND

Lake Taupo – the biggest lake

Mount Ruapehu – a volcano

NEW ZEALAND

6 _____

SOUTH ISLAND

5 _____

Wellington – the capital city

1 _____

2 _____

3 _____

0   300 km

4 _____

Module 5: Preparation, exercise 2, page 48

Group A

Witnesses

Last Saturday afternoon you came home to your apartment building. At the same time, thieves stole some diamonds from one of the apartments. The police believe that you were in the lift at the same time as one of the thieves, and they want you to give a description of this person. Turn to page 140 to see a picture of the man you saw. You have two minutes to look at the picture and remember the man's face. Then, discuss in a group how to describe him. Think about:
- age • face • skin • hair
- clothes • build

Module 14: Reading, exercise 2, page 125

Answers to Money Facts Quiz

1 25
2 2
3 150
4 100,000,000,000,000,000,000
5 17th
6 2002
7 34
8 1929
9 100

Module 8: Real life, exercise 5, page 77

Student A

Look at the map and ask Student B for directions to:

- a bank.
- a book shop.
- a car park.
- the Odeon Cinema.
- Rosehill Park.
- Fast Save Supermarket.

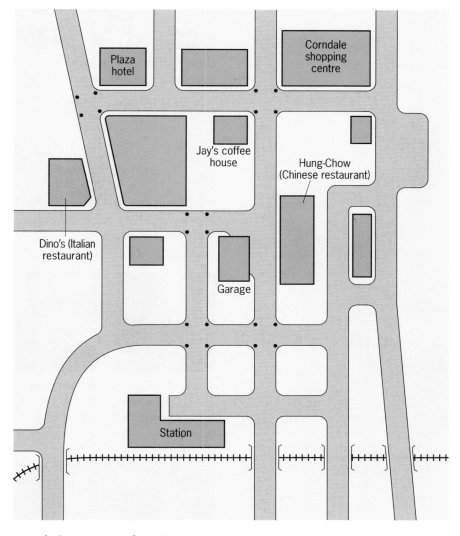

Module 9: Wordspot, exercise 3, page 86

Student A

Read the following statements to Student B. He/She should answer using a phrase with *if*.

1 Do you know if Wasim is coming tonight?
2 Do you mind if I open the window?
3 Do you think I should tell Cristina what happened?
4 Do you want to have your lunch now?
5 You can go now if you like.
6 Is Mark still upstairs?
7 I wonder if Carla would like a lift home.
8 Will you drive me home later?

Module 10: Task, exercise 1, page 94

Group A

Simon Roland / ten years old / one day play on the beach near home / young man jump into water

a few minutes later / hear shouts / the young man drown / Simon decide to help

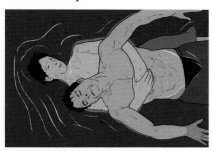

Simon swim
100 m / reach young man / young man unconscious / Simon pull him back to the beach

later / young man recover / ambulance take him to hospital / thank Simon for saving his life

Module 8: Task, page 76

Student B

1 Look at the map below. Answer Student A's questions.

2 Student A has a map with information about South Island. Find out where the following places are and why they are important. Mark them on your map.

- Bay of Islands
- White Island
- Lake Taupo
- Mount Ruapehu
- Auckland
- Wellington

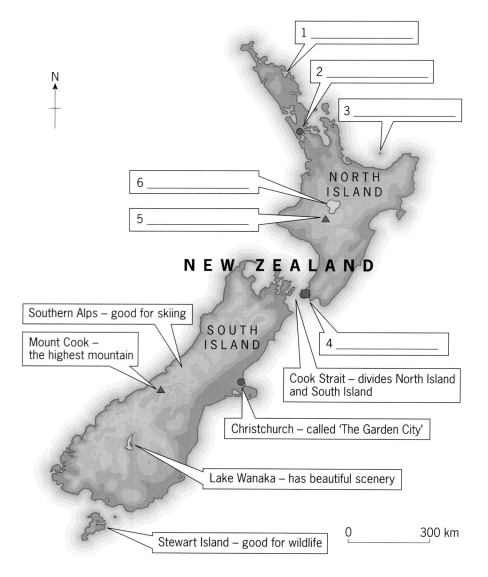

N

1 _____

2 _____

3 _____

NORTH ISLAND

6 _____

5 _____

N E W   Z E A L A N D

Southern Alps – good for skiing

Mount Cook – the highest mountain

SOUTH ISLAND

4 _____

Cook Strait – divides North Island and South Island

Christchurch – called 'The Garden City'

Lake Wanaka – has beautiful scenery

Stewart Island – good for wildlife

0   300 km

Module 10: Task, exercise 1, page 94

Group A

Shirley Yeats: on holiday on cruise ship / sail / near Malaysia

one day / go back to her cabin / could smell burning / look around / see smoke

immediately telephone the captain / then go for help / soon fire out of control / captain decide to leave ship

Shirley help passengers get into life boats / give first aid to other passengers / one of the last passengers to leave / 1,100 passengers get off safely

Module 12: Vocabulary, exercise 1, page 106

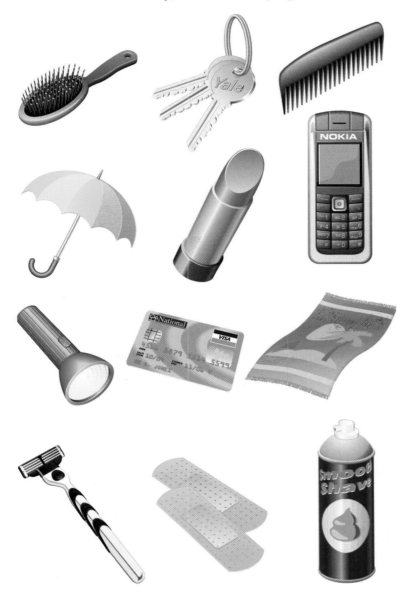

Module 5: Preparation, exercise 2, page 48

Group B

> ### Police officers
>
> Last Saturday afternoon some thieves stole some diamonds from an apartment. You know that one of the thieves used the lift just before the diamonds were stolen. You are going to interview a witness who was in the lift at the same time as the thief. You need an exact description of the man. In your group, discuss what questions you will ask the witness. Think about:
> • age • face • skin • hair • clothes • build

Module 13: Wordspot, exercise 3, page 119

Student A

a Complete the questions using a phrase with *how*.

1. How _____ do people run in a Marathon race?
   a **40 km**
   b 45 km
   c 50 km
2. How _____ legs do spiders have?
   a four
   b six
   c **eight**
3. What's the best answer to the question *How _____ you?*
   a Good idea!
   b **I'm fine. And you?**
   c I'm going home.
4. _____ tall is the world's tallest man?
   a 2.26 m
   b **2.36 m**
   c 2.46 m
5. How _____ was Princess Diana when she died in 1999?
   a 26
   b 30
   c **36**
6. Sudan is the biggest country in Africa. _____ big is it?
   a 1.5 km^2
   b 2.0 km^2
   c **2.5 km^2**

b Read the questions and the three possible answers to Student B. He/She must guess the correct answer (in bold).

Module 8: Real life, exercise 5, page 77

Student B

Look at the map and ask Student A for directions to:

- a garage.
- a good Italian restaurant.
- The Corndale Shopping Centre.
- a good Chinese restaurant.
- Jay's Coffee House.
- the Plaza Hotel.

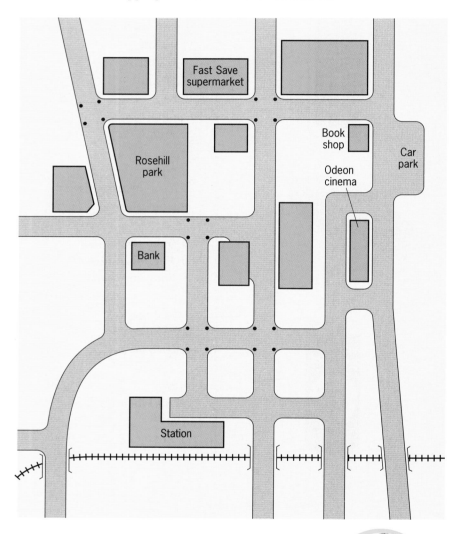

Module 13: Task, exercise 1, page 121

Student B

SIMONA CALLAS

Simona is famous in the pop industry as one of the most successful and intelligent managers. She can also be very hard. When she saw SPOTS! on the TV show Star Search three years ago, she said, 'They can't sing, they can't dance, and they're all ugly.' Since she quit the show a year ago, she has been looking for a group to work with. She is optimistic. 'Talent isn't important in the pop world. All you need is the right manager. I'm the right manager.'

Module 13: Wordspot, exercise 3, page 119

Student B

a Complete the questions using a phrase with *how*.

1. How _____ you spell the word *height*?
   a **H-E-I-G-H-T**
   b H-I-G-H-T
   c H-I-T-E
2. How _____ does a room cost per night in the world's most expensive hotel?
   a **$25,000**
   b $50,000
   c $100,000
3. What's the best answer to the question *How _____ going out tonight?*
   a Yes, I will.
   b Yes, I'd like it.
   c **Yes, good idea**.
4. How _____ have people used euros?
   a **since 2002**
   b since 2003
   c since 2004
5. What's the best answer to the question *How _____ you do?*
   a I'm fine. And you?
   b **How do you do?**
   c Not bad.
6. How _____ can a cheetah (the world's fastest animal) run?
   a up to 100 km an hour
   b up to 150 km an hour
   c **up to 200 km an hour**

b Read the questions and the three possible answers to Student A. He/She must guess the correct answer (in bold).

Module 5: Task, exercise 2, page 48

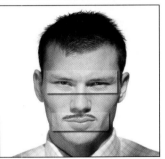

Module 8: Vocabulary and reading, exercise 2, page 75

Solution to puzzle.

a			I	C	E		
b			B	O	R	D	E	R
c			L	A	K	E	
d		D	E	S	E	R	T
e			S	T	O	R	M
f			I	S	L	A	N	D
g			C	L	I	M	A	T	E
h			C	A	N	A	L
i	R	I	V	E	R		

Module 11: Reading and vocabulary, exercise 6, page 99

Solution to puzzle.

a	H	E	R	O				
b		O	B	S	E	S	S	I	O	N
c		C	O	S	T	U	M	E
d		C	E	R	E	A	L
e	G	I	F	T	S
f	D	E	S	P	E	R	A	T	E
g	W	E	I	G	H	T
h	A	F	F	O	R	D

Module 13: Task, exercise 1, page 121

Student A

ROLAND BUNTING

After a career as a male model, Roland joined the boy band *Shake That*. Two years ago, he retired. He said, 'I've got everything I need, I never want to leave my home again.' Since then, he has been spending all his time in a €10 million house in Ireland with his wife and children. He now says he needs a new interest in his life. 'SPOTS! are my new hobby,' he says.

Module 1

A Question words

To ask about:	We use:
a thing	**What**'s that under the table? **Which** is your coat?
a time	**When**'s your next holiday?
a place	**Where** do you go at Christmas?
a person	**Who**'s your favourite film star?
the way you do something	**How** do you make bread?
the reason for doing something	**Why** do you always wear black?
a period of time	**How** long does the programme last?
the number of times you do something	**How often** do you see Maria?
the cost of something	**How much** does it cost?

We use *what* if there are many possible answers.
***What**'s your name?*

We use *which* if there are only a few possible answers.
***Which** do you prefer: coffee or tea?*

Some other expressions with *what* and *which*

***What sort / kind of** car have you got?*
***Which places** do you want to visit?*
***What time** does the restaurant open?*
***Which part of** Mexico is Monterrey in?*
***What colour** are her eyes?*
***What size** are your shoes?*

B Word order in questions

1 *be*

With the verb *be* we 'invert' the subject and the verb.

***They are** in the kitchen.*   ***Are they** in the kitchen?*

***You were** late for class.*   ***Were you** late for class?*

2 Modal verbs

With modal verbs (*can, will, might*), we also invert the subject and the verb to form the question.

***Erika can** ride a motorbike.*   ***Can Erika** ride a motorbike?*

***Tomas will** be here tomorrow.*   ***Will Tomas** be here tomorrow?*

3 Other verbs

a   With other verbs, we put the auxiliary verb *do* or *does* before the subject.
   They play basketball.   ***Do** they play basketball?*
   Jamie lives near the school.   ***Does** Jamie live near the school?*

b   The question word comes before the auxiliary verb.
   ***Where** do you play chess?*
   ***How often** do you go to the gym?*

C Present simple

Positive form	Negative form	Question form
I / you / we / they **know**	I / you / we / they **don't** (= do not) **know**	**Do** I / you / we / they **know**?
he / she / it **knows**	he / she **doesn't** (= does not) **know**	**Does** he / she **know**?

1   We use the Present simple for:
   a   habits or things we do regularly.
      *I **go** for a run before breakfast.*

   b   things that are generally or always true.
      *They **live** in a small village.*

2   These are the spelling rules for *he / she / it*.

Verb	Rule	Example
ends in a consonant + -y *(fly)*	change -y to -ies	This airline **flies** to Hong Kong.
ends in -s *(miss)* -x *(fix)* -ch *(catch)* -sh *(wash)*	add -es	She **misses** him. Mike **fixes** old cars. He **catches** the train. She **washes** her hair every day.
do and *go*	add -es	He **does** all the shopping.
all other verbs	add -s	My sister **speaks** French.

D How often?

1 Adverbs

never   sometimes   often   usually / generally   always

0%   100%

a   With most verbs, we put the adverb before the main verb.
   *We **never go out** at lunchtime.*

b   With the verb *be*, we put the adverb after the verb.
   *He**'s always** late for class.*

2 Other phrases

every	day
once / twice / X times a	week month

a   We usually put these phrases at the end of the sentence.
   *We go swimming **every week**.*
   *Nadia visits her aunt **twice a week**.*

b   But we can also put them at the beginning of the sentence.
   ***Every day** I go for a walk in the park.*
   ***Once a month** we go out for a really nice meal.*

Module 2

A Past simple

Regular Past simple forms end in *-ed* in the positive form.
But many verbs have an **irregular** past form (see list on page 157).

Positive form	Negative form	Question form
I / you / he / she / it / we / they **started**	I / you / he / she / it / we / they **didn't** (= did not) **start**	**Did** I / you / he / she / it / we / they **start**?
I / you / he / she / it / we / they **won**	I / you / he / she / it / we / they **didn't** (= did not) **win**	**Did** I / you / he / she / it / we / they **win**?

1 We use the Past simple to talk about a finished action or state in the past. It can be something that happened once or many times. We often say **when** it happened.
*He **died** in 1980.*   (= once)
*My father always **took** me to school when I was young.*   (= many times)
*We **lived** in a very small house in those days.*   (= state)

2 For regular verbs, we add *-ed* (*watched*, *started*). But there are some exceptions.

Verb	Rule	Example
ends in *-e* (*like*)	add *-d*	I lik**ed** the film.
has one syllable and ends in vowel + one consonant (*stop*)	double the final consonant	They sto**pped** for lunch.
ends in consonant + *-y* (*carry*)	change *-y* to *-ied*	He carri**ed** the bags all the way home.
has two syllables and ends in one vowel + *-l* (*travel*)	double the *final* consonant	They trave**lled** at night.

3 The past of *be* is *was / were*.

Positive form	Negative form	Question form
I / he / she / it **was** late	I / he / she / it **wasn't** (= was not) late	**Was** I / he / she / it late?
we / you / they **were** late	we / you / they **weren't** (= were not) late	**Were** we / you / they late?

B Time phrases often used in the past: *at, on, in, ago*

1 *at, on, in*

We can use these time phrases in the present and future.
a *at +* time
two / three days
b *on +* day / date
c *in +* month
season
year / decade / century
d We do not use a preposition with *last* and *yesterday*.
*We went there last **year / yesterday**.*

at 12.15   *at eight o'clock*
at Easter   *at Christmas*
on Monday   *on July 2nd*
in June   *in December*
in winter   *in spring*
in 1988   *in the 1990s*
in the twenty-first century

2 *ago*

Ago means *before now*. We use it to show how far in the past something happened.
*I first met Jackie two years **ago**.*

We do not use *ago* after specific time periods with *the*.
I met him ⟍the summer ~~ago~~.
(in)

Module 3

A should, shouldn't

Positive form	Negative form	Question form
I / you / he / she / we / they **should** buy a dictionary	I / you / he / she / we / they **shouldn't** (= should not) worry	**Should** I / you / he / she / we / they come in now?

1 We use *should* to say that something is a good idea or the right thing to do. We use *shouldn't* to say that something is not a good idea or not the right thing to do.
*You **should** buy a new alarm clock.*
*You **shouldn't** leave your bag open on the bus.*

2 *Should* is not as strong as *have to*.
*We **have to** go now or we'll be late.*   (= it is necessary to go)
*We **should** go now or we'll be tired tomorrow.*   (= this is a good idea)

3 The forms below are often used for giving advice.
***Why don't you** look for a flat in the centre of town?*
***Try putting** an advertisement in the local newspaper.*

B can, can't, have to, don't have to

1 *can, can't*

Positive form	Negative form	Question form
I / you / he / she / we / they **can** speak English	I / you / he / she / we / they **can't** (= cannot) speak English	**Can** I / you / he / she / we / they speak English?

We use *can* and *can't* to talk about different kinds of possibility.
a ability
*Sue **can dance** quite well but she **can't sing**.*

b permission
*You **can't come** in!*   *Can we **go** home now?*

2 *have to, don't have to*

Positive form	Negative form	Question form
I / you / we / they **have to** go now	I / you / we / they **don't have to** go now	**Do** I you / we / they **have to** go now?
he / she / it **has to** go now	he / she / it **doesn't have to** go now	**Does** he / she / it **have to** go now?

a We use *have to* if something is necessary.
*We **have to** be at the airport by six o'clock.*

b *Have to* is very similar to *must*.
We **must** go now. (= it's necessary)
We **have to** go now. (= it's necessary)

c We use *don't have to* if it is not necessary to do something.
We **don't have to wear** a uniform at my new school.
(= it isn't necessary)

> **REMEMBER!**
>
> *Have to* and *must* are similar, but don't have to *is not the same as* mustn't.
>
> You **mustn't** take any photographs. (= you can't, it's prohibited)
> You **don't have to** take any photographs. (= it's not necessary)

Module 4

(A) Present continuous

Positive form	Negative form	Question form
I'm (= am) working	I'm not (= am not) working	Am I working?
you / we / they're (= are) working	you / we / they aren't (= are not) working	Are you / we / they working?
he / she / it's (= is) working	he / she / it isn't (= is not) working	Is he / she / it working?

1 We use the Present continuous for something happening at this moment or something happening in the present period, but perhaps not at this moment.
Sue**'s talking** to someone on the phone.
We**'re studying** French this term.

2 For *-ing* forms with most verbs, we add *-ing* (start**ing**, go**ing**, buy**ing**). But there are some exceptions.

Verb	Rule	Example
ends in one -e (*make*)	take away -e	mak**ing** leav**ing**
has one syllable and ends in vowel + one consonant (*stop*)	double the final consonant	sto**pp**ing ge**tt**ing
ends in -ie (*lie*)	change -ie to -y	l**y**ing
has two syllables, ends in vowel + one consonant, stress on the last syllable (*begin*)	double the final consonant	begi**nn**ing forge**tt**ing
has two syllables and ends in -l (*travel*)	double the -l	trave**ll**ing

3 We do not usually use some verbs in the continuous form. These are:
a describing mental states.
believe   know   understand

b verbs connected with likes / dislikes.
like   love   want

c verbs connected with possession.
have   own   possess

(B) Present continuous or Present simple?

> **REMEMBER!**
> We use the Present simple for actions which are generally or usually true.
> I **speak** four languages.
>
> We use the Present continuous for actions which are in progress now or around now.
> Who **is** she **speaking** to?

1 We usually use the Present simple with phrases like *always, never, every day, usually, normally*.

2 We usually use the Present continuous with phrases like *now, at the moment, today , right now*.

(C) Present continuous for future arrangements

1 We use the Present continuous to talk about what we have arranged to do in the future.
A: *What **are** you **doing** next weekend?* (= what have you arranged?)
B: **I'm taking** my son to the zoo on Saturday, then **I'm cooking** lunch for some friends on Sunday. (= I've arranged to do this)

2 When we use the Present continuous like this, we either give a future time (for example, *this weekend*) or we know from the situation that we are talking about the future.

Module 5

(A) Comparative and superlative adjectives

1 One-syllable and two-syllable adjectives ending in -y

Adjective	Comparative	Superlative	Spelling rule
young tall	younger taller	**the** youngest **the** tallest	most adjectives: + -er, the -est
nice large	nicer larger	**the** nicest **the** largest	adjective ends in -e: + -r, the -st
thin big	thinner bigger	**the** thinnest **the** biggest	one vowel + one consonant: double the consonant
pretty	prettier	**the** prettiest	change -y to -i

2 Other two-syllable adjectives and longer adjectives

serious sophisticated	**more** serious **more** sophisticated	**the most** serious **the most** sophisticated

But we usually use *-er* and *the -est* with two-syllable adjectives: *clever, quiet, simple, gentle*.

3 Irregular forms

good bad far	better worse farther / further	the best the worst the farthest / furthest

4 Prepositions in comparative phrases

I think she's **more attractive than** her sister.
Your eyes are very **similar to** your mother's.
Are these glasses very **different from** your old ones?
She **looks like** a businesswoman.
Her earrings are **the same as** mine.
He's **the tallest in** the family! (not ~~of~~ the family)

5 Making comparisons with nouns

We can also compare nouns using *more* and *the most*.
She's got **more** energy than me.
Our team has won **the most** games this year.

B Describing people

1   We use the question *What does he / she look like?* to ask about someone's physical appearance.
    What does your friend look like?   *He's tall, dark and handsome.*

2   We use the question *How is… ?* to ask about someone's health.
    How's your mother ?   *Oh, she's much better thanks!*

    We also use *How is / was …?* to ask about someone's work, or their day at school, or their journey.
    How was school today?   *I got an 'A' for English!*
    How was your journey?   *Fine. No problems.*

3   We use the question *What's he / she like?* when we mean *Tell me about …* We use this question to ask about someone's personality rather than their appearance.
    What are your neighbours like?   *They seem very friendly.*

    > **REMEMBER!**
    > We do **not** use like in the answer.
    > What's the new teacher like?   She seems ~~like~~ very nice.

4   We use the verb *be* in these questions
    (Age) *How old **is** she?*   *She's about thirty-five.*
    (Height) *How tall **is** he?*   *He's about average height.*
    ***Is** he tall or short?*   *He's very tall.*
    *What colour **is** her hair /*
    ***are** her eyes?*   *Brown.*

5   We use *have got* to ask about features such as hair, eyes, glasses, beard, etc.
    ***Has** he **got** a beard?*   *No, he hasn't.*
    ***Has** she **got** nice eyes?*   *Yes, they're beautiful!*

6   If we use more than one adjective, we put:
    a   *long / short,* etc., before 'colour' adjectives *(dark, fair, brown).*
        He's got short brown hair.

    b   'opinion' adjectives *(nice, lovely, horrible)* before other adjectives.
        She's got lovely blue eyes.

    c   We do **not** put *and* between the two adjectives.
        He's got long ~~and~~ blond hair.

Module 6

A Intentions and wishes

1 *going to, planning to*

Positive form	Negative form	Question form
I'm going to / planning to buy a car.	I'm not going to / planning to buy a car.	Am I going to / planning to buy a car?
You / We / They're going to / planning to buy a car.	You / We / They're not going to / planning to buy a car.	Are you / we / they going to / planning to buy a car?
He / She's going to / planning to buy a car.	He / She's not going to / planning to buy a car.	Is he / she going to / planning to buy a car?

a   We use *going to* to talk about what we intend to do in the future. It can be the near future or the more distant future.
    I'm going to be a famous actor.
    Are you going to see him again?

b   We normally use *planning to* when we have thought carefully about the plan and decided how to do it.
    What are you planning to say at the meeting?
    I'm planning to leave this company next year.

2 *would like to, would rather*

Positive form	Negative form	Question form
I / You / He / She / We / They 'd (= would) like to / rather stay at home.	I / You / He / She / We / They wouldn't (= would not) like to stay at home. I / You / He / She / We / They'd rather not stay at home.	Would I / you / he / she / we / they like to / rather stay at home?

a   We use *would like to* to say what we want to do.
    I'd like to travel round the world one day.

    It is less direct than *want to* and we often use it to be polite, especially in questions.
    Would you like to see the menu?

b   We use *would rather* to say we prefer one thing to another thing. After this form, we always use the infinitive **without** *to*.
    I'd rather go on a walking holiday. Beach holidays are boring.
    Would you rather sit inside or on the terrace?

    > **REMEMBER!**
    > We do **not** usually use would rather *in negative sentences.*
    >
    > I would rather go on a walking holiday.
    > I ~~wouldn't rather~~ go on a beach holiday.

B Predictions: *will* and *won't*

Positive form	Negative form	Question form
I / You / He / She / We / They**'ll** (= will) be here at six.	I / You / He / She / We / They **won't** (= will not) see him next week.	**Will** I / you / he / she / we / they **have** time to phone them?

1 We use *will* to say what we **expect** to happen. We use it when there is **no** particular plan or intention.
*The weather **will be** very hot in July.* (= this is what I expect)
***Will** there **be** a lot of people?* (= what do you expect?)

2 Notice the difference between *will* and *going to* here.
*We're **going to visit** the London Eye today.* (= this is what we intend / plan)
*It**'ll be** busy and we**'ll have to** queue.* (= this is what I expect)

3 We often use *will* with *I think* or *I don't think*.
*Do you **think** France **will win**?*
*I don't **think** she**'ll be** very happy when she hears about this.*

4 Notice that there are no *will* forms of *can* and *must*. We use *will be able to* and *will have to*.
*We**'ll be able to go swimming every day**.*
*If you go in March, you**'ll have to take** a warm coat.*

Module 7

A Present perfect

1 We form the Present perfect with *have / has* + past participle. Regular past participles end in *-ed* in the positive form. Many verbs have an **irregular** past participle (see the list on page 157).

Positive form	Negative form	Question form
I / you / we / they**'ve** finished / won	I / you / we / they haven't finished / won	**Have** I / you / we / they **finished / won?**
he / she / it**'s** finished / won	he / she / it **hasn't** finished / won	**Has** he / she / it finished / won?

2 We use the Present perfect to talk about the past and present together. It tells us something about the present.
*I**'ve met** Daniel before.* (= I know him now)
*They**'ve left** the country.* (= they are not in the country now)

B Present perfect and Past simple with *for*

1 We use the Present perfect with *for* to talk about an action or state which continues from the past to the present.
*I**'ve been** in New York **for** two weeks.*

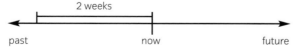

2 We use the Past simple with *for* to talk about a past action or state in a period of time which is finished.
*I **was** in New York **for** two weeks.*

C Present perfect and Past simple with other time words

1 Time phrases with the Past simple

We use the Past simple to talk about actions or states which are finished. We often use the following time words:

a days, dates, times, years.
in 2002   yesterday

b *last* and *ago*.
last** year   five years **ago

c questions and statements with *when*.
***when** I was ten years old*

2 Time phrases with the Present perfect

a Often, there is no time phrase with the Present perfect. We do not know exactly when the action happened.
*She**'s lived** in Italy, Egypt and France.*

b When we use time words with the Present perfect, they do not give a definite time.
*She's **just** had her first baby.* (= a short time ago)
*It's **already** sold a million copies.* (= before now / before expected)
*I haven't finished **yet**.* (= before now: only in questions and negatives)
*He's **never** been abroad.* (= not at any time)

c We also use the Present perfect with time phrases that refer to a time that is still in progress.
*I haven't seen him **this morning**.* (= this morning isn't finished)
*Barbara has done very well **so far**.* (= up to now)

Module 8

A Using articles

1 We use *a* or *an* the first time we mention something. When we mention it again, we use *the*.
*I saw **a** beautiful vase in **an** antique shop a few days ago. When I went back to **the** shop yesterday, **the** vase wasn't there any more!*

2 We do **not** use *the*:
a when we talk about people or things in general.
Dogs make very good pets.

b with the names of people and countries.
American people eat a lot of fast food.

c with many place names.

Continents	Africa, Asia	Countries	Thailand, Argentina
Cities	Madrid, Bangkok	Lakes	Lake Como
Mountains	Mount Fuji	Hills	Primrose Hill
Roads / Streets	Oxford Street	Islands	Easter Island

3 We use *the*:
a with some place names.

Oceans and seas	the Pacific Ocean, the Mediterranean Sea
Rivers	the River Danube, the River Thames
Mountain ranges	the Alps, the Himalayas
Countries which are republics or unions	the United Kingdom, the United Arab Emirates

b with superlative forms.
the longest river in the world

c when there is only **one** of something.
the Sun   the Earth   the Moon   the Sky   the Pope

4 Other phrases with *the*
at **the** bottom, at **the** top
in **the** east, in **the** west, in **the** south, in **the** north
in **the** centre, in **the** middle
in **the** morning, in **the** afternoon, in **the** evening
on **the** left, on **the** right
on **the** coast, on **the** border

5 Other phrases without *the*
at home, at school, at university, at work
at night
in bed, in hospital, in prison
on holiday

B **Quantifiers with countable and uncountable nouns**

Countable nouns have a singular and a plural form.
building / buildings   bank / banks   museum / museums

Uncountable nouns do not have a plural form.
traffic   scenery   nightlife

Some, any and other quantifiers

With plural nouns and uncountable nouns
some (not) any no a lot of
(not) enough

With plural nouns	With uncountable nouns
(not) many too many a few	(not) much too much

1 S*ome* means *an indefinite number / amount* (we don't know exactly how many / much). We use it in positive sentences.
*I'd like **some** information, please.*

We also use *some* in questions when we think the answer will be *yes*.
*Did you buy **some** milk, like I asked you?*
*Would you like **some** more tea?* (= offer)

2 We use *any* before countable or uncountable nouns in:
a negative sentences.
*There aren't **any** Italian restaurants near here.*

b questions where the answer could be *yes* or *no*.
*Are there **any** shops near here?*

3 *No* means the same as *not any*.
*There's **no** food in the fridge.*

> **REMEMBER!**
> We only use no with a positive verb. We do **not** say:
> There ~~isn't no~~ food in the fridge.

4 *A few* means *a small number of*. We usually use it in positive sentences.
*There are **a few** things I'd like to discuss with you, if that's OK.*

5 We usually use *a lot of* (also *lots of*) in positive sentences to mean *a large number of*.
*There are **a lot of** nice places to eat around here.*

6 We use *much* and *many* in negative sentences or questions.
*I haven't got **much** time today. How about tomorrow?*
*Are there **many** tourists at this time of year?*

7 *Too much* and *too many* have a negative meaning. We use them to mean *more than the right amount*.
*I can't work here. There's **too much** noise.*
*There are **too many** people in this classroom.*

8 *Not enough* also has a negative meaning. We use it to mean *less than the right amount*.
*There are**n't enough** chairs for everyone to sit down.*

Module 9

A *may, might, will definitely*, **etc.**

1 *will definitely*

We use this phrase when we are sure something will happen.
*We **will definitely** be out tomorrow evening.*
The negative of this phrase is *definitely won't*.

2 *will probably*

We use this phrase when we are fairly sure something will happen.
*We **will probably** be out tomorrow evening.*
The negative of this phrase is *probably won't*.

3 *may / might*

We use these verbs to say that it's possible something will happen.
*We **may / might** be out tomorrow evening.*
The negative of these verbs is *may / might not*.
*I **may not / might not** be able to see you.*

B **Present tense after *if, when, before* and other time words**

1 'The first conditional'

if clause   main clause
If we have time, we'll go and see Sarah.

a Notice that we use a present tense in the *if* clause and a future form in the main clause. This form is often called *the first conditional*. We use this for something that might happen in the future.

b We can also use other future forms or a modal verb in the main clause.
*If the weather's good, **we're going to** play tennis later.*
*If you're very good, I **might** buy you an ice cream.*

c We can change the position of the *if* clause and the main clause.
*I'll tell you **if** anything unusual **happens**.*

2 when, as soon as, before, etc.

a   We also use a present tense after *when* and *as soon as* to talk about things we are sure will happen in the future.
When we **get** home, I'll show you our new kitchen.

b   **when / as soon as**
I'll phone you **as soon as** we arrive.   (= I will do this immediately)
I'll phone you **when** we arrive.   (= it is not so urgent)

c   **before / after**
Remember to turn off all the lights **before** you **go**.
After I **graduate**, I'll take time off to think about my future.

Module 10

Ⓐ *used to*

Positive form	Negative form	Question form
I / You / He / She / We / They **used to** walk to school.	I / You / He / She / We / They **didn't use to drive**.	**Did** I / you / he / she / we / they **use to** go by train?

1   We use *used to*:
a   for actions that happened many times in the past (habits).
He **used to wait** for me at the school gates.

b   for feelings, thoughts, ideas, etc., in the past.
I **used to be** afraid of the dark.

c   Notice that the habit or state is probably not true now.
We **used to have** a dog called Tilly.   (= we don't have the dog now)

Or it may be true now.
I **didn't use to** like sport at school.   (= but I like it now)

2   We can always use the Past simple instead of *used to*.
We **had** a dog called Tilly.   I **didn't like** sport.

3   We do **not** use *used to* for actions that happened only once.
I **went** to Spain on holiday in 1999.   (not I ~~used to~~ go)

Ⓑ Past continuous

Positive form	Negative form	Question form
I / he / she **was travelling**	I / he / she **wasn't travelling**	**Was** I / he / she **travelling?**
we / you / They **were travelling**	we / you / they **weren't travelling**	**Were** we / you / they **travelling?**

1   We use the Past continuous to talk about actions in progress:
a   at a certain time in the past.
I **was driving** home at 6.30 this evening.

driving home   6.30

past   now

b   when another (completed) action happened.
I **was driving** along when I saw a friend of mine.

driving home   saw a friend

past   now

2   We often use the Past continuous to describe the background situation in a story. For the main events, we use the Past simple.
The sun **was shining** and everyone **was getting** ready for the party that afternoon. Then my phone **rang** …

3   Sometimes the other action in the Past simple interrupts the action in the Past continuous.
I **was crossing** the road when I **slipped** on some ice.   (= I stopped crossing the road)

4   When two actions happen one after the other, we use the Past simple for both actions.
When I **heard** the crash, I **ran** to the end of the street.

> **REMEMBER!**
>
> We do **not** use state verbs in the continuous form.
>
>   knew
> I ~~was knowing~~ her when we were children.

5   We use *when, while* and *as* to join Past continuous and Past simple parts of a sentence.
I saw Karl **when / while / as** I was waiting at the bus stop.

Module 11

Ⓐ Gerunds (-*ing* forms) after verbs of liking and disliking

1   Gerunds (-*ing* forms) are like nouns or pronouns. We use them:
a   as the subject of the sentence.
Spending time with my friends is very important to me.

b   as the object of the sentence.
I find **washing** up really relaxing.

c   after prepositions.
She's crazy about **shopping**.

2   Many phrases expressing likes and dislikes are followed by a gerund.
He's **crazy about** play**ing** chess.   I **don't like** buy**ing** clothes.
I **really enjoy** shopp**ing**.   They **can't stand** los**ing**.
I **love** gett**ing** presents.   I **hate** gett**ing** up early.
She's **keen on** travell**ing**.

Ⓑ *like doing* and *would like to do*

1   We use *like* to talk about things that we enjoy.
My little brother **likes** horror films.

If we put another verb after *like*, we use the -*ing* form.
I **like** stay**ing** in bed late.   He **doesn't like** ly**ing** on the beach.

2   We use *would like* to talk about things we want. *I would like* is more polite than *I want*.
I'd like a new tennis racket for my birthday.

If we put a verb after *would like*, we use the infinitive with *to*.
I'd like to speak to the manager, please.

> **REMEMBER!**
>
> We often use Would you like …? for an offer.
> **Would you like** some coffee?
>
> Notice that the answer is:
> Yes, please. or Yes, I'd love to. (*not* Yes, ~~I'd like~~. or Yes, ~~I'd love~~)

3　Other verbs with gerunds / infinitives follow a similar pattern.

a　Verbs which express general likes / dislikes take the -ing form.
*She loves **horse-riding**.*

b　Verbs that express particular wishes for the future take the infinitive form.
*I**'d love to come** with you.*
*She **hopes to do** a course in computer science.*

Module 12

Ⓐ Present simple passive

We form the present simple passive with the subject + *be* + past participle. Regular past participles end in -ed. For a list of irregular past participles, see page 157.

Positive form	Negative form	Question form
I **am** made	I**'m not** made	**Am** I / he / she / it made?
he / she / it**'s made**	he / she / it **isn't made**	
you / we / they **are made**	you / we / they **aren't made**	**Are** you / we / they **made?**

1　We use the passive when the person who does the action is:

a　not important or unknown.
*The chocolate **is made** in Switzerland.*　(= it's not important **who** makes it)

b　unknown.
*Hundreds of cars **are stolen** every week.*　(= we do not know who steals them)

c　'people in general'.
*His face **is recognised** all over the world.*　(= people in general recognise his face)

2　If we want to say who or what is the 'doer' of the action, we use *by*.
*All my clothes are designed **by** Federico Pirani.*

3　Active or passive? Compare the following examples.
a　*Martine **makes** all her own bread at home.*
b　*The bread **is made** in a large bakery outside town.*

In sentence a, we use the active because we are more interested in **who** makes the bread, so Martine is the subject of the sentence. In sentence b, we use the passive because we are more interested in the bread, not in who makes the bread.

Ⓑ Past simple passive

We form the Past simple passive with the subject + *was / were* + past participle.

Positive form	Negative form	Question form
I / he / she / it **was seen**	I / he / she / it **wasn't seen**	**Was** I / he / she / it **seen?**
you / we / they **were seen**	you / we / they **weren't seen**	**Were** you / we / they **seen?**

1　As with the Present simple passive, we use the Past simple passive when the action is more important than the person who did it.

2　The Past simple passive is common when we are speaking formally, or in written reports.
*We **were told** to report to the police station as soon as possible.*
*More than thirty people **were injured** in the explosion.*

Module 13

Ⓐ Present perfect continuous with *how long*, *for* and *since*

Positive form	Negative form	Question form
I / you / we / they**'ve been working**	I / you / we / they **haven't been working**	(How long) **Have** I / you / we / they **been working?**
he / she / it**'s been working**	he / she / it **hasn't been working**	(How long) **Has** he / she / it **been working?**

1　We use the Present perfect continuous to talk about actions that started in the past and continue to the present.

She's been working as a doctor for forty years.

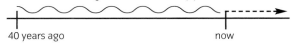

　40 years ago　　　　　　　　　　　now

2　We use *for* and *since* to talk about periods of time from the past to the present.

a　We use *for* to talk about periods of time. It answers questions with *how long*.
for *forty years*　　**for** *five hours*　　**for** *six months*　　**for** *a minute*　**for** *500 years*

He's been teaching for ten years.

　　　　　　　10 years ago　　　now

b　We use *since* to talk about points of time. It answers questions with *how long*.
since *1965*　　**since** *last year*　　**since** *2004*　　**since** *Tuesday*　**since** *six o'clock*　　**since** *October*

He's been teaching since 1996.

　　Since 1996　　　　　　　　now

> **REMEMBER!**
> We do **not** use a present tense to talk about actions that started in the past and continue into the present.
>
> I ~~am learning~~ English since last year.

3　The following phrases often occur with the Present perfect continuous but do not need *for* or *since*.
all day　　*all my life*　　*all morning*　　*all month*　　*all week*　　*all year*

B Present perfect continuous and Present perfect simple

1 In many cases, we can use the Present perfect simple and the Present perfect continuous with *for* and *since* with no real difference in meaning.
I've been living in this house for over a year.
I've lived in this house for over a year.

2 But if a verb describes a state (for example, *like, love, be, have, see, know*), we cannot use the continuous form.
They have ~~been knowing~~ each other for more than fifty years.

Module 14

A Past perfect

We form the Past perfect with *had* + past participle. Regular past participles end in *-ed*. Many verbs have an **irregular** past participle (see list on page 157).

Positive form	Negative form	Question form
I / you / he / she / it / we / they **'d** (= had) finished	I / you / he / she / it / we / they **hadn't** (= had not) finished	**Had** I / you / he / she / it / we / they **finished?**

1 We use the Past perfect to show that one action happened before another in the past, and that the first action finished before the second action started.
He had been to the bank and he was on his way home.

had been to the bank   on his way home
        past   now

2 We often use the Past perfect with *because* to explain a past situation.
Patrick felt ill because he'd eaten so much.

3 To show that two actions happened at the same time, we use the Past simple.
He woke up when the telephone rang.

4 If the sequence of actions is clear from the context, it is not necessary to use the Past perfect.
A robber appeared and pointed a gun at him.

B Past time words: *already, just*, and *never ... before*

already and just

1 If we want to emphasise that something happened before a particular time, we use *already*.
When we got there, the film had already started.

2 If we want to emphasise that something happened only a short time before, we use *just*.
Unfortunately, the train had just left when we got to the station.

3 Notice the position of *already* and *just*: between the auxiliary verb *had* and the past participle.

never ... before

If we want to say that it was the first time something happened or someone did something, we can use the Past perfect with *never ... before*.
It was a very interesting meal. I had never eaten Mexican food before.

Module 15

A Conditional sentences with *would*

if + Past simple + would(n't) + infinitive without to

    if clause   main clause

If I **became** president,   I **would build** more roads.
                    I **wouldn't** accept money.

We use conditional sentences with *would* to talk about imaginary, impossible or unlikely situations. The verb in the *if* clause is in the Past simple, but we are **not** talking about the past and we are not talking about a specific time.
If I had a ticket, I'd come with you. (= I haven't got a ticket)
If you lived in the country, you'd soon get bored. (= you don't live in the country)

Notice that:
1 we can change the order of the *if* clause and the main clause.
You'd soon get bored if you lived in the country.

2 we can use *were* instead of *was* after *I, he / she* and *it*.
If my brother were here now, he'd know what to do.

3 we often use *If I were you, I'd ...* to give advice.
If I were you, I'd look for someone else.

4 we can use *might* or *could* instead of *would*.
If you worked hard, you might pass the exam.
If I borrowed Mum's car, I could give you a lift.

B will and would

if + present + will / won't + infinitive without to

                       we**'ll go** for a picnic.
If the weather **stays good** tomorrow,   we **won't stay** at home.
                       will you **come** swimming?

1 We use *if* + present + *will / won't* + infinitive without *to* to talk about real possibilities in the future.
If Ben phones, I'll tell him you want to see him.

2 We use *if* + past + *will / wouldn't* + infinitive without *to* to talk about imaginary situations.
If I had more money, I'd buy a bigger house.

3 The choice of *will* or *would* sometimes depends on how we see a situation. Look at these examples:
a *If I get the job as manager, we'll go out to celebrate.*
b *If I were manager, I'd make a lot of changes.*

In sentence a, the speaker thinks it is a real possibility that he will get the job. In sentence b, the speaker is imagining himself in the job. He doesn't think he'll get it.

Verb	Past simple	Past participle
be	was / were	been
beat	beat	beaten
become	became	become
begin	began	begun
bend	bent	bent
bite	bit	bitten
blow	blew	blown
break	broke	broken
bring	brought	brought
build	built	built
burn	burned / burnt	burned / burnt
burst	burst	burst
buy	bought	bought
can	could	been able
catch	caught	caught
choose	chose	chosen
come	came	come
cost	cost	cost
cut	cut	cut
dig	dug	dug
do	did	done
draw	drew	drawn
dream	dreamed / dreamt	dreamed / dreamt
drink	drank	drunk
drive	drove	driven
eat	ate	eaten
fall	fell	fallen
feed	fed	fed
feel	felt	felt
fight	fought	fought
find	found	found
fly	flew	flown
forget	forgot	forgotten
forgive	forgave	forgiven
freeze	froze	frozen
get	got	got
give	gave	given
go	went	gone / been
grow	grew	grown
hang	hung	hanged / hung
have	had	had
hear	heard	heard
hide	hid	hidden
hit	hit	hit
hold	held	held
hurt	hurt	hurt
keep	kept	kept
kneel	knelt	knelt
know	knew	known
lay	laid	laid
lead	led	led
learn	learned / learnt	learned / learnt

Verb	Past simple	Past participle
leave	left	left
lend	lent	lent
let	let	let
lie	lay	lain
light	lit	lit
lose	lost	lost
make	made	made
mean	meant	meant
meet	met	met
must	had to	had to
pay	paid	paid
put	put	put
read / riːd /	read / red /	read / red /
ride	rode	ridden
ring	rang	rung
rise	rose	risen
run	ran	run
say	said	said
see	saw	seen
sell	sold	sold
send	sent	sent
set	set	set
shake	shook	shaken
shine	shone	shone
shoot	shot	shot
show	showed	shown
shut	shut	shut
sing	sang	sung
sink	sank	sunk
sit	sat	sat
sleep	slept	slept
slide	slid	slid
smell	smelled / smelt	smelled / smelt
speak	spoke	spoken
spend	spent	spent
spill	spilled / spilt	spilled / spilt
spoil	spoiled / spoilt	spoiled / spoilt
stand	stood	stood
steal	stole	stolen
stick	stuck	stuck
swim	swam	swum
take	took	taken
teach	taught	taught
tear	tore	torn
tell	told	told
think	thought	thought
throw	threw	thrown
understand	understood	understood
wake	woke	woken
wear	wore	worn
win	won	won
write	wrote	written

Module 1

A Complete the questions with one word only.

1 _____ do you spell that?

2 How _____ players are there in a football team?

3 _____ is your coat – the black one or the white one?

4 Where _____ your sister live now?

5 'How _____ do you see your grandparents?'
'About once a week.'

6 How _____ does the show last?

B Write the verb to make a leisure activity.

7 _____ chess

8 _____ for a run

9 _____ a video/DVD

10 _____ swimming

C Complete the text with the correct form of the verb to complete the passage .

Terri [11]_____ (live) in a small apartment in the centre of town. She [12]_____ (have) a car, but she [13]_____ (not / use) it very often. She usually [14]_____ (go) to work on foot – although she sometimes [15]_____ (catch) the bus if it's raining!

D Cross out the word or phrase which is not correct.

16 My sister always / every day / never goes to bed before midnight.

17 How long / What time / When does the film start?

18 I check my e-mail always / every day / once a week.

19 How long / When / Where were you born?

20 What / Where / Which part of London do you live in?

/20

Module 2

A Complete the sentences with the Past simple form of the verbs.

1 The film _____ (cost) millions of dollars to make.

2 Where _____ (be) you at seven o'clock?

3 I _____ (watch) television in my bedroom.

4 We _____ (buy) some food on the our way home.

5 _____ (feel) tired when you arrived home?

6 The lesson _____ (begin) a few minutes late.

B Underline the correct word to complete the sentences (ø = no preposition).

7 The shop opened at / in / on/ ø 1998.

8 Did you go out at / in / on / ø last night?

9 The film started at / in / on / ø eight o'clock. We're late!

10 He was a famous film star at / in / on / ø the 1930s.

11 There are no lessons at / in / on / ø Friday afternoon.

12 I last saw my cousin at / in / on / ø about a month ago.

C Find three pairs of opposites in the box.

bored	disappointed	embarrassed
excited	expensive	fed up
in a good mood	nervous	popular
relaxed	sad	

13 _____

14 _____

15 _____

D Complete the sentences with the correct form of the words.

16 Do you feel like _____ (go) for a walk later?

17 I hope you're feeling _____ (good) than yesterday.

18 We were very _____ (disappoint) that the concert was cancelled.

19 The room _____ (feel) very cold when I woke up.

20 I was very _____ (worry) when you didn't phone me.

/20

Module 3

A Complete each sentence with should, shouldn't, can, can't, have to or don't have to.

1 You _____ shout at the children. It frightens them.

2 I'm sorry, but you _____ bring your dog in here: it's forbidden.

3 You _____ get a visa before travelling to the United States. It's the law.

4 You _____ work in the library till ten o'clock. It's open all evening.

5 You _____ think very carefully before you sell the house, I think.

6 Teachers at this school _____ wear a tie, but they can if they want.

B Complete the jobs for the definitions.

7 Someone who designs and plans buildings.   a _ _ _ _ _ _ _ t

8 Someone who drives a taxi.   t _ _ i d _ _ _ _ r

9 Someone who looks after you in hospital.   n _ _ _ e

10 Someone who serves you in a shop.   s _ _ p a _ _ _ _ _ _ _ t

11 Someone who writes for a newspaper.   j _ _ _ _ _ _ _ t

C Choose the correct alternative.

12 Can you turn away / off / up the lights before you go out.

13 I need to wake off / out / up at seven tomorrow morning.

14 'Can I ask a question, please?' 'Sure, go ahead / off / up.'

15 The alarm went away / off / up at 5.30 a.m.

D Complete the sentences with the correct form of do.

16 You don't have _____ any homework tonight.

17 Here's some advice: try _____ your homework without the TV on!

18 _____ you mind if I leave the lesson early?

19 Why _____ you come and sit on the terrace?

20 Is it OK if my friend _____ the rest of this?

/20

Module 4

A Complete the sentences with the correct form of the verb.

1 '_____ (enjoy) your meal?' 'Yes, thanks. It's lovely, thank you!'

2 Joe always _____ (have) a party on his birthday.

3 I _____ (not / work) on Sundays. It's my day off.

4 'What _____ (read)?' 'It's the new novel by Stephen Craig.'

5 Mariana isn't here today. She _____ (spend) the day with her family.

6 All my friends _____ (come) to my birthday party next week.

B Choose the correct alternative.

7 Doing / Having / Making a party is a popular way of celebrating your birthday.

8 'We've just got engaged!' 'Cheers! / Congratulations! / Happy anniversary!'

9 Let's wish Olga a happy birthday! Many happy returns / thoughts / wishes!

10 I forgot to exchange / send / have my father a card for Father's Day … again!

11 I'd like to wish everyone a Funny / Happy / Merry New Year. Cheers!

C Choose the correct alternative.

12 You look tired. Why don't you take a day at / off / out work?

13 Statistics show that people eat off / out / up much more than ten years ago.

14 It was nice to see you. Thanks about / for / of coming!

15 Everybody's going away / off / out for a meal on Friday. Would you like to come?

16 Carnival is a good time for everyone to dress off / out / up and enjoy themselves.

D Complete the sentences with a(n), the, or ø (ø = no article).

17 Freddy was here _____ other day to say hello.

18 Our anniversary is on the 24th of _____ October.

19 Most people work five days _____ week.

20 The course began _____ day before yesterday.

/20

Module 6

A Choose the correct alternative.

1 I'll give you a ring when I get at home / to home / home.

2 Hi Mum! Here are we / we are / we come in Spain!

3 Are you planning to visit / visit / visiting the museum this afternoon?

4 Can / Do / Will you be able to come to our meeting?

5 Is your grandmother feeling / feel / feels better now?

6 The shop be / will / going to open again tomorrow.

B Complete the sentences with the correct form of the word in brackets.

7 Our _____ leaves at 6.30 on Saturday morning from Heathrow Airport.   (fly)

8 It's very _____ at this time of year.   (peace)

9 I find sitting by the swimming pool very _____ .   (relax)

10 It's one of the most _____ hotels in the Middle East.   (luxury)

C Complete the sentences with the correct preposition.

11 We want to be close _____ the beach.

12 My grandparents have decided to go _____ a cruise this winter.

13 We're staying _____ a really lovely hotel.

14 I'll see you next week! Bye _____ now!

D Complete the questions by adding one word only at the beginning.

15 _____ this your first time in London?

16 _____ you here on holiday?

17 _____ you have a good weekend?

18 _____ you got any plans for today?

19 _____ you like to join us for coffee?

20 _____ you rather go by car or by bus?

/20

Module 7

A Complete the sentences with the correct form of the verb.

1 I _____ (never / go) to Thailand but I'd like to go there one day.

2 My friend is only twenty-two, but he _____ (already / visit) more than thirty countries!

3 I _____ (begin) learning English when I was six years old.

4 My brother _____ (not / come) to visit me yet.

5 We _____ (move) to this apartment in 1999.

6 He _____ (always / be) very happy here, so there's no reason to move.

B Complete each sentence with a(n), the or ø (ø = no article).

7 I'd really love to travel round _____ world.

8 I'm hoping to go to _____ university to study economics.

9 He left this house _____ year ago.

10 Jo finished her university course _____ last year.

C Correct the words in bold in the sentences.

11 Why did you **became** a doctor?

12 He has **wrote** more than twenty books.

13 My sister has **spend** all her money.

14 When I was young, I **dream** of being a ballet dancer.

15 Did you **bought** anything interesting?

D Choose the correct alternative.

16 We decided to appear / become / go abroad for a few months.

17 It's Gary's ambition to become / get / learn how to famous one day.

18 He worked very hard to earn / start / win enough money to buy a holiday villa.

19 Have you decided what you like / want / wish for Christmas yet?

20 I'm still expecting / going / waiting for a reply to my message.

/20

Module 8

**A   Complete the gaps with *the* or *ø*
(ø = no article).**

The Sultanate of Oman is a country at the
entrance to the Persian Gulf. It has
borders with three other countries:
Yemen, Saudi Arabia and
[1]_____ United Arab Emirates.
In [2]_____ north, the
temperature can reach 45°C in summer.
Most of [3]_____ country is
desert, but [4]_____ visitors can
enjoy many fine beaches and luxurious
hotels on [5]_____ coast.

**B   Cross out the quantifier which
does not belong in each sentence.**

6   There aren't any / many / no foreign
    students at my university.

7   Do you need a few / any / some
    more time to decide?

8   There isn't enough / much / some
    time before we have to leave.

9   A few / Any / Some letters came for
    you while you were away.

10   There are a few / a lot of / too much
    mistakes in this exercise.

**C   Complete the missing words in
the sentences.**

11   A d_____ is a dry place where it
    never – or almost never – rains.

12   A b_____ is the imaginary line
    between two countries.

13   An i_____ is a piece of land
    which has water on all sides.

14   The c_____ is what the weather
    is like over a long period.

D   Complete the sentences.

15   Excuse me. I'm _____ for
    Warren Street.

16   Excuse me. How can we _____
    to Manchester Square, please?

17   _____ left at the traffic lights.

18   After you come out of the station,
    _____ the road.

19   _____ walking until you come to
    a set of traffic lights.

20   _____ off the bus at the last
    stop.

/20

Module 9

**A   Complete the compound nouns
after the definitions.**

1   A written message sent by mobile
    telephone. _ _ _ _ _ message

2   A system which makes a building
    warm. central _ _ _ _ _ _ _

3   A system which keeps a building cool.
    air _ _ _ _ _ _ _ _ _ _ _ _

4   A place where you can buy things in
    the open air. street _ _ _ _ _ _ _

5   a machine where you put dirty
    clothes. _ _ _ _ _ _ _
    machine

**B   Put the word in brackets in the
correct position in the sentences.**

6   My friends won't be here before six
    o'clock. (probably)

7   I definitely go out with her again.
    (won't)

8   It'll probably sunny again tomorrow.
    (be)

9   I not be able to come tomorrow.
    (may)

10   We know the answer when they
    telephone. (will)

C   Choose the correct alternative.

11   There might not be / being / to be
    enough food for everyone.

12   We'll probably go out if it stops /
    stopped / will stop raining.

13   I promise to phone you as soon as I
    get / 'll get / got there.

14   I wouldn't tell anybody about it if I
    am / were / will be you.

15   Make sure you turn off the lights
    before you are leaving / leave / 'll
    leave.

**D   Complete the sentences with one
word only.**

16   I'd like to pay by credit _____ ,
    please.

17   You can use the hotel swimming pool
    if you _____ .

18   Do you _____ if I ask a personal
    question?

19   Send me a text _____ if you get
    lost.

20   I'll ask her _____ she wants
    some more water.

/20

Module 11

**A   Complete the table with a word
from the word family.**

Verb	Noun	Adjective
to obsess	[1]_____	obsessed
to weigh	[2]_____	
	desperation	[3]_____
[4]_____	collection	

B   Choose the correct alternative.

5   assist at / go to see / visit a musical

6   collect / put on / play stamps

7   do / make / play chess

8   do / make / play a model aeroplane

**C   Complete the sentences with one
word only.**

9   _____ you like to come to our
    house for dinner next week?

10   My mother _____ like ironing,
    so my father does it.

11   I don't like this music at all: it
    _____ like cats fighting!

12   _____ you like living in the city
    centre?

13   Unfortunately, I _____ afford
    that new computer game.

14   '_____ does your new teacher
    look like?'
    'She's small and dark.'

D   Choose the correct alternative.

15   I'm the only person in my family who
    isn't keen about / in / on sport.

16   Angela is absolutely crazy about / of /
    with all kinds of pop music.

17   Simon really looks as / like / same
    his father.

18   How is / What was / Did the weather
    like while I was away?

19   I'm not / can't / don't stand dogs –
    they frighten me!

20   I real / really / very enjoy going to
    the cinema. How about you?

/20

Module 12

A Underline a word in B which makes the correct combination with A.

	A		B
1	hair	a	bag / brush / comb
2	hand	b	bag / brush / foam
3	sun	c	glasses / stick / torch
4	lip	d	bag / foam / stick
5	tooth	e	bag / brush / stick

B Complete the sentences with the correct form of the verb in bold.

6   The house was **build** more than 200 years ago.

7   The car **be** found a few kilometres from her house.

8   The book was **write** by a famous Russian author.

9   How much was the designer **pay** for his idea?

10   Twenty people **be** arrested at the demonstration.

C Choose the correct alternative.

11   The money stole / is stolen / was stolen about a week ago.

12   When did / was / were you buy that lovely necklace?

13   The tickets are sent / send / sent to you automatically.

14   These skirts wear / wore / were worn by many people in the 1990s.

15   I lose / lost / was lost my identity card a few days ago.

D Complete the suggestions with the correct form of go.

16   How about _____ out for a pizza this evening?

17   We could _____ out for lunch now, if you like.

18   Shall we _____ home now?

19   Why don't we _____ for a walk this afternoon?

20   Let's _____ outside. It's very hot in here.

/20

Module 13

A Complete the sentences with the correct form of the word in brackets.

1   All the players will be very _____ for this game. (motivation)

2   Nathalie is a very _____ child and she loves reading.   (imagination)

3   Ivan is so _____ – he never does any work at all.   (laziness)

4   My teacher was very _____ when I told him about my problem. (sympathy)

5   He has always shown a very _____ attitude to his work. (commit)

B Complete the phrases with *for* or *since*.

6   _____ twenty minutes

7   _____ I was ten years old

8   _____ yesterday

9   _____ last year

10   _____ fifteen years

C Complete sentences in the Present perfect simple or Present perfect continuous, using the verb in brackets.

11   How long _____ Olga _____ a teacher?   (be)

12   My mother _____ a cat for about three years.   (have)

13   How long _____?   (rain)

14   I _____ Dorota for a very long time.   (know)

15   I _____ wait for the phone to ring for ages.   (wait)

D Choose the correct alternative.

16   'How high / tall / much is your sister?' 'About normal height.'

17   He's been keen on cycling for / from / since he was ten years old.

18   How far / long / much is London from Paris?

19   This job is a great advantage / attitude / opportunity for me to travel.

20   How are / can / do you do? It's very nice to meet you.

/20

Module 14

A Choose the correct alternative.

1   I always buy a lottery ticket, but I never earn / win / spend anything.

2   Most children would like to get more pocket currency / money / salary.

3   The school can't / don't / won't afford new computers at the moment.

4   We paid €100 for tickets and the show was awful. What a loss / spend / waste of money!!

5   The police stopped us for speeding and we had to pay a change / fine / tip.

6   What is the change / currency / exchange rate for US dollars?

B Complete the sentences with the correct form of the verb in brackets.

7   I'd like _____ (change) this money into US dollars, please.

8   Can we _____ (have) the bill, please?

9   We had only been there for a few minutes when the restaurant _____ (close).

10   He was so horrible to me, he nearly made me _____ (cry).

11   'Have you decided, madam?' 'Yes, please. I _____ (take) this pair, please.'

C Put the words in brackets in the correct place in the sentences.

12   How much this pair of shorts cost? (does)

13   I felt very annoyed because I just lost all my money.   (had)

14   When we arrived at the stadium, the match had started.   (already)

15   I was very surprised that I had met him before.   (never)

D Complete the sentences with the correct preposition.

16   I don't spend very much money _____ clothes.

17   Marcus is going to borrow some money _____ his brother.

18   If you want to buy a new car, you'll have to save _____ .

19   I don't think it's a good idea to lend money _____ your friends.

20   I hope we can pay _____ credit card!

/20

161

TAPESCRIPTS

Module 1

Recording 1

Many people think that young people nowadays don't get enough exercise. But the survey shows that isn't true: only 11% say they like playing video games while 28% go for a run or go to the gym at least once a month.

It seems that people still like going to the cinema when they want to watch a film. 46% say they go to the cinema more than once a month, but only 40% rent a video or DVD.

There are two activities which everybody – or nearly everybody – says they do. Everyone who took part in the survey says they read a newspaper or magazine and 93% say they go for a walk – though they don't say if it's a long walk!

Going to a restaurant was one of the most popular leisure activities, according to the results of the survey. 64% of people say they regularly eat out.

It seems that many more people like listening to music than playing it. 71% say they regularly listen to the radio, but only 8% say they can play a musical instrument.

Recording 2

a The letters NBA mean National Basketball Association – the body which controls basketball in the United States.
b Argentina have won the World Cup twice, England and France have won once each – but Japan have never won the World Cup.
c The modern Olympic Games took place in Sydney, Australia, in the year 2000.
d A rugby ball is similar to the ball used in football, but there is one important difference: the shape. A football is round, but a rugby ball is oval, like an egg.
e The Winter Olympics happen every four years.
f The sport of judo is now popular all over the world, but it began about 120 years ago in Japan.
g There are twenty-one spots on a dice.
h The white player always starts in a game of chess.
i No one really knows why there are fifty-two cards in a normal pack – but one idea is that there is one card for every week of the year.
j A soccer referee signals the end of a game by giving three long blows on his whistle.
k An ice hockey match has three periods of twenty minutes – that's sixty minutes in all.
l The leader of the Tour de France wears a yellow shirt.

Recording 5

Toshi, a nineteen-year-old, from Nagasaki, in Japan, wants to become a sumo wrestler. Toshi, who weighs over 175 kilos, and is 1 metre 95 tall, lives in a special training camp, called a Heya, with thirty other sumo wrestlers. Their training is very hard. Even before breakfast, they normally practise for four and a half hours! It is important that Toshi doesn't lose weight, so he always has a large lunch of rice, meat, fish and vegetables with lots of beer, and sometimes he eats extra pizzas and burgers. After lunch he goes to sleep for a few hours. One day, Toshi hopes to be famous – and rich – but at the moment he doesn't earn much money, so each month his parents send him money to help him.

Ania, who comes from Lublin in Poland, is a champion gymnast. She's seventeen years old and lives in a small apartment with her mother. She trains very hard – usually about eight hours every day, except Sunday, when she rests. She normally gets up at about seven in the morning and practises for three or four hours. Then she rests in the afternoon, before practising for another four hours in the early evening. Like most gymnasts, Ania is very small – only about 1 metre 50, and she weighs very little too – around 40 kilos.

This is very important for a gymnast, so she doesn't eat very much – although her mother makes sure she has a healthy diet! Ania doesn't earn very much money, but she enjoys her lifestyle very much.

João, from São Paolo in Brazil, is a professional footballer with a big Italian football club. He lives with his Italian girlfriend in a large villa in the mountains near Milan. Although he's only twenty-three years old, he earns around $50,000 a week. He spends his money on fast cars, Italian designer clothes and goes to all the best restaurants and clubs in Milan. But João has to live a healthy life – he never smokes and only occasionally drinks alcohol, and most days he lives on a special diet of pasta and vegetables. Most mornings, before he goes to train with the rest of the team, he runs about eight kilometres.

Recording 6

WA: WAITER; WO: WOMAN

1 WA: Can I help you, madam?
   WO: Yes, where are the toilets, please?
   WA: Over there, next to the bar.
   WO: Thanks. And then can we have the bill, please?
   WA: Certainly, madam.
2 A: Excuse me. Do you speak English?
   B: A little bit.
   A: Where's the nearest underground station – do you know?
   B: Over there, next to the cinema. Can you see it?
   A: Oh yes. Thank you.
   B: Where are you from?
   A: Ontario, Canada.
   B: That's a long way. What are you doing in Warsaw?
   A: Oh, I'm just here on business.
   B: And how long are you going to stay?
   A: Just a week, but I'm having a great time!
   B: Oh well, good luck and enjoy your stay.
   A: Thanks, bye.
3 A: Excuse me. How much does this cost?
   B: Twelve ninety-nine.
   A: OK, right … I'll take it then.
   B: Anything else?
   A: No, that's it thank you.
   B: How do you want to pay?
   A: By credit card, if that's OK.
   B: Sure …

Recording 7

a Where are you from?
b What time is it?
c What's your date of birth?
d How long have you been in England?
e How long are you going to stay?
f How do you spell your name?
g How much does this cost?
h Where's the nearest bank?

Module 2

Recording 1

a The first person to appear on TV was William Taynton – a young Englishman who worked with Scottish inventor, John Logie Baird, the inventor of television.
b Many people call Vladimir Zworykin, a Russian who went to live in the United States in 1919, 'the father of television'. He invented the first 'electronic' TV in 1929.

c In 1936, the BBC (the British Broadcasting Corporation) made its first TV programmes. Not many people watched them as not many people had a TV!

d Cookery programmes were popular even in the1930s. Frenchman Marcel Boulestin became the first TV chef in 1937.

Recording 2

a The first TV soap opera began in 1947. Its name was *A Woman to Remember*.

b The first TV advert – for a Bulova clock – lasted just twenty seconds and it cost only $9 to make!

c Colour TV came to Europe in the 1960s. The first colour TVs were very expensive, so not many people bought them.

d The Japanese company JVC made the world's first VHS video recorders in the mid-1970s.

Recording 5

a When's your birthday?
b What time does this lesson finish?
c What time did it start?
d When did you last watch TV?
e Which month does it usually start to get hot in your country?
f What time do you usually go to bed?
g In which year were you born?
h In which decade did your parents grow up?
i When did your grandparents get married?
j When is your next holiday?

Recording 6

a A: The dentist will see you now, Mr Williams.
  B: Oh … er … right … I'll um … OK I'll, I'll be right um …
b A: I'm very sorry. All the tickets for the Friday concert are sold.
  B: Oh no! I really wanted to see that!
c A: Didn't you know? Tom and Barbara are going to get married!
  B: Really? Tom and Barbara? I don't believe it!
d A: So, if I get a ticket coming back tomorrow, will it cost the same as a ticket …
  B: Oh come on! There's only two minutes till my train leaves!
e A: Hello. Well did you win?
  B: Yes! We won 7-0!
f A: I think you've made a mistake … I'm not a shop assistant. I don't work here.
  B: Oh, I'm so sorry … how stupid of me … I'm really sorry.
g A: Two years later, there was another important change in the constitution, and this was agreed by the Parliament only after …
  B: Oooohh … thirty minutes till lunchtime …
h A: What's the matter?
  B: It's nearly eight o'clock. I don't know why John hasn't phoned. I hope he's OK.

Recording 7

angry disappointed embarrassed excited impatient
in a good mood nervous relaxed surprised worried

Recording 9

HELEN:
I particularly remember my first day at secondary school … um … It's very clear in my memory … I was very, very nervous in the morning … and my friend and I, we went out of our house because we lived next door to each other, and we were walking down the road, it was a Monday morning, um … in September … how long ago? 1990, it was …. um … and my mother came

outside with me and she took out a video camera and filmed me as I walked down the road, and I turned round and waved … um … I was very nervous but I had a big smile … um … I got to school and everything was fine, but recently she has shown me the video that she took and it was very embarrassing.

JOSH:
Well, one thing I'll never forget is the first time I met the woman who became my wife. I was working in a ski resort in Yugoslavia and we had a get together for the staff. I was shy, you know, I didn't like to go up and meet people … It was a crowded room and, well, I saw this woman standing on the other side of the room surrounded by a crowd of people. I really wanted to go up and speak to her but I just couldn't – well, I felt strange … I didn't know what to do so I just stood there and then she happened to turn around and so I smiled … that was all I could do, and she smiled back … and well … twelve years ago. Ten years ago we got married.

Module 3

Recording 1

1 He should tidy up his books.
2 He shouldn't smoke so much.
3 He shouldn't put his food on his notes.
4 He should empty the ashtray.
5 He should switch off his computer game.
6 He shouldn't chat on the phone when he's studying.
7 He shouldn't drink so much coffee.
8 He shouldn't read the paper when he's studying.

Recording 2

I = INTERVIEWER; M = MAYO
I: So, Mayo, you're studying here in London, is that right?
M: That's right.
I: … and you're studying something pretty unusual …
M: Maybe. I'm doing a course in Circus Studies, I want to be a circus entertainer. I want to be an acrobat.

Recording 3

I = INTERVIEWER; M = MAYO
I: So, how did you get on the course?
M: Well, I did some work in the theatre before this course, but I was more and more interested in circus work. It's my dream to work in the circus. You don't have to have any specific qualifications but it's really very hard work, so you have to be very enthusiastic.
I: And what do you study on the course?
M: You have to learn about theatre … about dance … and acrobatics, of course.
I: OK, so how about an average day? How many hours do you normally have to study?
M: Normally it's from nine, nine in the morning … till four in the afternoon … five days a week. If you want to, you can stay later in the evenings, you can do extra training …
I: And how about holidays?
M: We have a month at Christmas, one month at Easter … and … er … five weeks in the summer.
I: What kind of work do you have to do to graduate?
M: Well, you have to do some written assignments. As part of your graduation, you have to do a solo performance. I'm going to do an acrobatics show as part of my graduation.
I: What kind of people come on the course?
M: Oh, all kinds really … English, Swiss, German … people come from all over. You have to speak English because we are in England … there are a lot of Spanish people, but I can't speak Spanish … I think it helps if you can speak Spanish!

Recording 4

1 Can you understand what he's saying?
2 I can't believe that.
3 Can you help me with this?
4 I can see much better now.
5 We can't hear what you're saying!
6 They can speak three languages fluently.
7 I think we can help you.
8 You can't do that here!

Recording 5

a Hi. My name's Morgan and I'm from Australia ... from a place called Brisbane. I'm still at high school. I love all the usual things really ... like music, going to the movies ... but most of all I love people, I'm really interested in people and making friends. One day, er, my ambition is to do something that can really help people, I'd like to study for that.

b Well, I'm Luke. I'm from England ... I'm twenty years old ... yeah, money is quite important to me when it comes to work. Also I'd like to work for myself. I ... I don't want to work in an office, I'm not really into computers and that. I like to be more independent, I don't want to be in one place all the time ...

c My name is Carmen and I come from Mexico. I'm at college right now studying English and French ... I want to meet people from all over the world, that's why I study languages. I like reading too ... and meeting people ... I want to go to every continent, maybe learn some more languages ... maybe Chinese or something ...

d Hi. I'm Jong. I am twenty-three years old, from Seoul in South Korea, and I am studying hard right now. I am studying real hard and trying to improve my English ... When I finish my studies, I hope I will get a good job. I want to maybe become a millionaire one day ... I like to work hard, I'm a very ambitious person.

Recording 6

a Yeah, ultimately I want to become a psychologist and maybe help people that way.
b I'm doing a course to become a plumber, and I'd like to have my own business one day.
c I want to be a translator.
d I'd like to work as a trader on the stock market ... make a lot of money ... I hope!

Recording 7

1 A: Yeah?
  B: Hello, could you turn the music down, please? It's one o'clock and I'm trying to sleep.
  A: Oh, sorry. Is that better?
  B: Yes, thanks. Perhaps I can get some sleep now. Good night.
2 A: I'm sorry, is it OK if I leave early today? I'm going to take my cat to see the vet.
  B: You're going to take your cat to the vet? What's the matter with her then?
  A: Him. I don't know. That's why I'm going to take him to the vet's.
  B: Oh, I see. Sure, go ahead. Thanks for telling me.
3 A: David, do you have your mobile phone with you?
  B: Um ... yes. Why?
  A: Can I borrow it, please? I need to make a quick call to my mother.
  B: OK, here you are.
4 A: Do you mind if I change seats?
  B: Yes, all right. What's the problem?
  A: I can't see because of the sun.
  B: OK, then. Why don't you sit there, next to Andrea.

Recording 8

a Could you turn the music down, please?
b Is it OK if I leave early today?
c Can I borrow it, please?
d Do you mind if I change seats?
e Could you spell that for me, please?
f Is it OK if I take a photo?
g Can I close the window, please?

Module 4

Recording 1

1 Chinese New Year is either at the end of January or the beginning of February.
2 St Valentine's Day is on 14th of February.
3 In Britain, Mother's Day is at the beginning of March, usually the first Sunday in March.
4 Easter is usually between the end of March and the middle of April.
5 May Day is on 1st May. In some countries this is called Labour Day.
6 In Britain, Father's Day is in the middle of June.
7 American Independence Day is on the 4th July.
8 Halloween is on the 31st October.
9 Christmas Day is on the 25th December.
10 New Year's Eve is on the 31st of December.

Recording 3

a August 23rd	f May 22nd
b January 10th	g June 14th
c December 12th	h October 16th
d March 19th	i February 28th
e September 20th	j November 30th

Recording 4

KAREN:
Um ... one of the most important days for me really is New Year, because New Year in Scotland is really very, very important ... in fact, it's not so much New Year's Day, the first of January, but it's the evening before, New Year's Eve ... so on the thirty-first of December, at about seven o'clock in the evening, the cleaning begins, and I remember when I was a child, my mother spending hours cleaning the house to make sure that everything would be special, and ready for the New Year ... and then when it gets to twelve o'clock, and the bells start to ring, the first thing my mother does is go to open the door to let the New Year in ... and then everyone has something to drink and we wait for the first foot. The first foot is the first person who comes to your house in the New Year, and they're very, very special because they bring you your luck for the whole year, and the first foot has to bring three very important things. They bring shortbread, which is a special kind of biscuit, they bring coal, for warmth, and they bring something to drink ...

JOHNNY:
Chinese New Year is never on the same day every year because we follow a special calendar which follows the Moon. So sometimes it's at the end of January and sometimes it's at the beginning of February.
At Chinese New Year we like to wear our new clothes and we also like to eat special food which has special meaning, such as Chinese mushrooms and oysters and delicious sweets; hopefully they bring us lots of good luck and lots of money.
Now, it's special for children because they get little red envelopes of money from adults, so what they do is they go to adults, they say 'Happy New Year' and they get a little red envelope and because I'm not married, I get the little red envelope, too.

Recording 7

1 February … yes, well I put February 14th, Valentine's Day. I always send my boyfriend a valentine … and he sends me one too … If not, I'll kill him.
2 This is a most important date in Ireland – St. Patrick's Day – March 23rd. That's the national day in Ireland, the national day of celebration of all things Irish. It's the time when everyone can be Irish for a day!
3 May 8th is a day I'll never forget … It's the day I passed my driving test … finally!
4 June … I put Father's Day. I think it's the 20th this year, something like that … Everyone always remembers Mother's Day but I always get my dad a card for Father's Day and give him a ring if I can.
5 July 15th. I wrote July 15th because we're going on holiday … we're renting a villa on the beach. It's gonna be fun!
6 Well, the first day I put was September 7th … which is very, very important because it's my birthday. I'm hoping for lots of presents!
7 For October, I chose the 23rd because that's my wedding anniversary. It'll be our fourth wedding anniversary this October in fact … mustn't forget!
8 Of course, I had to choose Christmas Day, December 25th. It's always a big family day and every Christmas morning we all give our presents and then my father makes us go out for a long walk … even though it's always freezing cold.

Recording 9

a Well, it's happened! I'm thirty years old … today.
b I've got some news for you. James and I are getting married!
c Well, I think that's everything … a beer for you, André, and a glass of wine for you, Elisa.
d And I brought this for you Leonardo, I hope you like it. I made it myself.
e (Sound of bell striking twelve. Sounds of a party.)
f I'd better go now. I've got my exam tomorrow morning.
g … anyway, I've decided not to come out tonight. I've got a really awful cold, and I just want to go home to bed!
h Ben, we've got to go now, but thanks for a lovely party.

Module 5

Recording 1

supermodel   dangerous   attractive   powerful   athletic
enormous   gentleman   perfume   fashionable
important   traditionally

Recording 2

a This is a very casual look obviously … the T-shirt and jeans make her look very natural … She looks quite young in this picture, I think.
b It's hard to believe this is the same person … Obviously, her whole look is very different from the other picture, Picture A … the glasses make her look much more serious, much more mature … and the hairstyle, too … In fact, she looks like a senior executive or something like that, something in the business world.
c Hmm … I'm not sure about this one … the hair makes her look younger, doesn't it? Personally, I think her hair is better in the other pictures … and I think she looks prettier in Picture A, to be honest. That tracksuit isn't the most elegant outfit in the world, I must say. It makes her look heavier, definitely … I'd say she looks better in Picture A, definitely.
d You can see how the dress makes her look taller than in the other pictures. This is definitely the most sophisticated of the four pictures … it's the hairstyle, isn't it? It gives her a very elegant, sophisticated appearance … nice. I think this is the best picture, I really do.

Recording 3

(missing words only)

1 more serious / more mature
2 younger
3 prettier
4 the most elegant
5 better
6 taller
7 the most sophisticated
8 best

Recording 4

a My father is <u>older</u> than my mother.
b I'm very different from my sister.
c Her hair is very similar to mine.
d She's <u>the nicest</u> person I know.
e Her nose is the same as mine.
f I look like my father.
g Who's <u>the oldest</u> person in your family?
h She's the same age as me.

Recording 5

1 Well, he's quite tall … he's got fair hair … a bit longer than the others. I think he's quite good-looking, actually.
2 He's got a little beard … and a little moustache, too.
3 He's got a shaved head. He's very well-built.
4 I think he must have dyed hair … it's dyed blond. It's very, very short.
5 He's black. He's about average height and build, I'd say.
6 I suppose he's in his mid to late twenties … longish dark hair … he's wearing a scarf round his neck.

Module 6

Recording 2

a I'm planning to go abroad.
b She's going to find a job.
c We'd rather stay at home.
d We'd like to pay now, please.

Recording 3

Part 1

R = ROSA; M = MARK

R: So anyway, we decided to have a really good holiday – a 'dream holiday' in the Caribbean, because we'd always wanted to go there. So we saved our money up for months and months, and booked this holiday in a place called San Antonio. It cost over a thousand pounds each, but we wanted to do something really special so we booked it for two weeks in May, because all the brochures said that the weather's beautiful there in May …
M: We were flying from Gatwick airport, and the flight was overnight … leaving Gatwick late at night, and arriving in San Antonio the next morning, or that was the idea, anyway! But when we arrived at the airport they told us that because of bad weather in the Caribbean, the flight was delayed until the next morning. So we had to spend the night at the airport, sleeping on the floor, and we finally got on the plane the next morning twelve hours late!
R: But that was just the beginning. On the plane they told us that the bad weather over the Caribbean was actually a hurricane – Hurricane George – and that we couldn't fly to San Antonio. We had to go to the capital city instead, and stay in a hotel there for the night, until the hurricane passed. Anyway, we weren't too worried, we thought – well it's only one night … and they told us that we were going to

a five-star hotel, next to the beach, with a swimming pool, so we were quite happy at that point ...

Recording 4

Part 2

M: Anyway, we arrived at the hotel, the Hotel Paradiso it was called, what a joke! They said it was a five-star hotel, but I wouldn't give it one star! It was just awful. I don't know how to describe it ... it was an awful building, yes, it was next to the sea, but it wasn't a beach! Just a few rocks, and the sea was so dirty you couldn't swim in it. There were big ships travelling past, and the sea was all polluted and brown, it looked horrible.

R: So we went to look at the swimming pool, but that was no better. It wasn't a nice blue colour, like you'd expect. It was a sort of greeny-black colour and as we looked at it we could see things moving about in it, and we looked more closely and we realised it was full of frogs. There were hundreds and hundreds of frogs in it. So after that, obviously, we didn't use it.

M: And then there was the food. Do you remember the food?

R: I'll never forget it! The first morning, we went downstairs for breakfast, expecting to have you know, the usual things you get in hotels, bread, marmalade, fruit, coffee, and we were very surprised instead to see lots of different types of vegetables: carrots, peas, cabbage and a big bowl of lettuce! But anyway, I was really, really hungry so I decided to have some of the lettuce until I saw that it was moving! The leaves of lettuce were slowly moving around the bowl, and I looked a bit more closely and saw that the lettuce bowl was full of ants, hundreds of them, and there were so many that they were actually moving the lettuce leaves! After that, we didn't eat in the hotel again. We didn't want to.

M: The worst part though, was when the hurricane arrived. That was really frightening. It was a fifteen-storey hotel so you felt really terrified with all that wind, and rain, and the windows banging, and the trees crashing outside. It was terrible.

R: And then they told us that because of the hurricane, there were no flights to San Antonio, and that we had to stay there for another three days, three more days in that place! There was nothing to do! Nowhere to go! We couldn't eat the food! It was noisy and dirty. We just couldn't believe that it could happen.

M: So when we finally arrived in San Antonio, we were five days late. And the worst thing was that Hurricane George had never arrived there. The weather had been perfect in San Antonio all the time!

Recording 6

a You'll have a great time!
b We'd like some more water, please.
c She'd like to go home now.
d Would you like another one?
e They'll be here soon.
f It'll be very crowded
g We'd rather go by car.
h I'll see who it is.
i Will you be there this evening?
j You'll have to ask him.
k I'd rather stay where I am.

Recording 7

a A: Morning!
   B: Oh, morning! How are you?
   A: I'm fine, I'm fine. Nice day, isn't it?
   B: Yes, it's lovely.
   A: So, have you got any plans for today?
   B: No, nothing special. We might go to the park later, what do you think?
   C: Yes, Mummy.
   B: How about you?
   A: Well, my granddaughter's coming over later ...
   B: Oh, that's nice.
   A: Yes, well she's just come back from ...
   C: Mummy ...
   B: Yes, darling, I'm just talking.
   C: Mummy, can we go to the park now?
   B: Listen, I'd better get on. I hope you have a nice day.

b A: Oh, hello ... You all right?
   B: Oh, hello ... Yes, I'm fine. How are you?
   A: Oh, not so bad ... working hard, y'know. So have you been away, then?
   B: Yes, we have, actually. Just for a few days.
   A: I thought so. I thought I hadn't seen you for a while. Did you go anywhere nice?
   B: Yes ... well, only to stay with Richard – that's my husband – Richard's mother up in Scotland ... She's been ill.
   A: Oh, dear. Is she feeling better now?
   B: Yes, she's much better now, thanks.
   A: Oh, good. Did you get nice weather?
   B: Um ... no, not really. It rained most of the time, actually.
   A: Oh, well ... Are you happy to be back, then?
   B: Yes I am, actually. It's always nice to get home.
   A: Yeah ... So that's £18.92, please. Thank you ... and here's the change. Nice to see you!
   B: Nice to see you. Take care.

c A: Afternoon.
   B: Good afternoon.
   C: Hi there.
   B: Where are you going?
   A: It's the, er, Caledonian Hotel, please, it's in ... Princes Street.
   B: Caledonian Hotel, I know it, all right. So are you here on holiday?
   A: Right, yeah. We're here on holiday. How did you know?
   B: Oh, I can always tell. Where are you from, America is it?
   C: No, we're Canadian. We're from Toronto.
   B: Canada, eh? Well, well, that's a long way to come. Is this your first time in Edinburgh?
   A: Yes, it's our first time here, but I have family here.
   B: Is that right?
   A: Yes, my family came from near here. They moved to Canada.

d A: Hi.
   B: Hello there.
   A: Did you have a good weekend?
   B: Yeah, it was OK. I didn't do much, really, just sat at home relaxing, y'know. How about you?
   A: Yeah, oh I had a fantastic weekend, great yeah.
   B: Oh really. What did you do?
   A: Oh well, nothing really.
   B: Oh right. Like me then.
   A: Yeah, I suppose so.
   B: Did you see the football on Sunday?
   A: Oh, yeah, fantastic, wasn't it? That goal was brilliant!
   B: Did you think so? I wanted United to win, actually. I thought they were a bit unlucky.
   A: What do you mean unlucky! They were lucky they only lost 1–0, and that was definitely a penalty ...
   B: Nah! He just fell over.

Recording 8

(missing questions only)

a Nice day, isn't it?
b So, have you got any plans for today?
c Is she feeling better now?
d Are you happy to be back, then?
e Is this your first time in Edinburgh?
f Did you have a good weekend?
g Did you see the football on Sunday?

Recording 10

AK = ANDY KING; FK = FIONA KING; TA = TRAVEL AGENT

AK: We'd like to get away for a little bit, you know … last-minute holiday, you know, just a quick break.

TA: OK. So if I can just ask a few questions …

AK: OK.

TA: … just to find out the kind of thing you're looking for and then I can feed in your details into our database and see what we can offer you … Right … so, when would you like to go?

FK: Well, well … I think it'll have to be the last week in June.

TA: The last week in June? Oh, I see, quite soon. Next week, in fact, isn't it?

FK: Yes, well …

TA: OK, no problem. And how long are you planning to go away for?

FK: Oh, just a week … we haven't got that much time, y'know …

TA: Right. OK … So what kind of place would you like to go to? Have you got any ideas?

AK: Well … I thought maybe Spain, so we don't have to go too far. Spain perhaps, or Greece maybe … as long as it's hot, I don't mind.

TA: Right … so is it a beach holiday you want, or something else?

FK: Yes, I think we'd like to be near a beach really …

TA: Are you looking for somewhere quiet?

AK: Fairly quiet …

FK: … but not too quiet. I think we'd prefer it if there was somewhere to go in the evening.

TA: Oh, right. I see. So how many people are going to travel?

AK: Just the two of us.

TA: I see.

FK: You know, I think I'd like to go somewhere a bit more exotic … somewhere like Thailand or somewhere … you know, a bit more exciting.

TA: Right, OK. Well, of course, we have plenty of holidays there … but the price is obviously going to be higher. How much would you like to pay?

FK: Well, I'm not sure … maybe £500 each …

AK: How much?

FK: Well, maybe £500 per person …

TA: Right … well … of course, it also depends on the accommodation. Do you want self-catering or would you rather stay in a hotel?

AK: Self-catering. Definitely.

TA: Right. So self-catering it is … now let's see what we can come up with …

Module 7

Recording 1

Some celebrities always knew what they wanted in life. *Titanic* star Kate Winslet made her first TV appearance at the age of only eleven in an advert for breakfast cereal. And at the age of sixteen, Catherine Zeta-Jones asked if she could miss her school exams to appear in the theatre. 'Go!' replied her headmaster,

'You're going to be a star, not a professor!'

But not all Hollywood stars knew what they wanted to do so early on in life. Until he was fifteen, Irish actor Colin Farrell wanted to be a professional footballer like his father and his uncle. At first Farrell's dad laughed when Colin told him his plans. 'I remember my dad saying "An actor? Is that a real way for a man to make a living?" But now he couldn't be happier!' he says.

Farrell isn't the only Hollywood star who had sporting ambitions as a child. Renée Zellweger dreamt of fame as an international gymnast. But others trained for more serious occupations. Actor Tom Cruise spent a year in a Franciscan monastery training to become a priest, and rock star Sting taught at a primary school before becoming a singer.

Failure at school and a series of low-paid jobs was also a feature of many stars' early life. Keanu Reeves dropped out of high school at the age of seventeen and worked in an ice rink and in a pasta restaurant. And Academy Award winning actor Tom Hanks worked as a bellman in the Hilton Hotel in Los Angeles in the 1970s, an experience which he says helped prepare him for acting. 'You put on your bellman suit and then play the role of a bellman,' he told a magazine. 'You make good tips and a nice wage, working three, four days a week.'

So next time you're in your local restaurant eating spaghetti, or walking past a big hotel in the centre of town, take a good look at the people working there. You never know – they might become world-famous one day!

Recording 2

a I've had my car for about six months.
b I've been a student for two years.
c I've been at secondary school for six years.
d Before that, I went to primary school for six years.
e I've lived in London for ten years.
f I've known Anna for about eight years.
g My grandparents have been married for over fifty years.
h My mother has worked as a doctor for twenty years.
i Helen has been a teacher for three years.
j Before that, she was a translator for two years.

Recording 4

BILL:

My surname is O'Driscoll, which is originally an Irish name, and I know that my family came over from Ireland sometime at the end of the nineteenth century and settled in the States and … well I've never been to Ireland and my ambition is to go back there and rediscover my family roots. Maybe find some of my long-lost cousins over there … So that's my ambition: to rediscover the Irish side of my family … yeah, I'd really like to do that.

RALPH:

Well, looking back, I'd say my greatest achievement was a sporting one really … When I was about eighteen, I was very keen on football and I actually played one match for my local team where I scored three goals and I was the hero for a week or two. I still look back on that with a lot of pride … As for my dream, I still have one real ambition which is to visit the Taj Mahal in India. I suppose I'm getting a bit old now, but you never know – one day!

DEB:

Well, I've always, always wanted to own a car. I don't have a car at the moment because I can't afford one … also because I can't drive … but anyway, it's my ambition one day to own a car – but not just any old car. It has to be a Ferrari … and a red Ferrari at that. I don't know why … I suppose I ought to learn to drive first … but that's what I really want, yeah, to own a lovely red Ferrari.

IAN:

My biggest ambition is one day to buy an enormous house which is in the middle of the countryside, in the mountains somewhere, but you know, really miles from anywhere … and it has to have lots and lots of space, enough space so that I can invite all my friends and all my family for a big party … and then they can all go away and I can just enjoy the peace and quiet … that's my ambition.

SWATI:

Yes, well, my greatest achievement was actually to get in to university, where I'm studying medicine now, and my ambition is to really help people in some way … Not necessarily to be a famous surgeon or anything like that, but to make some medical discovery that really helps people. A drug that can cure some disease or something like that … so that my name is remembered … I think that would be a really great thing to do.

Recording 6

1 How long have you lived in your house?
2 What do people usually do when they're late for a bus?
3 What do you want for your next birthday?
4 What advice would you give someone who is looking for a job?
5 What did you eat for breakfast this morning?
6 What food is good for you?
7 Are you ever late for class? Why?
8 What's the best place in your town to go for a walk?

Module 8

Recording 1

a If you're at home, maybe. I think a lot of people have a cup of tea around then. But most people are at work, or on their way home, so, no, I don't think it's true, really.
b Well, in my family it's true, yes. We eat pasta at home every day. I think Italian people eat a lot of pasta, it's very common in my region at least. So, I think maybe yes, it's true.
c I've lived in Moscow for a few years now. In the winter, I can tell you, yes … it's really, really cold. Minus twenty degrees, and of course, at night it's even colder. But you know, in the summer it's sometimes very hot, maybe twenty-five degrees … so no, it's not always cold. Definitely not.
d Maybe in the south it's more popular, but I think most people in Spain nowadays aren't really interested in bullfighting. They even tried to stop it completely in one city, in Barcelona. I don't like it myself … so I think this is a myth, really.
e I think it's true, yes. We always try to show good behaviour in public. We don't like it when people are rude or shout. Yes, I think it's true for Japanese people.
f Definitely, definitely … people in Argentina love football. It's a passion for them, a great, great passion.
g I don't think it's true. People have the impression that we just eat burgers and fried chicken and that kind of fast food, but there's a whole lot of other stuff which people enjoy. We eat all kinds of things really.
h Yeah, I'd say it's true. Most Australian people live on the coast or near the coast, so the weather's always OK … so it's nice to eat outside, invite a few friends round …
i Well, I live in Dubai, and in the city you don't often see camels, but if you go out into the desert, sure you see plenty of camels … there are even camel races sometimes.
j Well, you do see Scottish people wearing kilts, but only on special occasions … weddings maybe, or when the Scotland rugby team or football team is playing. But generally, no … you don't see people wearing kilts normally.

Recording 2

1 Asia is bigger than Europe.
   True. Asia makes up 30% of the world's land mass, and is by far the biggest continent.
2 New York is the biggest city in the world.
   False. New York has a population of fourteen million people and it is certainly the biggest city in the United States. But there are at least five cities (including Tokyo, Mexico City and São Paolo) which are bigger.
3 Mount Fuji is in Japan. It's the highest mountain in the world.
   False. At 3,776 m, Mount Fuji is certainly the highest mountain in Japan. But other mountains in Asia – such as Mount Everest and K2 – are more than 8,000 m high.
4 The Queen of England lives in Downing Street.
   False. Number ten Downing Street is the official home of the British Prime Minister. The Queen's official London home is Buckingham Palace.
5 The Mediterranean Sea is bigger than the Pacific Ocean.
   False. The Mediterranean Sea has an area of just two and a half million square kilometres compared to the Pacific Ocean's 166 million square kilometres.
6 The Sun is smaller than the Moon.
   False. The Sun is of course much bigger than the Moon: approximately 400 times bigger, in fact!
7 The Himalayas are in Asia.
   True. The Himalayas are in Asia. They stretch from India in the west to China in the east.
8 You can always see the Moon in the sky at night.
   False. Of course this isn't true! The Moon is only seen when the sky is clear, and before it sets.
9 The Mississippi River is in the United States.
   True. The Mississippi River passes through the cities of St Louis, Memphis and New Orleans. It's the longest river in the United States.

Recording 3

I = INTERVIEWER; S = STUART
I: So, Stuart, you live in Switzerland, don't you, in Zürich …
S: I do, yes.
I: Did you know it was voted 'the world's best city to live in'?
S: I didn't, actually … no. Well, well …
I: Why do you think that is … I mean, do you agree?
S: Um, well … I don't know about the world's best, but, yeah, it's a pretty good place to live. I like it, yeah …
I: Why specifically … I mean, what's so good about it?
S: Well, a number of things really. I mean, the setting for one thing. You've got the lake, and you drive for a few minutes and you're in the mountains. There's some really beautiful scenery around the city … fantastic mountains, with snow in the winter, skiing and everything. It's a nice city to walk in, it's quite a relaxed place … it's quite small, really, and there isn't much traffic in the centre because the public transport is so good. You don't need a car really …
I: Right. And what else … It's a big business centre, isn't it?
S: Yeah, I mean, when people think of Zürich, they think of banks and money and, sure yes, it's an important financial centre. There are a lot of banks here, but it's not like London or New York – there are no enormous skyscrapers. Everything's much more human, really.
I: And how about entertainment, nightlife?
S: Oh, it's good. People have told me that there weren't many places open late a few years ago, but it's certainly changed now … I mean, it can be a bit expensive, but there are all kinds of restaurants: Italian, Chinese, Mexican … anything you like really … and lots of bars and stuff … so yeah, it's really lively. The only problem is, I don't have enough time to try them all!
I: And how about the way of life? Is there anything you find …

Recording 4

1 There's some really beautiful scenery around the city.
2 You drive for a few minutes.
3 There isn't much traffic in the centre.
4 There are a lot of banks.
5 There are no enormous skyscrapers.
6 There weren't many places open late a few years ago.
7 I don't have enough time to try them all.

Recording 7

New Zealand is in the South Pacific Ocean. The nearest country to us is Australia … but we're not really close neighbours, I think we're more than 2,000 km apart. We have two islands, which are called North Island and South Island. It's really not a very big country … it's about the same size as Great Britain, just a little bit bigger in area … but we have a much, much smaller population, only about three and a half million. We have two official languages, English and Maori, which is the language of the original people here.

I suppose now for a lot of people, when they think of New Zealand, they think of *The Lord of the Rings* which, of course, they filmed here … And people think of the fantastic scenery in the film … some people say it's the most fantastic scenery in the world … I don't know about that, but it's certainly an amazing place to visit. There are so many different types of scenery and climate. In the north, you've got fantastic beaches, mountains, volcanoes and even a small area of desert. The climate is very pleasant, mostly very warm … the average is around twenty-five degrees in the summer, while in the south it's a bit colder, especially in the winter, and the scenery is like Norway or Canada … lots of glaciers and fjords and snow-covered mountains where you can go skiing. There are so many things to see and do …

Recording 8

1 A: Excu … excuse me?
B: Yeah?
A: Can you help me? I'm looking for Church Street.
B: Church Street … Church Street … Sorry, I don't really know … Do you know where Church Street is?
C: Where?
A: Church Street.
C: Church Street? Oh right, yeah … You go down to the end here, down to this set of traffic lights, and turn left at the lights, that's Renton Street. And when you come to another set of lights, go straight on … and then the next right is Church Street. There's a big garage, you can't miss it.
A: So it's left at the lights … then second right where the garage is.
C: That's it.
A: OK then. Thanks a lot.
C: Cheers.
2 A: Hi! It's me!
B: Oh, hi. Where are you?
A: I just got off the train. I'm at the station.
B: Oh, right. Well, we're all here. We're just about ready to start …
A: OK, I'll be with you in a minute, but there's just one problem – I'm not sure how to get to you.
B: Oh, right.
A: Can you give me some directions?
B: Sure … OK. You're at the station, yeah?
A: Yeah. I'm just at the entrance.
B: Right, so if you look to your right, you'll see a big cinema … The Odeon … got it?
A: Yeah, yeah I can see that.

B: So just carry on past the cinema and … cross the road and you walk along Finlay Street for about 100 metres and then you'll see a building on your left called The Factory. We're in there. On the first floor. Just ring the bell.
A: OK, I'll be there in about five or ten minutes then.
B: OK, just give me a ring if you get lost.
A: I will, don't worry. See you in a minute.
B: See you in a minute.
3 A: Excuse me. Excuse me …
B: Yes, madam.
A: How can we get to Central Station, please?
B: Central Station … what, are you walking or … er …?
C: Er … how long does it take to walk?
B: Well, from here? It's about … oh, I dunno … about twenty, twenty-five minutes, I suppose.
C: It's quite far for us …
B: Or you can get a bus … any bus will take you there. Can you see the bus stops on the other side of the road, just on the corner?
A: OK, yes.
B: Any bus going that way will take you to Central Station.
A: I see.
B: Just ask the driver to tell you when to get off …
A: OK. Thank you.
C: Thank you.
B: My pleasure.

Recording 9

(missing words only)
1 help / looking
2 know / is
3 Can / give
4 can / get

Module 9

Recording 2

computer game   shopping mall   fast food   washing machine
mobile phone   vacuum cleaner   text message   electric fan

Recording 3

(missing words only)
a definitely   b probably   c probably   d definitely   e may
f might

Recording 4

1 They should try to bring more homes to the area as soon as they can … single people, young families, it's very difficult for them to find the right type of accommodation, so I think the flats idea is the best solution. Besides, if they build new flats, it might help other businesses in the area.
2 Well, if you ask me, after they finish demolishing the old power station, they should wait for a few months to give people a chance to think about the best way forward. Personally, I think the hotel scheme is the best one for the area. Unemployment is quite high around here and if they build a new hotel on the site, there will definitely be more jobs for local people.
3 Well, I'm not sure, really I'm not. I hope they ask local people what they want before they make a decision, because we'll have to live with it, after all. The area will change completely if they put a new shopping centre there. We have plenty of small shops around here, and a shopping centre will make things very difficult for local businesses.
4 If they decide to put a cinema here, it's going to create very serious parking problems. There aren't enough parking spaces for local people as it is. All this … I'll be glad when the work is over! The noise is going to be terrible!

Recording 5

(missing words only)

a build / will definitely be
b decide / going to create
c build / might help
d will change / put
e make
f can
g finish / should wait
h 'll be / is

Recording 6

(missing phrases only)

a ... this programme finishes.
b ... the weather's not too bad.
c ... I get dressed.
d ... I can find something else.
e ... I get back.
f ... we have enough money.

Module 10

Recording 1

1 Well, if you burn yourself on anything, you certainly shouldn't put butter or oil on it – that is the worst thing you can do, because it will make the burn hotter. You want to cool it down, so put it under cold water ... under the tap for about five or ten minutes – that's the best thing to do, and certainly don't put a plaster on it – if it's a bad burn and you need to go to hospital, you can cover it loosely with a clean cloth, but certainly no plasters!

2 If you've got a temperature, again you really need to cool down ... and the best thing to bring down your temperature is aspirin or paracetamol or something like that. Don't put a lot of warm clothes or blankets on, but of course you can lie down and have a rest if you feel bad.

3 You don't need to take the pills at exactly the same time every day, but you should take them at more or less the same time, because you need to maintain the level of antibiotic in the body, and certainly you should continue taking them until you've finished all the pills, that's really important, even if you feel better. As for alcohol, well it can make you feel ill if you drink alcohol with some antibiotics, but otherwise it's not really a problem – it doesn't stop the antibiotics from working.

4 If someone faints, you certainly shouldn't pour cold water over their face, and you certainly shouldn't shake them and try to wake them up. You should just leave them to come round, and of course, yes ... make sure they are comfortable.

5 If a bee stings you, then it's a good idea to do something to take the sting away, so you could put some ice on it, or just put it under cold water. Normally that's all you need to do, certainly you don't need to put a plaster on it! Sometimes, though, people have bad reactions to bee stings, so if you feel dizzy and there's a lot of swelling, you should certainly phone the doctor quickly.

6 If you develop a rash after eating strawberries, yes it may mean you are allergic to them, so stop eating them and the rash should soon disappear. Don't put cream on it, but if it's getting worse and worse quite rapidly, you should speak to a doctor, you might have a serious allergy.

Recording 2

N = NURSE; P = PATIENT

N: Health Helpline, how can I help?
P: Yeah, I'm not feeling very well. I wonder if you might be able to help me ...
N: OK, sure. I'll just need to ask you some questions ... Now, what are your symptoms exactly?
P: Well, I'm just ... I don't know ... I'm not feeling too good ... just generally. My stomach is a bit ... you know ... I've got a pain in my stomach.
N: Right ... Have you got a temperature, d'you know?

P: I don't think so ... I haven't checked ... I haven't got a thermometer.
N: Any headache or anything like that?
P: No, not really.
N: Right. Are you taking any medicine at the moment?
P: No, nothing, no.
N: Right. And do you have any allergies that you know of?
P: No.
N: Have you had any serious illnesses at all?
P: No, I haven't. Nothing. I've always been really healthy ... usually.
N: Right. When did you last have something to eat or drink?
P: Lunchtime. I had a burger for my lunch ... well, a couple, actually ... three, in fact. And french fries ... large fries ... and, er ... a couple of milkshakes.
N: I see.
P: And, er, an ice cream dessert ... two of those, in fact.
N: Yeah.
P: And a large Cola ... two large Colas ...
N: Right. Well, it sounds like you've eaten rather a lot, haven't you?
P: Hmm ... yeah, I suppose so.
N: The best thing you can do is just have a lie down for a couple of hours. And if you have any further trouble, just give us a ring.
P: Yeah, maybe you're right. I think I'll feel better if ...

Recording 4

a Barbers used to extract teeth.
b Families used to be bigger.
c Many people didn't use to live very long.
d People didn't use to go to the dentist.
e Doctors used some dangerous methods.
f Barbers used a different type of razor.
g People didn't use soap.
h Doctors didn't use modern methods.

Recording 5

Part 1

Perhaps you've heard that cats have nine lives. Well, Frane Selak has had at least seven lucky escapes, making him the world's luckiest – or unluckiest – man!

Recording 6

Part 2

His first escape came when the train he was travelling on fell into an icy river. He managed to swim to the river bank with only a broken arm. A year later, as he was travelling on a DC-8 aeroplane, a door flew open and Selak fell out of the aircraft. Fortunately, Mr Selak landed safely, with only cuts and bruises.

Three years later, he had to swim for his life again – this time after the bus he was travelling in left the road and fell into a river. Accident number four came when his car caught fire while he was driving along the motorway. He escaped seconds before the petrol tank exploded.

'You could look at it two ways,' he says. 'I was either the world's luckiest man or the unluckiest. I preferred to believe the second one.'

But the accidents weren't over yet. Number five came when his car again caught fire and he lost most of his hair. Then a bus hit him, but once again his injuries were not serious. The following year he was driving in the mountains when he saw a truck coming straight for him. His car crashed through the barrier and over the edge. Mr Selak jumped out at the last minute and landed in a tree. Moments later, he saw his car explode 100 m below him.

His luck was no better in his love life: Mr Selak has been married and divorced four times.

'I suppose my marriages were disasters too!' he said.

But fate had not quite finished with Mr Selak. At the age of seventy-four, he bought a lottery ticket for the first time in thirty years.

Mr Selak won £600,000. He is now planning to buy a house, a car, a speedboat and marry his girlfriend, who is twenty years younger than him.

'I'm going to enjoy my life now. I feel like I have been re-born. I know someone was watching me all those years,' he says.

Recording 7

a … the train he was travelling on …
b … as he was travelling on a DC-8 aeroplane …
c … the bus he was travelling in …
d … he was driving along the motorway.
e … someone was watching me all those years …

Consolidation Modules 6–10

Recording 1

ELIZA:
Well, I live on my own now. I decided after my fourth husband died that I didn't want to marry again, and I like being independent. I still enjoy going to parties and meeting people – it's quite funny when I meet someone for the first time and they recognise me, but they can't remember the names of any of my films. They get embarrassed, but I don't mind. The last one was quite a few years ago, after all! I've lived here in Los Angeles for nearly forty years now, and I love the weather, and the people, but I feel I need a change, so maybe next year I'll do something exciting, like travel around the world. I've always wanted to go to Australia you know – so I should go, really, before it's too late!

PHILIP:
I used to be the director of a large finance company. I had a really good salary, nice house, big car, all those things, but I was just working all the time, and I never saw my wife, or had any time for my great passion – cooking. So, I decided, and one day – about three years ago – I just left my job, and we moved to a smaller house, got a smaller car, you know, and my wife and I opened a small restaurant. I did all the cooking at first, and it was very hard work – I thought 'I've made a mistake,' but then we started to make some money, and we got a chef, and it was easier. Nowadays, I decide the menus, and I go to the market every day, to get fresh vegetables, fish, and I do some cooking. We're certainly not as rich as we were, and we work long hours, but I think we're much happier. Maybe next year we'll have a holiday – our first one in three years!

CARLA:
I never go shopping myself – well, not very often – I really hate it. All those crowds of people, and you can never find exactly what you want. That's what gave me the idea for the Internet company, you know, buy clothes, things for the house, presents, etcetera over the Internet, and the things were cheaper, too, of course. I was so surprised when the business grew so quickly – I suppose there are lots of people out there who hate shopping too! I still can't believe that the company is only a year old and it's already worth one and a half million! I don't really think of myself as a businesswoman – it was just luck, really. I think I'll probably sell the company in two or three years' time. Then I can stop work and have that great big family that I've always wanted, and go and live in a huge house in the countryside.

Module 11

Recording 2

1 I love chocolate … I specially love white chocolate. It's very, very sweet, but it's fabulous.
2 Usually, I hate buying presents … If I know what I'm going to buy, it's OK – but my family have got everything, I never know what to buy and … I can't stand it!
3 I love watching some sports on TV. I'm crazy about Formula One, but I don't like football or tennis very much.
4 Well, I really enjoy sunbathing for two reasons: I like lying down, it's one of my favourite hobbies, and I'm very keen on reading … So put the two together and that's sunbathing for me.
5 I can't stand long car journeys because I get sick, but I love travelling by train and looking out of the window and watching everything go by.

Recording 3

1 A: Would you like to come to our house on Sunday? We're having a barbecue!
   B: Thanks, I'd love to! Did you know I don't eat meat?
   A: No, I didn't. Do you eat fish?
   B: Yes, I love it. That's great. We'll see you on Sunday, then.
2 A: Have you been to see *Naked Eye* yet?
   B: No, but I'd like to. I've heard it's brilliant. How about going to see it next week?
   A: To be honest, I don't really like action films.
   B: Oh well. Maybe there's something else you'd like to see?

Recording 4

a Would you like to come to our house on Saturday?
b How about going to see it next week?
c Would you like to go out for a meal?
d How about going out for a meal?
e Would you like to have an ice cream?
f How about having an ice cream?
g Would you like to go for a drive?
h How about going for a drive?

Module 12

Recording 1

1   What colour was the comb in the picture?
2   Was there an umbrella in the picture? What colour was it?
3   What was below the lipstick?
4   What was between the razor and the shaving foam?
5   Was the comb the same colour as the torch?
6   Was the lipstick next to the towel or the keys?
7   What colour was the towel you saw in the picture?
8   Was there a hairbrush in the picture? What colour was it?
9   How many keys were there?
10 What make was the mobile phone?

Recording 2

accepted   recognised   liked   connected   manufactured
produced   avoided   worked   designed   used

Recording 3

1   Dark glasses have been an important fashion item for a number of years now. But the first dark glasses had nothing to do with fashion and nothing to do with the sun. Glasses with dark lenses were worn by judges in China more than 600 years ago. They wore smoke-coloured lenses so people couldn't see their eyes – and therefore couldn't know what they were thinking!

2 The history of blue jeans goes back to the nineteenth century. A young immigrant called Levi Strauss designed the first jeans as clothes for people who worked long hours in the open air, such as gold miners and even cowboys! They didn't become fashionable until the middle of the last century.

3 Although the word *shampoo* comes from a Hindi word, the history of modern liquid shampoo is quite short. In the early twentieth century, a man called John Breck became the world's leading shampoo manufacturer and helped give the world shiny, healthy hair. Breck himself, however, lost all his hair and became completely bald.

4 Chanel No 5 was introduced by the French fashion designer Coco Chanel in the 1920s. Because she considered the number five to be her lucky number, the perfume was first presented on the 5th of May – the fifth month of the year.

Recording 4

(missing words only)

1	are sold	5	is known	9	is recognised
2	is pronounced	6	made	10	was created
3	was named	7	was paid	11	received
4	made	8	does not appear		

Recording 5

Well, from this list, there are one or two things that we can throw out straightaway, we definitely don't need them. You don't need a compass, 'cos you're not going to travel very far, digital camera no, mirror no, rope no, and a mobile phone … well, it's no good, you won't get a signal, and you don't need an umbrella, you're not in the middle of London, you're in a tropical rainforest … so also you don't need sunscreen, or sunglasses. It's hot and it's humid but there's no direct sunlight because of all the trees and the vegetation … it'll be pretty dark. Pencil and paper: not necessary unless you want to write a shopping list. Things you need, well number one, the most important thing to survive is water … you can take bottled water, that's OK, but it won't be enough so number two is water purification tablets … you've got streams and rivers but you've got to be careful … So as well as that, you'll have to eat … the best thing to take is energy bars, not very exciting but they'll keep you alive for three days. There are coconuts and fruit as well if you need them … leave the fishing rod at home, it's too dangerous with all the crocodiles. The biggest problems come at night. You've got insects and snakes and all kinds of things, so you must have a tent to sleep in, and a fire to keep the animals away … and for a fire you need matches – I don't think a magnifying glass is going to help you – and in case the fire goes out, a torch, with plenty of batteries. Also take some insect repellent – those mosquitoes can be pretty nasty – and you always want a good knife, there are a hundred reasons why you'll need it. So how many's that? That's nine … well, I'd say also you need some things to make yourself feel human. It's hot, it's wet and it can be pretty tough, so it's a good idea to take some clean clothes, a toothbrush and some toilet paper. They're not absolutely necessary, but you'll feel a whole lot better if you have them.

Recording 6

a A: Hi there!
  B: Hi. Everything OK?
  A: Yeah, I'm just … er … cleaning up.
  B: Good. Listen, I'm just in the supermarket. Shall I get something for dinner tonight?
  A: Mm, yes, good idea.
  B: What d'you fancy?
  A: Oh, I don't know … Why don't we have pasta? You know, with some of that seafood sauce. That's easy.
  B: OK, then. Do we need anything else?
  A: Er … let's have some of that ice cream, the double chocolate one.

  B: All right. I'll see you in about twenty minutes.
  A: OK. See you then.
b A: Are you OK there, sir? Do you need any help?
  B: Well, yes, actually. I'm looking for a Christmas present for my mother and I'm not sure what …
  A: I see, well, how about this perfume? It's called 'Heaven Scent'. It's very popular with the more mature woman.
  B: I don't think so, really. I'm never sure with perfume.
  A: Yes, it can be difficult, can't it? Now, let's see. You could buy her a really nice lipstick. Now this range has some lovely colours …
  B: Yes, maybe I'll do that. Which one do you think would be …
c A: … and I must get something to take back for Francesca. What do you think I should get?
  B: Er, how about one of those ashtrays we saw in that little souvenir shop by the bridge?
  A: Oh, come on, Ricky, be serious. They were horrible. And anyway she doesn't smoke!
  B: Well, I don't know. What about getting her a purse, a really good leather one.
  A: Good idea. Thanks!
d A: Now, here are the children's sports shoes. Oh, these are nice, look. <u>Why don't you</u> try these on?
  B: Oh, Mum. Nobody wears trainers like that. Can't I have these?
  A: Oh, they're much more expensive. Don't you want that backpack we saw?
  B: Yes, 'course I do!
  A: Well, you can't have that and the expensive trainers. So <u>shall we</u> ask the assistant for your size in these?
  B: I suppose so.

Module 13

Recording 1

imagine   imagination   imaginative   organise
organisation   organised   discipline   disciplined
talent   talented   commitment   committed
laziness   lazy   experience   experience   experienced
honesty   honest   motivate   motivation   motivated
sympathise   sympathy   sympathetic

Recording 2

I = INTERVIEWER; T = TANYA

I: Tanya, you run an agency called Vacation Express. Can you tell me what you do exactly?

T: Well, we have a large database of people looking for temporary jobs, mainly young people – a lot of them are students, in fact – and we match them to our database of jobs all over the world. Most of the jobs we have are summer jobs and many of them, the majority in fact, are in the tourist industry. But there are jobs in other areas like teaching English, which can be all year round.

I: What are the reasons people have for doing this kind of work?

T: Well, for a few people, the money is the main thing, even though, to be honest, in most cases the money isn't fantastic … but there are many other reasons for doing summer work, and these are really more important than the money you earn. Obviously, you learn a lot of new skills, for one thing, and also it's a great opportunity to see another culture, to meet new people … and, of course, all these things will look good on your CV later on.

I: What kind of things are you looking for in the people you employ?

T: The most important thing is a positive attitude and the ability to get on with people. That's really the main thing, with this kind of work anyway … although I have to say that languages – especially English – are a big, big advantage.

I: Tell me about some of the more unusual or attractive jobs you've got at the moment.

T: Well, let me see … we've got vacancies for jungle guides in Peru, so if you're keen on the rainforest, then this is for you. You've got to lead groups of tourists on jungle walks … That's for six months, starting in September. And also, if you like water sports, there's a nice job for a water sports teacher, a very nice job on the Spanish coast. Obviously, you need to have some experience for that one …

I: OK, and I believe you have some jobs for people who have some special talent or other and would like to do a bit of travelling?

T: Well, yes. If you're thinking of a career in the entertainment industry, or you're looking for experience, we've got a vacancy on a cruise ship for a children's entertainer. That's a very popular one, and it's a great way to see the world. Also there are a number of teaching jobs. We've got some jobs in Asia right now – that's great opportunity for people to see a different culture – and also, one thing that might be interesting is …

Recording 3

1 I have been waiting.   I've been waiting.
2 You have been working.   You've been working.
3 He has been working.   He's been working.
4 It has been raining.   It's been raining.
5 We have been waiting.   We've been waiting.
6 You have been sitting.   You've been sitting.
7 He has been coming   He's been coming.
8 I have been looking.   I've been looking.

Recording 4

a How long has Florence been living in England?
b How long has she been working as a teacher?
c How long has she been studying yoga?
d How long has she been teaching yoga?

Module 14

Recording 1

a $6,000   b 190   c 6.32   d £50 million   e 620   f 98.5
g 5 billion   h 8.2   i 49.8

Recording 2

(missing phrases only)
1 Thanks, Dad   2 I'm thinking   3 died and left me $10 million

Recording 3

(missing words only)

1	sent	5	discovered	9	had bought
2	was	6	had made	10	had sold
3	had arrested	7	had arrived	11	had
4	tried	8	thought	12	died

Recording 4

One day, I was at home and my little girl came to me – she's five – and she was crying and of course, I asked her, 'What's the matter?' She said that she was playing with a coin and then she lost it. She said she had dropped it down the back of the sofa and she couldn't find it and this made her very sad, because she had lost the money, and she thought she would be in trouble. So of course I said, 'Look, darling, don't worry. It's only money. Money isn't important.' And she said, 'What is important?' So, I don't know, I said the first thing that came into my mind. 'Love, of course, love is more important than money.' So she looked a bit happier. Then, about a week later, I had a bit of luck. I won some money in the lottery. It was quite a lot of money, actually, about a thousand euros. Of course, we were all very happy, and when I came home with the money, it was in my wallet, we had a little celebration, a little party for a few people, family and friends. I put the wallet with the money in it on the table, and we were all enjoying ourselves … and then I looked over to the other room and I saw my daughter. She was throwing all the money out of the window! It was everywhere! I couldn't believe my eyes, I was so horrified. When I saw her, I think she had taken nearly all the money out of the wallet. I said, 'What are you doing? Are you crazy?' And she said to me, 'But Daddy, you said money isn't important.'

Recording 6

a A: Excuse me, is there somewhere around here I can change money?
   B: Sure, we can change it for you here. Or, if you prefer, there's a bank in the main square.
   A: What's the exchange rate for US dollars?
   B: It's marked up here. It's 3.3 pesos to the dollar and there is a 5% commission.
   A: OK, I'd like to change this into pesos, please. It's 200 American dollars.
   B: Certainly, madam. If I could just see your passport …
   A: Sure.
   B: So that will be 660 pesos minus 5%, that's … 627 pesos. OK, so if you'd just like to sign here …

b A: Excuse me. How much are these earrings?
   B: Which ones?
   A: These ones here.
   B: They're £20.
   A: Oh, that's a bit expensive. How about these smaller ones.
   B: They're £12.
   A: OK, I'll take this pair, the smaller ones, these. Can I pay by credit card?
   B: Well, I prefer cash.

c A: Hello, I'm staying in England for a year. I'd like to open a bank account here. What documents do I need, please?
   B: Right, well, we need to see your passport …
   A: Yes.
   B: … and a letter from your employer or your place of study, if you're a student.
   A: OK. What else?
   B: Nothing else. That's all.
   A: Oh, right. I see. Oh, and one other thing: how long do I have to wait before I …

d A: … and, well, so I told him … Oh, there he is. Excuse me, can we have the bill, please?
   B: Together?
   C: Yes, please.
   B: OK. That's one mineral water, one fresh orange juice and er …
   C: One club sandwich …
   B: One club sandwich and one prawn salad, was it?
   A: That's right.
   B: OK. Just a moment.
   A: Thank you. So, I told him that if he doesn't get back to me soon, I'll have to look for someone else, which is a bit annoying when you think how long we've been …
   B: There you go.
   C: Thanks. Is service included?
   B: Er, no, it isn't.
   C: OK, thank you.

Do you think we should leave a tip?

A: How much is it?

C: It's £11.50. It's a bit expensive.

A: Oh, leave him a pound. He has been very nice.

Recording 7

a What's the exchange rate for US dollars?

b I'd like to change this into pesos, please. It's 200 American dollars.

c Excuse me. How much are these earrings?

d OK, I'll take this pair.

e Can I pay by credit card?

f What documents do I need?

g Can we have the bill, please?

h Is service included?

i Do you think we should leave a tip?

Module 15

Recording 2

(*missing words/phrases only*)

a continue / won't survive   b 'd go / had / 'd miss

c got / 'd go

Recording 3

a I'll see you later.   e You'd like him.

b I'll have a look.   f That'd be great.

c I'd love to.   g We'll be back soon.

d I'll think about it.   h I'd prefer not to.

Consolidation modules 11–15

Recording 1

a A: Excuse me!

  B: Yes, madam.

  A: I want to know, er, was my bedroom cleaned this morning?

  B: Yes, all the rooms are cleaned every morning, madam.

  A: Well. I have a bit of a problem, then.

  B: Oh dear, madam, is your room not satisfactory?

  A: No, it's not that. It's just that I can't find some earrings which I left on the table by the bed …

b A: Hi, Paul. How was your holiday?

  B: Oh, don't talk about it. It was really terrible!

  A: Oh no. Why? What happened?

  B: Well, the hotel was nothing like the photo in the brochure. The rooms were really small, the food was horrible, all the staff were rude …

  A: How awful! But the other people were nice?

  B: Well, they were nice, yes, but I don't think that any of them were under fifty.

  A: Oh dear. So you won't go there next year, then?

  B: You're right. I wouldn't go there again if you gave me £10,000! I'm going to stay here next year!

c A: Right then, madam, could you tell me exactly what happened?

  B: Well, I got home at about nine o'clock, and I went straight through to the kitchen, to make a cup of coffee …

  A: And you didn't notice anything unusual?

  B: No. I was quite tired you see, and I was thinking about work, but when I went to the cupboard I stepped on some broken glass and then I saw that someone had broken

the kitchen window. I was so shocked.

  A: Yes, a very unpleasant experience for you. So what exactly was taken, do you think?

  B: Well, all my jewellery, I'm sure from the bedroom, and some antique silver from a cupboard.

  A: Were all these things insured, madam?

  B: Well, I think so …

d A: Ah, Anita. Is the design for the conference centre ready?

  B: Er, no. I was …

  A: But you know I need it for tomorrow morning and I asked you to stop work on everything else until you finished it.

  B: I know, I've been working on it all day, but I haven't finished it yet. I'm sorry.

  A: Well, you'll just have to stay here until you finish it, then.

  B: Yes, of course. It'll be on your desk by nine o'clock.

Pearson Education Limited
Edinburgh Gate
Harlow
Essex CM20 2JE
England
And Associated Companies throughout the world.

www.longman/cuttingedge

First published 2005
Fifth impression 2007

ISBN 978-0-582-82509-3

Set in 9/12.5pt ITS Stone Informal and 10/13pt Congress sans.

Printed in China   GCC/05

Author acknowledgements

We would like to thank the following people for their help and contribution: Karen Adams, Tracey Archibald, Dave Butler, Helen Clark, Jill Craig, Hazel Dempsey, Pat Ryland, Pat Ryland, Simon Williams and Johnny Wong and Alma Gray (Producer) for making the unscripted recordings. Stuart Beaumont, Emma Ream, Jayne Silva, Emma Walton and Mayo Yanachi for their help and advice. We would also like to thank the publishing team for their support and encouragement, in particular Jenny Colley (Senior Publisher), Lindsay White (Project Manager), Tanya Whatling (Editor), Jonathan Barnard (Senior Designer) and Alma Gray (Producer).

The publishers and authors are very grateful to the following people and institutions for keeping user diaries:
Patrick Creed, IH Dublin; Caroline Gordon, Elite College, London; Michelle Ives, Waikato Institute of Technology, Auckland; Edina Varga, Novoschool, Budapest; Gabriella Heged s, ILS Nyíregyháza, Országzászló; Szilvia Páder, Nyelutanoda KFT, Veszprém; Timea Kovács, K rösy József Secondary School of Economics & Foreign Trade, Szeged; Natalia Isupova, Group of companies Mr English, Moscow; Svetlana Yu Gladtsyna, Foreign Language School of the diplomatic academy of the RF foreign Ministry, Moscow; Lydia Budaragina, State Language Courses N3, St Petersburg; Justyna Stadnicka, Silesian Technical University, Ksi enice; Alicja Smreczak-Kach, Wy sza Szkoa Bankowa, Wrocaw; Giovanna La Magna, Liceo Classico delle Lingue Straniere 'S Maffei', Verona; Clare Whitmell, Lead On, Rome; Francesca Capurro, British SRL, Genoa; Emma Lush, International Institute Australia, Brisbane; Beth McNally, International Institute Australia, Brisbane; Brian Swash, Language Link, London; Alex Waring, Language Link, London; Marcela del Campo, Universidad Javeriana, Bogotá; Cecilia Bonilla Gil, Pontificia Universidad Javeriana, Bogotá; Clara Inés de Diaz Granados, Universidad Sergio Arboleda, Bogotá; Mark Hamer, Tti School of English, London; Osmund Devlin, IH, Dublin; Tom Conway, The New School of English, Cambridge; Jeni Wilson, The School, Aranda de Duero; Darren Harbutt, British Council, Barcelona;Virginia Laura Pigretti, ITESL, Buenos Aires; Richard Sutton; London School of English, London; Iwona Kau na; Archibald, Warsaw; Laura Hayward, Embassy CES, Froebelcollege, London; James Arteaga, Embassy CES, Froebelcollege, London; Amanda Bailey, St Giles College, London.

and the following people for reporting on the manuscript:
Darren Harbutt, British Council, Barcelona; Steven Smith, Australian College of English, Perth; Iwona Kotula, Rybnik; Esin Catlayan, Izmir University of Economics, Izmir; Pauline Belimova, St Petersburg State University, St Petersburg; Caroline Antonuk Kings School Oxford.

We are grateful to the following for permission to reproduce copyright material:
Guardian Newspapers Limited for extracts from the article "Ewan McGregor: Questions from the floor" NFT Event, published on *Guardian Unlimited* 23 October 2002 © Guardian Newspapers Limited 2002; The Cincinnati Enquirer for an extract adapted from "PBS '1900 House' shows 'dirty, hard work'" by John Kiesewetter published on *Enquirer.com* June 11 2000; Allan Hall Berlin for an extract adapted from "The World's Luckiest Man Wins Lottery" published on *Ananova.com* 21st April 2004; CNET Networks UK Ltd for an extract adapted from "The silicon.com weekly round-up" by Will Sturgeon published on *Silicon.com* 25th April 2003 © 2004. All rights reserved.

We are also grateful to the following for permission to reproduce copyright song lyrics:
Music Sales Limited for the lyrics '(Marie's the Name) His Latest Flame' words and music by Doc Pomus and Mort Shuman © 1961 Elvis Presley Music, USA. Carlin Music Corporation, and the for the lyrics 'Imagine' words & music by John Lennon © Copyright 1971 Lenono Music. All Rights Reserved. International Copyright Secured; International Music Publications Limited for the lyrics 'You Are Everything' words and music by Thomas Bell and Linda Creed © 1971 Assorted Music, Bell Boy Music, USA, Warner/Chappell North America Music Ltd. All rights reserved.

Illustrations by:

Barbara Bellingham (Début art) pages 24-25, 98-99, 111, 124-125; Richard Morris page 67, 72, 142, 143 , 144 , 146; Matt Buckley (Chrome-Dome Design) pages 27 , 77, 88, 113, 145; Jonathan Williams pages 64, 65, 78, 94, 95; Martina Farrow (New Division) pages 14, 39, 57, 97, 112; Emma Brownjohn (New Division) pages 27; Dominic Li (The Organisation) pages 136-137; Yane Christensen (Sylvie Poggio) pages 21, 34, 35, 52, 128-129 ,141; Sue Webb pages 46, 140, 146; Melanie Barnes page 32; Mark Dickson (Folio) page 48; Gilles Boogaerts (The Art Market) page 44; Francis Blake (three-in-a-box) pages 8-9, 18, 28, 31, 93, 108; Gary Kaye page 30, 70, 84, 85, 126, 127, 134; Illustrated Arts page 83.

Photo acknowledgements

We are grateful to the following for their permission to reproduce copyright photographs:
Advertising Archives for page 17 top right; Alamy Images/Acestock for page10(a), /Jon Arnold Images/Demetrio Carrasco for page 58(3), /Bananastock for page 25 middle left, /Peter Bowater for page 80 top right, /Chris Cameron for page 76 bottom, /Nic Cleave Photography for page 11 middle, /Don Geyer for page 110 top right, /gkphotography for page 115 top right, /Vladimir Godnik for page 121 left, /Jeff Greenberg for page 59(5), /Robert Harding Picture Library for pages 22, 59(6), 72 middle, 72 bottom left, 74 top, /Dallas & John Heaton for page 55, /Chris Howes for page 110 middle left, /D Hurst for page 7 bottom, /Image 100 for pages 67(e), 72 top, /Image Shop for page 62 bottom right, /Image Shop-Zefa for page 27 top, /Image State for pages 11 right, 49, /Ingram Publishing for page 19(b), /Inmagine for page 80 bottom right, /Leisurepix for page 59(8), /Medioimages for pages 24 bottom right, 54 bottom, /Motoring Picture Library for page 67(a), /Photofusion/Bob Watkins for page 88, /PhotoLibrary Wales for page 116 top left, /Pictures Colour Library for page 58(2), /Plainpicture/TatjaB for page 7 middle, /John Powell for page 102 top, /Mervyn Rees for page 11 left, / Shout for page 62 top right, /Steve Skjold for page 29 bottom right, /Stock Image/Pixland-Jim Boorman for page 116 bottom left, /StockShot for page 7 top, /Tetra Images for page 38 top right, /Thinkstock for page 80 top left, /Travel Ink/Jeremy Richards for page 75 bottom, /David Wall for pages 60, 76 top, /Janine Wiedel PL/Jacky Chapman for page 115 top left, /David Young-Wolff for page 29 bottom left; Anthony Blake for page 38 bottom right; Associated Press/Kentucky Fried Chicken HO for page 107 top middle; Bridgeman Art Library/Bibliotheque des Arts Decoratifs, Paris, France for page 90(e); Camera Press for page 109 top; CEN for page 92; Corbis Images for pages 6 middle, 6 bottom, 42(a), 42(c), 58(1), 63(a), 63(e), 63(f), 90(d), 107 left, 107 top right, 107 bottom right, 110 bottom, 114 top, 114 middle left, 114 middle right, 114 bottom left, 132 bottom; DK Images for page 67(d), 75 top; Empics/EPA for page 10(b), /PA for page 17 top left, 54 top, 118; Eye Ubiquitous for pages 67(b), 94 middle; First Choice Holidays UK for page 115 bottom right; Getty Images/Image Bank for pages 89 left, 120 (Jacqui), 146, /John Peters for page 46 bottom, /Stone for pages 19(a), 36 left top, 54 middle, /Taxi for pages 74 bottom, 121 right; Ronald Grant Archive for page 66 top left; Ronald Grant Archive/Polygram Filmed Entertainment for page 66 top right; Robert Harding Picture Library for page 94 bottom; The Hutchison Library for page 42(b); Image Source for pages 36 left bottom, 58 left, 103 bottom right, 140, 147 left; Image State for pages 19 (f), 36 right middle, 36 right bottom, 56, 62 bottom left, 120 left bottom, /Bananastock for page 120 (Heather); Impact Photos for page 115 bottom left; Empics/ANP for page 10(c); Life File Photographic Library for page 90(a); Mary Evans Picture Library for page 90(b), (c); Natural History Museum PL for page 50; Photonica/Special Photographers/Alexandra Murphy for page 83; Popperfoto for page 133; Punchstock/Bananastock for pages 29 top right, , 46 top (top right), 46 top (top left), 103 bottom right, 114 bottom right, 120 (Chris), 120 (Justin), /Brand X for pages 6 top, 19(e), 45, 80 bottom left, /Comstock for pages 89 right, 117 bottom, /Creatas for pages 46 top (bottom left), 117 middle, /Digital Vision for page 62 top left, /Image Shop for pages 116 top right, 117 top, /IT Stock for page 29 top left, /PhotoDisc for pages 24 bottom left, 100 left, 100 right, 120 left top, /Rubber Ball for pages 19(d), 102 bottom, 116 middle right, 120 (Zoe), 147 right bottom, /Stockbyte for page 46(main), /Thinkstock for page 19(c); Redferns/Tom Hanley for page 132 top; Retna for page 94 top; Rex Features for pages 13 left, 13 right, 16 top, 17 bottom, 25 left, 42(d), 63(b), 63(c), 63(d), 63(g), 63(h), 66 bottom right, 67(b), 106, 107 bottom middle; Chris Ridley for page 81 left, 81 right, 82; South American Pictures/Tony Morrison for page 38 top left, bottom left; Superstock for page 36 right top; photo swiss-image.ch for page 72 bottom right; Topham Picturepoint for page 42(e); Travel Library for pages 58(4), 59(7).

The cover photograph has been kindly supplied by Getty Images.

Every effort has been made to trace the copyright holders and we apologise in advance for any unintentional omissions. We would be pleased to insert the appropriate acknowledgement in any subsequent edition of this publication.

Picture Research by Hilary Luckcock.

This book is dedicated to Joseph, Jessica and Isabel.